Crimes of Mobility

This book examines the role of criminal law in the enforcement of immigration controls since the mid-1990s in Britain. The criminalization of immigration status has historically served functions of exclusion and control against those who defy the state's powers over its territory and population. Since the mid-1990s, the powers to exclude and punish have been enhanced by the expansion of the catalogue of immigration offences and their more systematic enforcement.

This book is the first in-depth analysis of such criminal offences in Britain, and presents original empirical material about the use of criminal powers against suspected immigration wrongdoers. Based on interviews with practitioners and staff at the UK Border Agency and data from court cases involving immigration defendants, it examines prosecution decision making and the proceedings before the criminal justice system. *Crimes of Mobility* critically analyses the criminalization of immigration status and, more generally, the functions of the criminal law in immigration enforcement, from a legal and normative perspective. It will be of interest to academics and research students working on criminology, criminal law, criminal justice, socio-legal studies, migration and refugee studies, and human rights, as well as criminal law and immigration practitioners.

Ana Aliverti is an Assistant Professor at the University of Warwick School of Law.

Routledge Studies in Criminal Justice, Borders and Citizenship
Edited by Katja Franko Aas
University of Oslo

Mary Bosworth
University of Oxford

Sharon Pickering
Monash University

Globalizing forces have had a profound impact on the nature of contemporary criminal justice and law more generally. This is evident in the increasing salience of borders and mobility in the production of illegality and social exclusion. *Routledge Studies in Criminal Justice, Borders and Citizenship* showcases contemporary studies that connect criminological scholarship to migration studies and explore the intellectual resonances between the two. It provides an opportunity to reflect on the theoretical and methodological challenges posed by mass mobility and its control. By doing that, it charts an intellectual space and establishes a theoretical tradition within criminology to house scholars of immigration control, race and citizenship, including those who traditionally publish *either* in general criminological *or* in anthropological, sociological, refugee studies, human rights and other publications.

Crimes of Mobility

Criminal law and the regulation of immigration

Ana Aliverti

Routledge
Taylor & Francis Group

LONDON AND NEW YORK

First published 2013
by Routledge
2 Park Square, Milton Park, Abingdon, Oxon, OX14 4RN

Simultaneously published in the USA and Canada
by Routledge
711 Third Avenue, New York, NY 10017

Routledge is an imprint of the Taylor & Francis Group, an informa business

British Library Cataloguing in Publication Data
A catalogue record for this book is available from the British Library

Library of Congress Cataloging-in-Publication Data
Aliverti, Ana J.
Crimes of mobility : criminal law and the regulation of immigration /
Ana Aliverti.
pages cm
1. Criminal justice, Administration of–Great Britain. 2. Emigration and
immigration law–Great Britain. 3. Criminal law–Great Britain. I. Title.
KD7876.A955 2013
345.41'0237–dc23
2012049531

ISBN: 978-0-415-82090-5 (hbk)
ISBN: 978-0-415-83922-8 (pbk)
ISBN: 978-0-203-38593-7 (ebk)

Typeset in Times New Roman by
Keystroke, Station Road, Codsall, Wolverhampton

Printed and bound in Great Britain by
TJ International Ltd, Padstow, Cornwall

To Raja and Sophia

Contents

Statutes and legislation

Domestic statutes

European Community legislation

Legislation and regulations from other jurisdictions

Cases

Domestic cases

European Court of Human Rights cases

Cases from other jurisdictions

Figures

Series editors' preface

In recent years, a growing body of literature has begun to refer to the 'criminalization' of migration. Nonetheless, we know surprisingly little about the extent or nature of this phenomenon. Ana Aliverti's book, *Crimes of Mobility*, addresses this gap, documenting the changing legal landscape in the UK and exploring the impact of such changes empirically, in the courts. This approach enables Aliverti to examine the intricate dynamics between the expressive and the instrumental functions of criminal law, and to identify some surprising findings. Notwithstanding apparent legislative enthusiasm for criminalizing migration, relatively few of these offences are enforced in the courts. The legislative 'bark', in other words, often overstates its actual 'bite'.

Why and how immigration-related activities are punished lie at the heart of the transformations of criminal law under conditions of globalization. As such, *Crimes of Mobility* should be of interest to a variety of scholars, not only those with an explicit interest in criminal and immigration law, but also to students of criminology and migration studies, and those with an interest in globalization more generally. The proliferation of immigration crimes lies at the gist of ethical issues raised by the use of coercive sovereign power over migrant populations. It is therefore appropriate in many ways that *Crimes of Mobility* should be one of the first books in the *Criminal Justice, Borders and Citizenship* series. We hope and trust that the series will continue in this mode, both when it comes to the level of excellence and its thematic engagement with debates about the nature of contemporary justice, citizenship and rights.

Katja Franko Aas
Mary Bosworth
Sharon Pickering

January 2013

Acknowledgements

This book is based on my doctoral dissertation, which was completed at the Centre for Criminology, University of Oxford. During this time I benefited from the generous support of my supervisor, Mary Bosworth. She has been readily available throughout this project and has provided me with insightful and prompt feedback. She encouraged me to think critically and from different perspectives about my research findings. She has done much more than supervise my thesis. With great generosity, she has guided me along the path from being a student to becoming a young academic. It has been a privilege to have her as my dissertation adviser. Ian Loader was my supervisor and co-supervisor during the first stage of this research, and his comments contributed to its structure and gave shape to the project. This project was evaluated at various stages. I am grateful to my examiners for their sharp and thoughtful comments and suggestions, which enriched this study: Lucia Zedner, Matthew Gibney, Nicola Lacey, Bridget Anderson and Peter Ramsay.

Many other institutions and people supported me in this process. I am grateful to the Howard League for Penal Reform, which funded a one-year postdoctoral research fellowship at the Centre for Criminology at Oxford; this allowed me to work on my doctoral dissertation to turn it into this book. A number of scholarships from the Centre for Criminology, the Faculty of Law and Corpus Christi College provided me with the financial support needed to undertake this research. I am grateful to all of them for their generosity. I owe significant debts to my interviewees who kindly made time to be interviewed. The staff members at Uxbridge Magistrates' Court and Isleworth Crown Court were helpful and their assistance facilitated my work. My special thanks go to Umesh Mistry, at the Ministry of Justice, who helped me to get access to these courts. Earlier drafts of this book or parts of it were read by academics and colleagues: Lucia Zedner, Leanne Weber, Katja Franko Aas, Marie Manikis and Lea Sitkin. I am grateful to them for taking the time to read my work and providing me with critical comments, suggestions and information. I need to extend enormous gratitude to Lucia Zedner who, as my college tutor, has been always available to discuss my research and other academic matters.

My friends and family supported me in different ways. Particular thanks go to my friends Maía Cristina Dorado, Andrea Canales, Francesca Badocco, Jessie Gil, Mariela Barressi and Bárbara González, who broke the long periods of solitude that characterize research work and made this process less lonely. I am most grateful to my family. They helped me during the most pressing and stressful times, especially my youngest brother, Pablo, and my parents-in-law, Lalitha and Shankar. My parents, Omar and Angela, in particular, gave me academic guidance and advice. At a distance, they followed my progress, and were always prepared to talk, discuss and share my concerns and anxieties.

Without the support of Raja, this work would not have been possible. He encouraged me from the beginning to pursue a DPhil. He gave me his unconditional support in bad times and shared my accomplishments. His careful reading of my work and his comments challenged me to improve my writing and rethink my arguments. I am indebted to him for his perseverance and constant assurance. Sophia was born during my doctoral studies and experienced from early days the perils and rewards involved in this process. Both Raja and Sophia gave me their love and company, and in many instances, forced me to put aside my work and enjoy the cosiness of family life. I dedicate this book to you both.

———

The author and Routledge would like to thank Sage Journals for permission to reproduce material for which they hold copyright: a modified version of Chapter 6 originally titled 'Making People Criminal: The Role of the Criminal Law in Immigration Enforcement' (*Theoretical Criminology*, 16[4], 2012); and part of Chapter 4 originally published as 'Exploring the Function of Criminal Law in the Policing of Foreigners: The Decision to Prosecute Immigration-Related Offences' (*Social & Legal Studies*, 21[4], 2012).

Abbreviations

AA 1793	Aliens Act 1793
AA 1814	Aliens Act 1814
AA 1826	Aliens Act 1826
AA 1848	Aliens Act 1848
AA 1905	Aliens Act 1905
AIA 1996	Asylum and Immigration Act 1996
AIAA 1993	Asylum and Immigration Appeals Act 1993
AI(TC)A 2004	Asylum and Immigration (Treatment of Claimants, etc.) Act 2004
AO 1953	Aliens Order 195
APIs	Asylum Policy Instructions
ARA 1914	Aliens Restriction Act 1914
AR(A)A 1919	Aliens Restriction (Amendment) Act 1919
BCIA 2009	Borders, Citizenship and Immigration Act 2009
BIA	Border and Immigration Agency
BNP	British National Party
CAA 1981	Criminal Attempts Act 1981
CIA 1962	Commonwealth Immigrants Act 1962
CIA 1968	Commonwealth Immigrants Act 1968
CJA 2003	Criminal Justice Act 2003
CPS	Crown Prosecution Service
EC	European Community
ECHR	European Court of Human Rights
ECJ	European Court of Justice
EU	European Union
FCA 1981	Forgery and Counterfeiting Act 1981
FNP	Foreign national prisoner
FOI	Freedom of Information
HC Deb	House of Commons Debate
HL Deb	House of Lords Debate
IA 1971	Immigration Act 1971
IA 1988	Immigration Act 1988
IAA 1969	Immigration Appeals Act 1969
IAA 1999	Immigration and Asylum Act 1999
IANA 2006	Immigration, Asylum and Nationality Act 2006
IAS	Immigration Advisory Service
I(CL)A 1987	Immigration (Carrier Liability) Act 1987
ICT	Immigration Crime Team
IDCA 2006	Identity Cards Act 2006

IDIs	Immigration Directorate Instructions
IIIU	Illegal Immigration Intelligence Unit
ILPA	Immigration Law Practitioners' Association
IND	Immigration and Nationality Directorate
JCWI	Joint Council for the Welfare of Immigrants
LIT	Local Immigration Team
MP	Member of Parliament
NIAA 2002	Nationality, Immigration and Asylum Act 2002
RMJ	Refugee and Migrant Justice
SAC	Standard Acceptable Criteria
SIAC	Special Immigration Appeals Commission
SIACA 1997	Special Immigration Appeals Commission Act 1997
SOA	Sexual Offences Act 2003
UK	United Kingdom
UKBA	UK Border Agency
UKBA EI&G	UKBA Enforcement Instructions and Guidance
UN	United Nations
US	United States

1 Introduction

Background of the book

Being a foreigner today in a globalized world is perfectly normal. For many, it is much easier than it was decades ago to leave one's own country, venture into other cultures and study, work and settle in a country different from that of one's origin. It is estimated that around 214 million people currently live outside of their countries of origin, more than double the figure recorded in 1980 (United Nations 2008). In this context of global mobility, as Seyla Benhabib put it, 'individuals no longer enter their societies at birth and exit them at death' (1999: 719). As a consequence, receiving societies have not remained untouched. Along with the conflicts and tensions involved in the process of adaptation, they have become more open to accommodating newcomers and more cosmopolitan, incorporating elements of different cultures into their own (Benhabib 1999, 2002; Melossi 2003, 2005). For some foreigners, especially those who are well-off, educated and capable of quickly adapting to the vernacular society, this process is smoother than for others (Dauvergne 2004: 602). While the rapid expansion and modernization of the transnational transportation of people and goods, and the globalization of media outlets have brought different parts of the world closer and increased human mobility and communication dramatically, this process has not been equal (Aas 2011a). In fact, the experience of migration for some has become ever more difficult. While the 'best and the brightest' are still a sought-after category by countries imposing stringent controls on immigration – such as Britain[1] – many others struggle to reach the shores (Boswell 2003: 5). The images of people trying to cross the Mediterranean Sea in home-made boats, escaping political turmoil in North Africa in the first half of 2011, is but one example. Contemporary Western European societies enjoy relatively high levels of social and economic welfare and equality. Economic immigrants, refugees and expatriates are perhaps a constant reminder of an unequal world at Europe's doorsteps (Sassen 2002).

Recent practices and policies in rich countries suggest that the international mobility of people from poor regions of the globe is regarded as undesirable and to be avoided (Bigo 1994; Anderson 2000; Torpey 2000; Bigo and Guild 2005). Stronger border controls have made these journeys increasingly hazardous, exposing people to death (Weber and Pickering 2011). Even if they are seldom broadcast, their experiences of exile are dramatic and distressing.[2] So too is the reality that some of them face once they arrive in Europe. For those who manage to reach the shores, the response is to block, detain and eject them through practices that resemble those deployed by the police to punish outlaws and disorderly sections of the population. In European countries, these exclusionary policies – including the criminalization of immigration violations – are in part the result of the process of harmonization and coordination of European immigration and asylum policies, particularly after the Schengen Agreement and the Maastricht Treaty in 1985 and 1992, respectively (Bigo 2005; Sciortino and Pastore 2004; Guild and Minderhoud 2006; D'Appollonia and Reich 2008). Poor, low-skilled immigrants are increasingly considered a new underclass. As a consequence, the mechanisms and practices of the criminal justice system are being transposed onto the treatment of foreigners. In what Loïc Wacquant called the 'penal management' of foreigners, non-nationals fill the space of seclusion centres in many countries of Europe and are over-represented in their prison populations (Wacquant 2005: 40; see also Wacquant 1999, 2006; Melossi 2003; De Giorgi 2010).

This book aims at understanding the devices introduced by the British government to control the entry and stay of immigrants in the country. It examines the system of immigration enforcement and the juxtaposition of different regulatory regimes – administrative and criminal – to control immigration. Because of the transposition of the vocabulary, strategies and tools used in the criminal justice system, immigration enforcement has become increasingly hybrid, operating in between the administrative and the criminal regimes. This is what some authors have named the 'criminal administrative system' (Albrecht 2000: 146), the 'quasi-administrative, quasi-criminal' system (Pratt 2005: 23) or the 'hybrid crime/immigration system of social control' (Miller 2003: 666). I focus on a particular aspect of this system: the criminalization of immigration breaches – so-called 'immigration crimes'. 'Immigration crimes' is a category difficult to circumscribe because of its blurred contours. For analytical reasons, in this study I will consider immigration offences as those inserted in immigration and asylum legislation. These are offences purely related to one's immigration status and can be committed both by citizens and non-citizens (Demleitner and Sands 2002). I will particularly address immigration offences that can only be committed by non-nationals.

Despite the fact that the 'criminalization of immigration' as a theme is current in recent scholarly research, the formal conversion of immigration breaches into criminal offences remains under-researched – particularly in the United Kingdom (UK). This is surprising given the enlarged scholarship on immigration studies and the significant expansion of these offences in British legislation since the mid-1990s. It is also curious because the formal criminalization of immigration law is perhaps the most apparent facet of the criminalization phenomenon. In fact, it is in the proliferation of immigration crimes that the convergence of administrative and criminal regimes is becoming more visible.

Further, some of the literature on the criminalization or securitization is backed by thin empirical evidence about this phenomenon. This is probably one of the reasons why the novelty and strength of the criminalization phenomenon are often exaggerated.[3] In this research I demonstrate that while certain claims are undeniable – such as the deployment of criminal law control strategies and language in immigration enforcement – other assertions about the dramatic changes in the field of immigration and crime are quite overstated. Not only are immigration offences not new, but neither is this a generalized phenomenon. In fact, the use of criminal law against non-citizens is usually confined to specific cases, particularly when the option of executive removal is not available. Criminalization is, thus, an accidental, mundane, erratic and discretionary phenomenon rather than a planned strategy and a synchronized project to keep people behind bars.

This study is both a theoretical and empirical enquiry about the role of criminal law and the criminal justice system in the regulation of immigration. It sheds light on the unexplored field of 'criminal immigration laws' (Eagly 2010: 1297) by providing original empirical data on the decision-making process in cases involving people in breach of immigration rules and how these cases are dealt with by the criminal justice system. Theoretically, it critically analyses the function that the criminal law is called on to play in immigration enforcement. By examining immigration crimes in past and contemporary legislation, and the function they serve in present conditions, it assesses whether the justification for criminalizing immigration breaches is sound. In doing so, this study brings together recent criminal law theory and immigration studies in order to enrich the debate on criminalization in both fields.

Criminalization, immigration and 'crimmigration'

Because immigrants – and undocumented immigrants in particular – have become the main targets of state control both in public rhetoric and policy, it is not surprising that the devices to control the outsiders and marginalized within the state are increasingly applied to immigrants – including the criminal law. In this context, a number of scholars have argued that a process of 'criminalization' of immigrants and immigration policies is taking place in Western, liberal democracies (e.g. Wacquant 1999, 2005, 2006; Aas 2007; De Giorgi 2010; Cecchi 2011) – or in Juliet Stumpf's terms, 'crimmigration' (2007).[4] These authors have claimed that states are increasingly deploying the penal system – or indirectly, the representations and strategies used by the criminal justice system and its agencies – in the treatment of unwelcome foreigners. In this sense, the policies and practices that have the effect of criminalizing immigrants are partly different from purely 'restrictionist' policies – understood as those which curtail the enjoyment of rights and liberties of a particular population – in that the former appeal to criminal justice imagery, while the latter do not necessarily do so. Often, though, these policies overlap. As Jennifer Chacón (2007: 1840) showed, measures that restrict immigrants' access to health care, education and other welfare services are frequently backed by depictions of those immigrants as criminals and security threats, and are justified as crime prevention strategies (also Pratt and Valverde 2002).

Even though in strict terms the notion of 'immigrant' is broad, encompassing foreigners with different backgrounds (professional, ethnic, socio-economic, etc.), in public discourse and the media, it is increasingly circumscribed to a narrower category of non-citizens: non-white, poor, unskilled workers from developing countries. Robin Cohen (1994: 189) called this group 'third world immigrant' or 'helots'; that is, those immigrants who, in addition to being deprived of many rights enjoyed by citizens – principally, the right to vote and be elected – are in a much worse situation than other foreigners in a given receiving country because they belong to an ethnic minority, are unskilled, and are poor. The difference between foreigners coming from poor and rich countries is also manifested in the enforcement of controls over borders: states do not distribute the burden evenly. Foreigners coming from different parts of the globe are treated differently concerning formal and informal practices – visa requirements, restrictions on the right to entry and stay, enjoyment of civil rights, and judicial and extrajudicial treatment (De Giorgi 2006: 112). Further, not all 'third world' foreigners are treated alike. Katja Franko Aas (2011a: 336) pointed to a further stratification within this group, between 'crimmigrants' (suspected terrorists, people with criminal convictions, undocumented immigrants, etc.) and 'bona fide travellers' (defined as the globally privileged population). This classification is rooted in the different functions that the European Union (EU) border surveillance systems perform: while they act as a 'gate opening' for frequent flyers, they block the entry to unwanted foreigners.

As the foregoing analysis suggests, not all foreigners are 'immigrants'. Those so designated are often represented in the tabloid media as a 'dangerous' class and their social, cultural and sometimes ethnic differences in the receiving society render them as 'outsiders'. However, the link between immigration and crime is not new (Melossi 2000). As I will show in Chapter 2, in Britain, immigrants have been in many instances linked to criminality, social unrest and public disorder. Elsewhere, in the late nineteenth and early twentieth centuries, large flows of immigration – mainly Jewish, Southern European, Irish and Chinese people escaping from hunger and wars – became a great concern for receiving countries in South and North America, not only because of their numbers but also because of their origin. They were accused of bringing disorder and crime to the 'new continent', and anarchist and socialist ideas to agitate the masses. Early criminological research in countries that hosted the newcomers both in the North and the South – such as the United States (US) and Argentina – addressed this relationship, sometimes reinforcing it, at other times disputing it (Park 1928; Burgess [1925] 1967; Melossi 2002; Valier 2003; Rodriguez 2006).

Perhaps because of the long history of linking immigrants to disorder and crime, it is not surprising that current immigration policies enacted in receiving countries – particularly in the 'advanced West' – are increasingly resorting to strategies traditionally used by law enforcement agencies to deal with offenders and crime in order to control immigration (Bosworth 2007). According to the criminalization thesis, economic migrants, refugees and asylum seekers are increasingly portrayed by the media and politicians in Europe, North America and

Australia as dangerous and criminal; and as cheats and unscrupulous, seeking jobs that are scarce and benefits that they do not deserve (Pratt and Valverde 2002; Pastore 2004: 90; Pratt 2005; Broeders and Engbersen 2007: 1594). Such characterizations are being institutionalized through legislation, policies and administrative practices that seek, on the one hand, to strengthen the external borders; and on the other, to introduce ever more intrusive controls on those who manage to cross them. The first set of measures pre-emptively targets migrants before they even reach the external borders by making entry more difficult, while the second aims to ensure a smoother and easier process for spotting, punishing and removing undocumented immigrants (Weber and Bowling 2004; Weber 2007; Bosworth and Guild 2008; Bosworth 2008, 2011a).

According to Loïc Wacquant (2006: 99, italics in original), what characterizes the criminalization of immigration is 'the vastly *greater capacity and propensity of the state to deploy its penal resources* at both the national and the supranational levels to "resolve" the problems they pose or embody' and this phenomenon is crystallized in three features of contemporary immigration practices: limited legalization schemes, expanded border control, and mass deportation. He also related the over-representation of 'extra-communitarians' behind bars in European prisons in comparison to the share of foreigners in those societies to the criminalization phenomenon. This disproportion, he suggested, cannot be solely explained by higher crime rates among minority groups. In addition, other factors are at play. First, law enforcement agencies differentially target immigrants and courts apply legal standards that make it difficult for foreigners to obtain bail – such as the requirement of a stable job and residence. Second, a large number of crimes for which immigrants are confined can only be committed by non-nationals – the so-called 'immigration crimes' such as unlawful entry or overstay (Wacquant 2006: 88; see also Wacquant 2005). Likewise Alessandro De Giorgi (2010: 158, italics in original) referred to the 'unusual *intensity* of penal practices' deployed against immigrants by European states through, for example, the criminalization of immigration status.

In terms of how this 'criminalization' phenomenon concretely works, other authors have gone further by showing the different intersections between immigration and crime-control fields. Mary Bosworth (2007), for example, drew striking parallels between the confinement of immigrants and offenders in Britain. She observed that the borrowing by the British Immigration and Nationality Directorate (IND) of practices and staff from the criminal justice system ultimately reveals that immigrants are considered as actual or potential criminals. Further, both prisons and immigration detention centres operate as 'exclusionary zones' that mark the physical and symbolic borders of British society. Jonathan Simon (1998: 590) examined the systematic imprisonment of immigrants in the United States from the 1980s onwards as a response to the massive population flows from Latin America. He suggested that the use of imprisonment – a 'specialized penal system' – was a governmental strategy to regulate the global flows of people in a flexible, cost-efficient way. In what she calls 'crimmigration', Juliet Stumpf (2007: 14) noticed an overlapping of immigration law and criminal law, both in terms of substance (the type of wrongs sanctioned and the measures imposed), and in terms of the procedure followed to enforce those norms.

Others scholars have called attention to the institutional parallels in the contexts of immigration and crime control. Border patrols and other immigration authorities, which have acquired powers to detain and arrest non-citizens, are frequently involved in criminal investigations and overlap with criminal law enforcement agencies (Miller 2005: 1116; see also Tumlin 2004). Similarly, the police perform tasks that go beyond crime control and include immigration controls (Bigo 2005: 83). Other authors (Bloch and Schuster 2005; Gibney and Hansen 2003; Gibney 2008) have documented the extensive use and the 'normalization' of deportation and detention to control immigration, and the 'outsourcing' of these controls to private actors. For instance, in the US, Huyen Pham (2008, 2009) noted that a number of laws make the requirement of proof of legal immigration status paramount not only for crossing the borders, but also for enjoying a range of rights and benefits once inside the country. Concomitantly, they impose on private parties a duty to check entitlement to these rights and benefits, thus burdening transportation companies, employers and landlords with immigration enforcement tasks.

As part of the criminalization of immigration, other authors have discerned a link between tougher immigration regulations and anti-terrorism measures. They state that the terrorist acts in Western countries – notably in New York, Washington, DC, London and Madrid – and the measures put forth afterwards reinforced this relationship (Tumlin 2004; Miller 2005; D'Appollonia 2008; D'Appollonia and Reich 2008). In the same line, Aas (2007: 288) explained that the link between immigration and terrorism was reinforced after the 9/11 attacks with the consequence of an increase in deportations of foreigners and the extensive use of cross-border surveillance networks on immigrants (Aas 2011a, 2011b). With specific reference to the European Union, Didier Bigo (2005: 75) considered that the measures to close the borders and to keep out third-country nationals illustrate the attempt by European bureaucrats to control what is considered a chaotic outside. Immigrants from the 'third world' are depicted as potential offenders and thus those measures seek pre-emptively to eliminate the risk they embody (Bigo 2005: 88). These measures, Bigo explained, were toughened by post-9/11 counter-terrorism policies as terrorism, organized crime and illegal immigration were placed together as a continuum of security threats (Bigo 1994: 164).

The impact that counter-terrorism measures has had in recent legislative reforms and public debates on immigration in Western Europe should not be over-stated, though. Since the 1980s, such countries have sought to limit immigration – a trend reinforced by the 'Europeanization' of immigration policies. Restrictive policies, then, have not been solely generated after the attacks, but rather there has been continuity in the line of policies enacted by these European states.[5] Neither at the public discourse level nor at the policy-making one is there enough evidence to affirm that terrorism has had an impact on how states deal with immigrants (Boswell 2007, 2008; see also Neal 2009). Further, the control of immigrants is mostly exercised through measures that are not directly linked to counter-terrorism. At least in Britain, there is a greater concern reflected in the government's policy papers about law breaking (particularly immigration law violations) and social disorder, the abuse of welfare services by those who do not contribute to the tax system, and the disruptive impact that the arrival of large groups of migrants may have in local communities. In their analysis of parliamentary debates on immigration policies after the terrorist attacks, Jef Huysmans and Alessandra Buonfino (2008) found that immigration is often linked to security through a more mundane and managerial discourse about deviance, incivilities and minor offences in order to justify restrictions on immigration (also Huysmans 2006). In the American context, where the link between immigration and terrorism seems clearer, Chacón (2007, 2008) considered that post-9/11 immigration measures merely continued restrictive measures of the preceding decade. While attempts to strengthen border controls allegedly for national security purposes after the attacks did not result in an increase in the removal of non-citizens on security grounds, they boosted the removals related to crime and immigration controls (Chacón 2007: 1875; see also Demleitner 2004: 567).

The body of work reviewed above has encouraged a fruitful debate about the different ways in which immigration and criminal regimes are converging to police non-nationals, in what Leanne Weber and Benjamin Bowling (2004: 195) have called an 'emerging punitive regulatory system'. While some of this literature is rich with rhetoric, it falls short on a detailed, legal analysis of the 'symptoms' of the criminalization trend. Particularly in Britain, there is not much work done on the reliance on criminal law to enforce immigration norms, despite the increase of these offences since the mid-1990s. Some scholars have called attention to the existence of immigration offences in Britain and other European countries, and the parallel system of administrative and criminal sanctions for dealing with immigration offenders (e.g. Albrecht 2000: 147; Weber and Bowling 2004: 204; Wacquant 2006: 88; Zedner 2010: 381; De Giorgi 2010: 158). Apart from the literature on trafficking in human beings and illegal employment,[6] there are few academic works dealing with the formal criminalization of immigration breaches and their enforcement.

On the other side of the Atlantic, US scholars have paid more attention to this phenomenon. Some years ago, Maria Isabel Medina (1997) examined the criminalization of unauthorized labour and marriage fraud. She assessed that enforcement agencies and US society are morally ambivalent about these offences and this attitude may explain their low enforcement. Teresa Miller (2003) documented the increased enactment and enforcement of immigration crimes since the mid-1980s – particularly illegal entry and illegal working – (see also Morris 1997; Chacón 2007: 1837; Stumpf 2007: 16). In a recent article, Stumpf (2009) traced the history of immigration-related sanctions in US legislation and showed that these offences are older than sometimes thought, even though they were seldom enforced. They can be found in laws of the late eighteenth century. She also noted that removal and deportation are relatively new immigration sanctions. Instead, 'criminal penalties including incarceration, fines and hard labor were the first tools the US Congress chose to enforce its new immigration laws' until the turn of the twentieth century (Stumpf 2009: 1711). While the enforcement of immigration offences remains relatively low compared to the large number of undocumented migrants caught by enforcement agencies, some authors have evidenced a steady rise in the number of prosecutions for these offences in recent years, along with the increase in the number of these offences (Demleitner and Sands 2002: 247; Legomsky 2007: 479; also Coutin 2005).

This work takes the literature on the criminalization of immigration as a starting point. My purpose is to enrich this debate by focusing on a particular aspect of the criminalization of immigration: the formal conversion of immigration/administrative violations into crimes and their enforcement. In addition, this research contributes to the expansion of the topics of enquiry in criminal law and criminology. Criminal law scholars have concentrated on the criminal justice system and institutions. Along with others (Garland 2001; Ericson 2007; Simon 2007; Bosworth 2008; Aas 2012; Valverde 2010), I consider that as societies change their 'control cultures', the themes of contemporary criminological and criminal law research should be expanded to explain those changes.

Content and structure of the book

This book consists of six chapters and a conclusion. A discussion of the methodology used is provided in the Appendix to the book. Chapter 2 describes the foundations of Britain's immigration controls from the late eighteenth century to the 1990s. It traces the first sets of regulations in the construction of the British immigration system and its development in the twentieth century in order to understand the origins of and rationale for recent policies. It shows that since the 1790s, criminal law provisions have been introduced to enforce immigration legislation. Unfortunately there is limited empirical evidence of their actual use. It also illustrates the harsh controls imposed over foreigners through war-time legislation and the progressive expansion of the category of 'exclusionable aliens' to cover Commonwealth citizens. Post-war years were dominated by the debate on how to manage Britain's colonial past and restrict migration from former, poor colonies to the UK. The government's immigration imperatives shifted in the 1980s following growing concerns about an influx of asylum seekers. The chapter shows that criminal law had a symbolic as well as a practical role in the drawing of national boundaries and the policing of non-citizens.

In Chapter 3, I analyse the proliferation of 'immigration crimes' in British legislation and their enforcement, particularly since the mid-1990s. The White Paper *Fairer, Faster and Firmer* (Home Office 1998) announced an integral overhaul of the British immigration system and set the tone for subsequent reforms. I take it as a base to analyse the multiple reforms of the system during Labour's 13-year tenure. I identify three main features of this period. First, there was a huge expansion of immigration legislation including the growth of the catalogue of immigration crimes. Second, there was an enhanced and more systematic enforcement of such legislation and a greater reliance on the criminal justice system. Third, I map an institutional convergence between criminal and immigration enforcement with the creation of a police-like immigration enforcement agency – the UK Border Agency (UKBA). These policy developments sought to tackle abuses in the asylum system and address loopholes in the enforcement of immigration controls during a period in which the border force and the immigration system as a whole were subject to increased public pressure to deliver.

Chapters 4 and 5 look at how the criminal–immigration system works in practice. These chapters draw on empirical data from records and hearings at criminal courts, and interviews with key actors in the enactment and practice of immigration legislation. Interviews conducted with practitioners and policy makers show that many of the numerous immigration-related crimes on the books are barely enforced (such as overstaying, illegal entry, obstruction or assault of an immigration officer, etc.) and when caught, offenders are still often administratively removed rather than criminally prosecuted. On the other hand, the examination of court cases reveals that a handful of these offences are prosecuted in certain circumstances and against certain offenders, and that criminalization is a relatively frequent experience for some (undocumented) immigrants.

Chapter 4 analyses the decision to prosecute immigration offenders. Enforcement officers have a number of options when dealing with breaches of immigration laws. They can treat the matter as a criminal or as an administrative case. This chapter shows that in the absence of clear guidelines, immigration officers and the police have broad margins of discretion in the decision to proceed against immigration offenders. Because there is no legal constraint on the use of criminal law powers, practical considerations are generally taken into account in this decision. One of the most important factors is whether or not the offender can be summarily removed from the country. When this is not an option, criminal prosecution often follows. The practice of prosecuting undocumented migrants is then contrasted with policy statements which emphasize that criminal law should be reserved for the most harmful and serious crimes. This chapter shows that criminal law in the immigration field is used instrumentally. It serves the goals and imperatives of immigration enforcement of restricting and excluding those with no right to be in Britain. As such, its primary function of censuring serious wrongs is disrupted.

Once a criminal prosecution is initiated, the normal criminal process follows. In Chapter 5, I examine those immigration crime cases predominantly reaching the criminal justice system. I look at whether and how the immigration case and the immigration status of the defendant influence the criminal case. I analyse the handling of these cases by defence lawyers and prosecutors. In particular, I notice that exemptions to punishment based on the asylum or immigration background of the defendant are barely raised and defendants are often advised to plead guilty. Conversely, the immigration status of the defendant is central to the bail determination and to the choice of sanction if convicted, as people with weak ties to the country and with irregular status are inexorably refused bail and punished with custodial sentences. Because immigration defendants are subject to a bureaucratic-like process characterized by short hearings – a cursory examination of the facts and the mechanical application of the law – the complexities of these cases are obscured, individual suffering is erased and the imposition of sanctions goes largely uncontested.

In Chapter 6, I explain the causes and consequences of the use of criminal law in immigration enforcement. I discuss the origins of the use of criminal law for regulatory purposes and how this 'legal tradition' of backing non-penal norms with criminal sanctions has had an effect on the contemporary criminalization of immigration laws. I argue that the reproduction of criminal provisions in immigration laws in recent years is as much a result of the attempt by the British government to reassert its sovereign powers to control non-citizens as an outcome of the pragmatic and strategic use of criminal law in everyday enforcement practices. The first explanation points to the deployment of criminal regulation for expressive purposes – to be seen as having immigration flows under control. The second one is far from the high world of 'grand politics' and grounded in the everyday practice of immigration controls. The expansion of immigration crimes is explained as a necessary outcome of a dual system of immigration and criminal sanctions which is driven by convenience and efficiency. In this latter perspective, criminalization is motivated by an instrumental logic which conceives criminal law as an additional tool with which to enforce compliance with administrative norms. I then assess the consequences of the criminalization of immigration legislation and the role of criminal punishment in the policing of non-citizens, and show that the normative justification of punishment in these cases remains weak.

The concluding section of the book reflects on the nature of criminal sanctions attached to immigration breaches and the consequences of using criminal law for immigration control purposes. Criminal offences have been historically considered a necessary corollary of immigration enforcement. They back immigration powers and are conceived of as an additional means of intervention. The sanctions attached to immigration breaches are, however, not merely regulatory. The ultimate goal behind the use of criminal punishment against immigrants is their expulsion. As such, there is a distinctive rationale at play which is neither purely regulatory nor purely punitive. Criminal law serves immigration policy objectives by supporting enforcement officers in their work, particularly in the expulsion of unwelcome foreigners. So too is the punishment of immigration transgressors driven by the goal of bringing down unwanted immigration rather than aimed at punishing serious wrongs. The role of criminal law in this context is strictly related to the prerogatives of the state to exclude non-members, and can only be understood if criminal law is considered as part of the assemblage of the hybrid system of penal/administrative regulation. The distinctive function of criminal sanctions in the immigration field is thus to increase the flexibility and to widen the reach of immigration controls. Beyond this categorization, criminalizing immigration breaches and bringing immigration into the criminal justice forum make possible the bypassing of limiting criminal law principles – such as proportionality, last resort and harm – and certain due process protections, and contribute to the expansion of criminal regulation. These issues also cast doubts upon the instrumentality of the criminalization approach to achieve immigration control imperatives.

This work will help readers to understand how the exercise of the state's sovereign powers – to control who enters and stays, and to punish – are becoming blurred, and what the consequences of this blurring are. In liberal democracies, these sovereign powers have been progressively restricted by human rights norms and standards. However, there are still 'rightless zones' where those rules are not fully available to non-citizens, and this book will shed light on these. In the next chapter, I look at the history of the British immigration system and show that from early days, criminal law was an important enforcement tool to control population flows. That system, which heavily relied on criminal law and punishment, became the foundation for the regulation of immigration for decades to come.

2 Tracing the history of immigration controls in Britain (from the late 1700s to the mid-1990s)

Britain has a long and established history of immigration. It has been a point of arrival for people from many latitudes, cultures and places. French insurgents, Jews, Irish, Polish, old and new Commonwealth citizens have all arrived at different times and in large numbers. Britain has one of the largest migrant resident and naturalized populations in Europe, and is still an important destination for asylum seekers (Gibney and Hansen 2003). This chapter traces the first pieces in the construction of the British immigration system and its development in the twentieth century in order to understand the origins of and rationale for recent policies. I will, therefore, provide a brief historical background of immigration legislation and debates before discussing more recent policies in this field. British immigration legislation, since the early twentieth century, established harsh controls over non-nationals and continuously expanded the category of 'exclusionable' foreigners. In contrast to the more widely accepted view in criminology (e.g. Albrecht 2000; Miller 2003; Wacquant 2006; De Giorgi 2010; Sklansky 2012), I will demonstrate that the criminalization of migration is not new. Immigration-related offences or 'immigration crimes' – some of them punishable by imprisonment – have been incorporated in immigration statutes since the late 1700s.

The development of British immigration controls

> *[A]nd the East End of London was being swamped by aliens who were coming in like an army of locusts, eating up the native population or turning them out.*[1]

In the late eighteenth century, there was an influx of French *émigrés* to Britain, following the radicalization of the French Revolution which led to the formation in France of the Committee of Public Safety during the 'Reign of Terror'. The British government suspected that many of those French people were involved in the Revolution and feared that they would advocate for 'atheist' and 'anarchist' ideas once in Britain (Troup 1925: 142; Cohen 1994: 41). As a response, in 1793, Parliament passed the Aliens Act (AA 1793).[2] This is the first act authorizing the executive to exclude foreigners from the country during peace time (Dinwiddy 1968). Furthermore, the act included a plethora of sanctions to be imposed against 'aliens'[3] who failed to comply with regulations regarding their entry to and residence in the country. It contained rules on their landing, their registration, their residence and their obligation to carry a passport issued by the British authorities. It not only imposed fines ranging from £10 to £100 on masters or commanders of ships and vessels and on 'housekeepers of dwelling houses' who in any way failed to comply with those rules. It also subjected foreigners in breach of those rules to detention and imprisonment upon conviction. For instance, foreigners who did not exhibit their passports when so requested were liable to up to a month in prison if convicted for that crime, and were ordered to depart from the kingdom at the expiration of the sentence. In the case of non-compliance with such an order, convicted foreigners were liable to be 'transported for life'.[4] Alternatively, foreigners accused of such an offence could be 'discharged' or directed to depart from the country.[5] The act also punished non-compliance with the sentence of transportation for life with the death penalty:

> [I]n case any Person ordered or adjudged to be transported, shall be found at large within this Realm after Sentence of Transportation [is] pronounced, he shall be guilty of Felony, and shall suffer Death as a Felon; without Benefit of Clergy.[6]

At the time there was no organized police force so the enforcement of the act was left to magistrates (Troup 1925: 142).

Although it was passed as a temporary law, the AA 1793 was renewed by subsequent acts until 1826 when it was allowed to lapse. After the French wars, the British government started to use its power to deport foreigners more sporadically. Moreover, such power was subject to mounting criticisms by the opposition who claimed that it placed foreigners 'at the mercy of the executive' (Dinwiddy 1968: 207). The main target of the critics was the deportation power contained in the act. By contrast, the introduction of criminal sanctions against foreigners and 'third parties' attracted less condemnation. In fact, although the AA 1793 was repealed in 1826, already the Aliens Act 1814 (AA 1814) contained some of these offences.

Legislation on the entry and residence of foreign nationals passed during the nineteenth century incorporated further criminal offences.[7] While they did not constitute a comprehensive system of controls, these laws established a set of rules to govern 'aliens' and formed the legal basis for the system of immigration controls in the early twentieth century. Under these rules, illegal entrants were subject to arrest and detention without bail.[8] The master of a vessel faced criminal punishment if he neglected or refused to make a declaration, or made a false declaration, about whether he had any 'alien' on board and if such a foreigner had disembarked in the country.[9] Other provisions relating to control over the arrival of non-nationals, their whereabouts once in the country and their exit from British territory punished any breach with a fine or imprisonment. These rules established a system of registration of foreigners with the police.[10] Foreigners were obliged to state in a written document – a certificate, declaration or proclamation – their place of residence during their stay in the country. Refusing or neglecting to make a statement or making a false one or 'knowingly and willingly dwelling or residing or being found to be or having been' in a different place, in breach of their established residence, constituted a criminal offence punished with fines of up to £50 or imprisonment of up to six months.[11]

An offence penalizing any forgery of a residence certificate, a passport or other documents was also part of this catalogue, as was overstaying, which was subject to two months' imprisonment.[12] Residents in the country for seven years or more, or foreigners under 14 years old, were exempted from these provisions. Similarly, people who were not allowed to remain or disembark in the country, or were found in the UK contrary to any such order, were subject to arrest without bail until they were 'sent out'. In case of return without authorization, a person could be convicted and 'transported for life'. The penalty for the first offence was up to one month of imprisonment and for the second, up to two months. Authorities had the option of deciding whether the convicted person should be imprisoned or sent out.[13] In cases where the person to be expelled was considered dangerous to the security of the country, detention without time limits was authorized.[14]

The Aliens Act 1848 (AA 1848) 'to authorize for One Year, and to the End of the then next Session of Parliament, the Removal of Aliens from the Realm' permitted for that limited period the 'removal' of foreigners from the country if authorities had reasons to believe that this was necessary for the 'Preservation of the Peace and Tranquillity'. Failure to comply with such an order constituted a misdemeanour and carried for the first offence imprisonment of up to one month, and for subsequent offences, imprisonment of up to 12 months.[15]

A brief review of late eighteenth- and nineteenth-century legislation shows how widespread the criminalization of immigration laws was. Perhaps because of the absence of a comprehensive system of immigration control, criminal law was a key enforcement tool in the regulation of immigration to Britain. While the existence of these criminal law provisions on the books does not necessarily mean that they were enforced in practice, the number and variety of offences included in immigration laws reveal an early reliance on the criminal law in this field. Even though data about the use of criminal powers are not available,[16] between the mid-nineteenth and early twentieth century, Britain witnessed a period of lax controls over foreigners when powers of expulsion were seldom used against them. Bernard Porter (1979: 4) described Victorian Britain as a period in which 'the British government deliberately denied itself any control over immigration, and appeared indeed for the most part to take no interest in it' (see also Craies 1890: 39; Feldman 2003: 167).

The first system of controls to restrict the arrival and settlement of foreign populations was created in 1905. Prompted by the enforcement of the May Laws of 1882 by Czar Alexander III, a number of Jews were expelled from Russia and Eastern Europe. Many went to the UK. The arrival of Jewish immigrants was not without controversy. Confrontation and xenophobic expressions from the general public and the press were widespread. As a consequence, the government appointed a Royal Commission on Immigration to work on a proposal for a bill

(Holmes 1988: 73; Dummett and Nicol 1990: 102). The outcome of the Royal Commission's work formed the basis for the Aliens Act 1905 (AA 1905), the first comprehensive legislation on immigration controls. Parliamentary debates on the bill concentrated on the problems that aliens – particularly Polish Jews – caused to the native population in terms of overcrowded housing, unemployment rates and labour competition, the reliance on public services by the poor among them, and their impact on crime rates and the expansion of sweating diseases. There was also a concern among Members of Parliament (MPs) about the country being used 'as the refuse heap of the whole of Europe' with reference to the provisions in the bill recognizing the right to request refuge in Britain.[17]

The act stipulated that non-British subjects – or 'alien immigrants' – might only cross the borders through specific ports and that authorized immigration officers could deny entry to those considered 'undesirable', and entitled the Secretary of State to issue an expulsion order against them.[18] This law, however, was not systematically enforced and few were denied entry or expelled after arrival (Pellew 1989: 384). The AA 1905 also incorporated criminal sanctions against immigration violations. It penalized the unauthorized landing of an immigrant, being found in the UK in contravention of an expulsion order, and making a false statement or representation to an immigration officer, medical inspector, immigration board, or to the Secretary of State,[19] among others. Penalties ranged from fines to a term of imprisonment and hard labour. A foreigner landing in contravention of the act was 'deemed a rogue and vagabond within the meaning of the Vagrancy Act, 1824, and [was] liable to be dealt with accordingly as if the offence were an offence under the section four of that Act'.[20] The sanction prescribed by the Vagrancy Act was confinement in a house of correction with hard work for up to three months.

In an early example of the regulation of carriers' liability, the act also punished ship masters who allowed the unauthorized landing of foreigners or failed to comply with an order to return them.[21] Ship masters were liable to pay a fine for bringing 'undesirables' to the British shores and were obliged to pay the costs of their return.[22] Only third-class or 'steerage passengers' were subject to these controls. By contrast, 'cabin passengers' were exempted from them (Pellew 1989: 373). The act was harshly criticized by the opposition because it imposed stringent controls over foreigners, and it was disliked by the government itself because it was deemed ineffective. Even though it established the Aliens Inspectorate to control the ports of entry, it was claimed that passengers very easily managed to evade entry controls (Troup 1925: 144).

A few years later, the outbreak of the First World War and a wave of displaced people throughout Europe prepared the ground for further legislation. In 1914, Parliament passed the Aliens Restriction Act (ARA 1914), first enacted as an emergency law during wartime. This act imposed a number of restrictions on foreigners who, in order to be admitted, had to possess permits issued by the Secretary of State.[23] It was particularly directed at enemy aliens – most notably spies. Under its provisions, a significant number of Germans living in Britain were deported.[24] The act granted the Home Secretary a wide range of powers to deport foreigners and control their movements while in British territory: prohibition from landing and imposition of restrictions or conditions on landing or on arrival; prohibition from embarking; requirements to reside and remain within a particular area or district; prohibition from residing or remaining in particular areas; requirement to register with the police, etc.[25] Failure to comply with such rules carried a fine of up to £100 or imprisonment for up to six months with or without hard labour. The exercise of these powers was not subject to appeal or review by the courts. So great were the powers conferred to the executive that an MP expressed astonishment: 'I find it hard to imagine any more absolute police power given over individuals than that which we are being asked to enable the Government to have by that Act'.[26]

The ARA 1914 was extended by one year after the end of the war by the Aliens Restriction (Amendment) Act 1919 (AR(A)A 1919). Though this act was initially passed as a temporary, exceptional measure, it was extended by annual expiring laws continuance acts until 1971 – when Parliament passed permanent legislation. The AR(A)A 1919 was aimed at regulating foreigners who were already in the UK, rather than their entry. In terms of criminal offences in section 13, the act incorporated two very broad provisions which criminalized any contravention or failure to comply with the act 'or of any order or rules made or conditions imposed thereunder', as well as assisting, abetting or harbouring those in contravention. In 1920, an order under this act authorized the Secretary of State to deport a foreigner if his or her presence in the country was not 'conducive to the public good', even if the person had never been subject to investigation or questioned before (Gordon 1985; Cohen 1994: 46); however, this power was exercised only under exceptional circumstances (Bloch and Schuster 2005: 494). People who were denied entry were detained while awaiting removal. At that time, there were no special facilities, so foreigners were confined in prisons (Cohen 1994: 108). The order, amended by Order of 12 March 1923 and Order of 11 August 1931, also incorporated the offence of 'being an alien to whom leave to land in the United Kingdom has been refused was found in the United Kingdom'.[27]

In 1953, the Aliens Order (AO 1953) replaced and consolidated the provisions on immigration controls, incorporating the requirement of work permits for those foreigners wishing to seek employment in Britain (Newsam 1954: 100; Gordon 1985: 11). This order also introduced a number of immigration-related criminal offences through a broad provision similar to that in the AR(A)A 1919. The reliance on the criminal law and its institutions to enforce immigration rules during the period reviewed was never subject to question, and it was considered as an inherent attribute of any legislation in order to be properly enforced.

Between the enactment of the AR(A)A 1919 and 1971, the entry and residence of foreigners into Britain were almost entirely regulated by orders in council over which Parliament exercised very limited review and scrutiny. Neither were the courts prepared to question the exercise of executive powers (Evans 1983: 10).[28] Until 1969, refusals of leave to enter and deportation orders were not subject to any appeal. While the AA 1905 provided for an appeal process against those decisions, it was suspended in 1914. Review was reinstituted in 1955, but it had a limited scope (Dummett and Nicol 1990: 152). Thus, emergency regulation which extended for over 50 years with limited judicial or parliamentary checks created a whole category of persons whose liberty was almost entirely subject to the discretion of the executive. When the need for permanent legislation was discussed in Parliament in relation to the AO 1953, the government representative Hugh Lucas-Tooth recognized that while the regulation of non-citizens by yearly renewable orders was 'an anomaly', it 'does not create practical difficulties and it has produced a flexible and useful piece of machinery' and he justified it as needed in a still unstable world.[29] While many MPs demanded an Act of Parliament, they had to wait almost two decades to see it passed.

The legislation that regulated the entry to and residence of foreigners in Britain in the nineteenth and early twentieth centuries bears some resemblance to the laws to control the 'outsiders within' – so-called 'poor laws' such as the laws of settlement and the vagrancy laws. The first ones imposed residence requirements in order to be eligible for 'pauper relief' and authorized the removal from a parish of unwelcome sojourners. Established during the seventeenth century, these laws inhibited the physical mobility of the 'working poor' in order to prevent a large influx of poor people – likely to be unemployed and thus a social burden – into more prosperous parishes (Taylor 1976: 55; Snell 1992: 152). Another example of the control of lower-class migration in early modern England can be found in the vagrancy laws against those who lacked permanent settlement and means of subsistence, many of whom were victims of restrictive settlement laws (Slack 1974). Vagrancy laws punished vagabonds for a broad set of loosely defined conducts – begging, idleness and moving from one place to another. Vagrants ranged from labourers in search of employment, casual workers and 'professional' tramps. Runaway apprentices and servants, and the Irish[30] were among the most noticeable groups caught by vagrancy laws (Slack 1974: 365; Feldman 2003: 173). Those deemed to be vagrants were placed in 'casual wards' where they were obliged to work and provided with shelter and food. Social relief was granted in order to prevent them from turning to criminality, begging or starvation, and thus it was a form of suppressing disruptive behaviour (Vorspan 1977). In view of the similarities between the poor laws and early immigration norms, it is no coincidence that the first comprehensive immigration legislation in 1905 penalized the unauthorized landing of immigrants with the penalties imposed on 'rogues and vagabonds' and vagrancy was one of the grounds for expulsion of foreigners from the British Isles.

Nineteenth- and early twentieth-century legislation gave government officials substantial powers over non-citizens and remained the same – except for minor changes – until the Immigration Act 1971 (IA 1971). Those provisions which had been envisaged for wartime remained in place well after the end of the war to ensure tight regulation of certain foreigners. By the mid-1950s, immigrants from Commonwealth countries, over whom British officials had little control, started to arrive in large numbers. In the post-war period, a number of reforms targeted the rights of Commonwealth citizens; these substantially modified their status as British subjects and the *laissez-faire* policy towards them.

Citizenship in post-war Britain from 1945 to 1960

[I]f the skins of the Irish had been green instead of white, they would have met a similar reception as the Asians are meeting today.[31]

Citizens of the British Empire and Great Britain were considered British subjects with equal rights under the protection of the Crown. However, due to the independence of many former British colonies and the decision by the Canadian government in 1946 to create a Canadian citizenship independent of the British one, it became increasingly important to differentiate between the independent Commonwealth countries, on the one hand, and Britain and its colonies, on the other. Therefore, the British Nationality Act 1948 (BNA 1948) introduced the category of 'Citizens of the United Kingdom and Colonies' (CUKC), while the independent Commonwealth countries adopted their own national citizenship. This was, however, just a formal distinction between the two. In fact, both UK citizens and Commonwealth citizens remained British subjects[32] – and thus British citizens – entitled until 1962 to enter freely and reside in the UK (Cohen 1994: 6; Hansen 2000). This *laissez-faire* policy, one of the most generous and liberal immigration policies in the world (Freeman 1994: 297), which allowed around one-quarter of the globe's population unrestricted rights to enter and stay in the 'mother country', was never aimed at attracting Commonwealth citizens and even less those from 'new' Commonwealth countries; i.e. from South Asia, Africa and the Caribbean. It sought, rather, to remedy the 'legal inconsistency' resulting from the introduction of Canada's citizenship, to preserve the well-regarded relationship with the Dominions and to prevent any nationalist outbreak in the former colonies (Hansen 2000: 37).

After the Second World War, in search of workers to rebuild British cities and re-establish the industrial sector, the government launched the European Volunteer Workers programme. This programme, though, was limited in scope and imposed restrictions on residence and family reunification rights. Faced with labour shortages, employers often turned to workers from Commonwealth countries who were free from these restrictions (Sivanandan 1976; Kay and Miles 1988). As a consequence, the number of citizens from the new Commonwealth rose significantly: from 3,000 in 1953 to 46,800 in 1956 and to 136,400 in 1961.[33] In 1952 and 1953, immigrants from the West Indies barely exceeded 2,000. In 1954, the total number rose to 9,000 and in 1961 to over 74,000. After that, the number started to fall. Similarly, the number of immigrants from the Indian subcontinent increased from around 11,000 in 1955 to between 70,000 and 100,000 by the early 1960s. After that, it declined to a total figure of 27,000. In the 1960s, the Indian subcontinent was the main source of non-white immigration (Tranter 1996: 30). Figure 2.1 (below) shows the gross increase of new Commonwealth immigration: from 1951 (202,000) to 1961 (571,000) it almost tripled. In 1971, the figure was 1.2 million – more than double the number in 1961 .

While newly arrived migrant workers from former colonies had in theory the same civil and political rights as British nationals, they occupied a subordinate position in employment compared to (white) British workers and were subject to

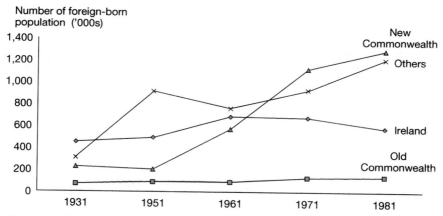

Figure 2.1 Birthplace of foreign-born population in England and Wales (1931–1981)
Source: Coleman and Salt (1992: Table 12.1). Reprinted with permission.

discrimination (Wrench 2000). Sections of the native population were concerned about these immigration flows. Until then, immigrants to Britain were predominantly white Anglo-Saxons and Europeans (Hampshire 2005: 10).[34] Non-white, non-European immigration was considered by many to be undesirable due to fears about the integration of newcomers, and because it was thought to undermine white racial hegemony and generate a range of social problems (crime, social unrest, unemployment and housing shortages, etc.) (Layton-Henry 1992: 28). It should be remembered, however, that before the arrival of people from the former colonies, the Irish and Jews met with similar hostile reaction from the locals. Even though they were white, they were considered to be ethnic minorities and were treated as racially different from the British/Protestant population (Dummett and Nicol 1990; Cohen 1994: 11, 41; Hickman 1998). Further, the assumption that non-white immigration to Britain was homogeneous neglects the differences between the multiple groups in terms of language, religion, education, economic and social position, and political culture. For example, because of their closer ties to Britain, Afro-Caribbean groups were less culturally diverse than South Asian ones from India, Pakistan and Bangladesh, and the former adapted more easily to Britain (Smith 2005: 67).

Immigration from the new Commonwealth to the UK thus generated public disaffection, prompting the government to adopt restrictive measures (Layton-Henry 1992: 36; Hansen 2000; Weber and Bowling 2004: 196).[35] As a response, the government initially tried to discourage these immigration flows from the former colonies through informal controls, such as information campaigns and controls over passports in the sending countries. In 1950, the Labour government established a special committee in charge of 'finding ways which might be adopted to check the immigration into this country of coloured people from British colonial territories'.[36] This committee concluded that such restrictions were not necessary as the numbers were too small to need to adopt legislative measures. So a decision was held up (Layton-Henry 1992: 30; Carter *et al.* 1996). Successive Conservative administrations faced the same dilemma.

Within the cabinet, there were opposing views and interests on the proposal of restricting the rights to entry to Commonwealth citizens. One of the main concerns – articulated most strongly by the Colonial Office in charge of foreign relations between Britain and the Commonwealth – was that a restrictionist approach would disregard the historical ties that linked Britain to its former colonies and damage diplomatic and economic relations with them. Additionally, within the Conservative Party there was a wing which favoured maintaining strong relations with the 'Old Dominions', and accepted as a necessary – but less desired – consequence the right to enter of new Commonwealth citizens, as a differentiation between the two groups was politically and morally unacceptable (Hansen 2000: 55). For example, in the Commonwealth Affairs Committee, the Chief Whip stated: 'Why should mainly loyal . . . and hard-working Jamaicans be discriminated against when ten times that quantity of disloyal . . . Southern Irish . . . come and go as they please?' (quoted in Carter *et al.* 1987: 8). On the other hand, a number of MPs – particularly those from constituencies with many newcomers – were concerned about the increasing number of British subjects coming from the former colonies and pushed for immigration reforms. The same position was held by the Ministry of Labour, which favoured a controlled policy towards admitting migrant workers.

The riots in Notting Hill and Nottingham in 1958 put the issue of racial discrimination and public outrage in the national spotlight (Panayi 1996; Paul 1997). These were racially motivated riots against Afro-Caribbeans residing in West London and Nottingham, organized by gangs of white, working-class youth with the slogan of 'Keep Britain White'. While there had been a number of isolated events against non-white British before, these are considered among the most violent riots in British history and illustrated the increasing tensions between white and ethnic minority groups at the time. In recently released police witness statements from an internal police enquiry on the Notting Hill riots, a policeman recounted that around 300 to 400 white people were shouting, 'We will kill all black bastards. Why don't you send them home?' Another official was told by this mob: 'Mind your own business, coppers. Keep out of it. We will settle these niggers our way. We'll murder the bastards' (quoted in Travis 2002a: n.p.).

Some MPs responded by proposing barriers against newcomers based on the argument that the arrival of people from different cultures generated unrest and instigated violence in the native population (Solomos 1989; Layton-Henry 1992: 39). Thus, in order to ensure harmonious racial relations, they argued that the number of Commonwealth citizens coming to Britain should be controlled. Labelled the 'numbers game' thesis (Solomos 1989; Cohen 1994; Layton-Henry 1994: 275; Hansen 2000), this approach gained currency within the cabinet in the early 1960s. While a minority of MPs – among others Enoch Powell, Peter Griffiths and Cyril Osborne – made incendiary speeches in favour of limiting entry to newcomers of alien cultures, their proposals permeated and contributed to shaping the immigration policies of both mainstream parties. Enoch Powell, a Conservative MP, advocated tighter controls and re-emigration, and is (in)famous for his 'rivers of blood' speech of 1968 where he warned about the transformation of the fabric of British society by the inflow of an 'alien element' into the country. Even if he was viewed with disdain in the Conservative Party (Hansen 2000: 73) and widely condemned inside the House of Commons, many of his colleagues also supported restrictions. Because of his support from a large section of the working-class electorate, Powell's rhetoric was taken up by others, albeit in a tempered fashion, in subsequent electoral campaigns.

Post-colonial immigration legislation in Britain was strongly dominated by fears of social fragmentation. Politicians worried about the impact on a predominantly white Britain of the arrival of people from different races, with different languages, customs and cultures, and the future of Britain as a multi-ethnic society. The racial issue was connected to other social and economic concerns about the pressures that newcomers might pose on housing, the welfare system and employment, and the social tensions arising at the community level in a period of steady increase of unemployment, as shown in Figure 2.2 below.

In the early 1960s, Britain experienced an economic recession which ended the era of prosperity driven by economic growth and full employment that characterized the post-war years and which set the base for the emergence of Britain as an 'affluent society' (Lowe 2005: 110). The economic downturn unleashed a political, social and cultural crisis, and exposed social divisions and inequalities (Seldon 1994; Fraser 2000). As Kenneth Morgan described it, from 1961 'paternalist one-nation Tory Britain began to sink into various forms of

Percentage unemployed

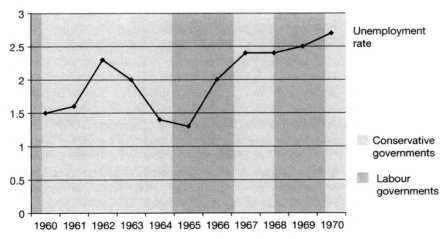

Figure 2.2 Unemployment rate in Britain between 1960 and 1970

Source: Global Financial Data. Available at http://www.globalfinancialdata.com/index. html (accessed 9 March 2011).

disarray'[37] (Morgan 2001: 198). In this socio-economic context, newly arrived immigrants encountered a hostile environment where allegations of 'parasitism' became prevalent. By the mid-1950s, negative coverage in the press contributed to generalize the view that Commonwealth citizens were taking advantage of the welfare system and represented a charge on public funds (Hampshire 2005: 96).

While the race issue is no doubt key to understanding this period and the response by the government, it is also important to consider these other factors which were closely related to race and on many occasions were used to veil the latter. Together they contributed to generate restrictionist immigration policies. During parliamentary debates on the 1962 Commonwealth Immigrants Bill, most of the interventions did not raise the race issue, but the social and economic impact that uncontrolled flows would have in an already 'thickly populated country'. Ultimately, as Cohen (1994) puts it, the immigration debates in this period reproduced the struggle of British people and their leaders to ascertain the frontiers of their identity. Skin colour was a salient feature – or to quote John Hall MP in his intervention during the debates on the Commonwealth Immigrants Bill 1968, 'an identifiable factor'[38] – of those who ought to be excluded from the new shapes of British identity. The restrictions introduced by 1960s legislation were not only about colour, though. They were also an attempt by the British government, in the context of the dismantling of the Empire, to prevent the 'hordes' from its poorer, third-world colonies coming to Britain.

Expanding exclusionable populations: the Commonwealth Immigrants Acts 1962 and 1968

Political interests against restricting Commonwealth immigration delayed the enactment of legislative measures. However, with the increase in the number of immigrants from the new Commonwealth in 1961, these political forces started weakening. Obstacles to restrictions on Commonwealth citizens were then lifted, and the new legislation found its way (Hansen 2000). The adoption of the Commonwealth Immigrants Act 1962 (CIA 1962) coincided with the end of a period of relative open-door policies towards immigration throughout Europe. Many European countries – particularly Germany and France – stopped their guest worker programmes when the post-war shortage of workers ended and the unemployment figures started to rise (Hollifield 1992; Huysmans 2006: 65).

The CIA 1962 made British subjects party to immigration controls, except for those born in the UK or whose passports were issued by British authorities. It restricted the right to entry and settlement in mainland Britain to certain British subjects without introducing any changes in the law of citizenship. Commonwealth nationals retained their British citizenship, yet lost certain citizenship rights. Thus, the act effectively created a second-class group of citizens who were not allowed to enter freely and stay in the country. Commonwealth citizens subject to controls needed an employment permit – or voucher – issued by the Ministry of Labour in order to migrate to Britain.[39] Those criminally convicted were also, for the first time, subject to deportation following the recommendation of a court.

The act also made the illegal entry of Commonwealth citizens a *criminal* offence.[40] This is the first time that an immigration-related offence was introduced in British legislation against Commonwealth citizens. The manipulation of citizens' rights through immigration laws made it possible to criminalize British subjects for their illegal entry to the country. However, this provision was not subject to scrutiny by Parliament. When he presented the bill to Parliament, Home Secretary Richard Butler briefly referred to the offences introduced: 'I need not trouble the House in great detail with Clauses 3, 4 and 5. Clauses 3 and 4 provide the necessary ancillary provisions for the enforcement of the scheme proposed.'[41] Historically, law makers have taken for granted the inclusion of criminal offences in immigration statutes as a necessary corollary to the control over foreigners. This 'legal tradition' of backing up immigration legislation with criminal sanctions has barely been subject to critical examination. During the debate on the CIA 1962, some MPs questioned the use of criminal law against those who helped illegal immigrants, which Labour MP Arthur Irvine called an 'unnecessary edifice of penal legislation'.[42] While the act introduced 14 different offences – most of them criminalizing Commonwealth citizens for their illegal entry and stay – it was the provision which criminalized harbourers that attracted most attention. Mr Irvine questioned it because it was unnecessary to achieve 'What the authorities are legitimately after[:] the apprehension of, and penalty for, the illegal immigrant'.[43] The harbouring offence was also criticized for its potential to damage racial and community relations. The new provision either would make people more cautious about assisting others – especially if they were non-white – due to the threat of being punished, or would provide them with an excuse to discriminate against non-whites.

In reply, and to reassure his colleagues in the House, the Attorney General, Sir Reginald Manningham-Buller, explained that the harbouring offence was necessary, but unlikely to be used because of the evidentiary difficulties involved in its prosecution:

> I doubt very much whether there will be any prosecutions under it, because the difficulties of proving that a particular individual has reasonable grounds for believing the man to be an illegal immigrant, or that he knows it, are not likely to lead to many prosecutions. At the same time, it is desirable that we should have this in the Bill so that if need be, in appropriate cases, a prosecution can be brought, and as a deterrent to those who might otherwise participate in the evasions of the provisions of the Bill.
>
> (Hansard, HC Deb 7/02/1962, col. 438)

Similarly, the Lord Chancellor, the Earl of Kilmuir, explained to his peers in the House of Lords that the harbouring offence 'should provide a deterrent to those who might otherwise participate in deliberate evasion of the basic control; and, if you have a control, you must be seen to have the machinery to enforce it'.[44] Both the Attorney General and the Lord Chancellor put in very clear and unusually frank language the rationale underlining most immigration-related offences. Still today they are, first and foremost, 'necessary ancillary provisions' of the legislation – if there is a law, there should be a mechanism to enforce it – which does not necessarily mean that they will be enforced in practice; and second, they serve as a deterrent to ensure compliance with immigration norms.

When Labour came into power in 1964, it ratified the principles underlying the CIA 1962. In particular, the White Paper *Immigration from the Commonwealth* published in 1965 anticipated the continuation and tightening of restrictions on Commonwealth citizens. It justified the need for immigration controls by appealing to the 'numbers game' thesis and claiming that in order to ensure good race relations and prevent ethnic conflict, it was necessary, first, to integrate those already in the country; and, second, to impose strict controls over the number of new arrivals. This dual interventionist strategy which consisted of pairing immigration controls with integration measures[45] depicted non-white citizens as a source of potential social problems and, therefore, legitimized the need for controls. From then on, the two policies became inextricably connected in the public agenda. As Labour MP Charles Pannell put it bluntly during the debates on the 1968 Bill:

> My plea is that we had better behave rather better to the people already here before we take on this extra-commitment. . . We shall have a sort of civic indigestion if we try to digest all this lot at one time.
>
> (Hansard, HC Deb 27/02/1968, col. 1284)

Among other measures, the White Paper proposed the reduction of the quota for workers and the elimination of the quota for unskilled workers. It also significantly restricted the right to family reunion.[46]

In 1968, under the Premiership of Labour's Harold Wilson, Parliament adopted the second Commonwealth Immigrants Act (CIA 1968). One of its main objectives was to prevent the Asian population living in Africa – particularly in Kenya – from migrating to Britain. As Kenya was a British colony in 1962, Kenyan citizens were issued passports by the colonial governor – and thus they were subject to immigration controls given the provisions of the CIA 1962. However, after Kenya's independence in 1963, passports to British subjects were issued by the UK's High Commission in Kenya – the direct representative of the British government – and therefore they were no longer subject to controls over entry and settlement in the UK (Hansen 2000: 171). After independence, East African governments, such as Kenya, Uganda and Tanzania, denied non-African populations automatic local citizenship, and most Asians, instead of applying for it, opted for British citizenship (Hansen 2000: 169).[47] 'Africanization' policies which discriminated against non-citizens adversely affected British Asians and provoked an important wave of emigration to Britain.[48] The CIA 1968 was the response of the British government to this situation and an attempt to prevent future movements of British Asians from Africa. As with the previous act, the CIA 1968 did not modify the law of citizenship. Instead, it recognized the British citizenship of East African Asians, but it ended their unqualified right to settle in

Britain: the fact that their passports were issued by British authorities did not exempt them from immigration controls any longer. British passport holders were only exempted from such controls if at least one of their parents or grandparents was born, adopted or naturalized as a British citizen in the UK.

Both the CIA 1962 and the CIA 1968 were aimed at tackling the increasing arrival of 'a large number of holders of United Kingdom passports who do not, "in common parlance belong" to this country',[49] in an attempt to manage one consequence of dismantling the Empire. In recently released secret cabinet minutes, Home Secretary James Callaghan justified the introduction of the bill in the following terms:

> It is sometimes argued . . . that we can take a less serious view of the scale of immigration and settlement in this country because it could be, and currently is being, more than offset by total emigration. This view overlooks the important point that emigration is largely by white persons from nearly every corner of the United Kingdom, while immigration and settlement are largely by coloured persons into a relatively small number of concentrated areas. The exchange thus aggravates rather than alleviates the problem.
>
> (quoted in Latimer 1999: n.p.)

The influence of the working-class movement and the trade unions on the Labour Party significantly shaped its policies towards immigration. The interest of the party to attract the vote of a large group of ethnic minorities and the party's liberal concern with minority rights clashed with the interest of the trade unions. In 1968, Labour was divided between those who wanted Commonwealth citizens to remain foreigners and those who advocated their full integration (Harrison 2010: 197). Labour's strategy to focus on race relations and integration while limiting incoming numbers of immigrants to the country attempted to reconcile the two opposing sectors of the party (Hampshire 2005: 31).

The CIA 1968 introduced the offence of landing without proper examination by an immigration officer in section 3. Commonwealth citizens were guilty of such an offence if they could not demonstrate that they were properly inspected upon arrival. This offence not only reversed the burden of proof, it also lacked the subjective or mental element (*mens rea*). The act made criminally liable the master of the ship or aircraft who allowed that landing. The period during which an illegal entrant could be subject to examination was extended from 24 hours to 28 days. One of the justifications given by some MPs for extending or eliminating altogether the 24-hours rule was that the police found it difficult to distinguish 'coloured' people from each other and required extra time to bring them to justice.[50] The offence of landing without submitting to examination and the extension of the 24-hours rule were directed at tackling the problem of people who were exempt from enforcement actions even though they entered illegally, because they were not caught during the 24 hours after their arrival. These provisions also sought to facilitate the swift return of illegal entrants at the port without keeping them in the country for prosecution and subsequent removal.[51]

The CIA 1968 provoked strong reactions and public demonstrations, especially from Asian communities. In response, Prime Minister Harold Wilson introduced the Immigration Appeals Bill which was passed in 1969 (IAA 1969). This was considered a progressive piece of legislation. It created a whole administrative system consisting of adjudicators and an Appeal Tribunal to review appeals against immigration decisions, which until then were not subject to any form of judicial or administrative re-examination.[52] While these administrative judgements were final and could not be appealed before the courts, it provided for the first time the possibility of reviewing decisions in a field where immigration authorities had broad margins of discretion (Hepple 1969). Even so, there were few trained lawyers operating in this field. A barrister practising immigration law at that time explained that the Joint Council for the Welfare of Immigrants (JCWI) was the only organization that filed appeals and had only two caseworkers working on them (Respondent 8, 17/05/2010). In 1970, the United Kingdom Immigrants Advisory Service (UKIAS), a publicly funded independent organization, was established to provide legal aid on immigration appeals.

Things only began to change in the mid-1970s when immigration law and practice started to grow as a separate field with courts, specialized practitioners, law reports and academics, and became an independent legal branch. Three decades later, immigration would be the lead subject in judicial review proceedings. The institutionalization of immigration law as an independent subject coincides with the enactment of the IA 1971 which is still in force and the basis for a much more complex legislative framework that regulates the field today.

Immigration Act 1971: the institutionalization of the immigration system and its legacy

In order to distance himself from Labour Prime Minister Harold Wilson and his liberal stance, Conservative candidate Edward Heath deployed thinly veiled rhetoric in his political campaign, appealing to 'the nation', 'the British people', and 'the national interest', promising that under his Premiership, 'the silent majority',[53] left aside by liberal politicians, would be listened to (Hall *et al.* 1978: 274). In his electoral manifesto, he had promised to reduce large-scale, permanent immigration, a pledge he honoured in the enactment of the Immigration Act 1971 (IA 1971). Even though numbers were in decline, the government justified the new legislation on migration-control grounds, as explained by Conservative MP John Hunt:

> [T]he argument is not only statistical but psychological, that it is a question of immigration not only being effectively checked but being seen to be effectively checked. That is why it is important to realize that the provisions of the Bill for conditional entry and, most important, for tightening control of illegal entry are important not so much for the net reduction in numbers which will result as for the reassurance which the measures will bring to those,

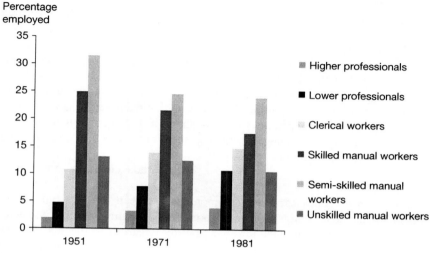

Figure 2.3 Changes in occupational classes (1951–1981)
Source: Routh (1987: 38). Reprinted with permission.

particularly in our large cities, who feel themselves in danger of being swamped and overwhelmed.

(Hansard, HC Deb 8/03/1971, cols 92–93)

The impact of further waves of arrivals on community relations was one of the reasons expressed during parliamentary debates and cabinet meetings. Additionally, there was a concern about the effect on already rising unemployment rates, particularly in low- and semi-skilled jobs due to changes in the occupational structure of the labour market, as Figure 2.3 illustrates.

The IA 1971 repealed the ARA 1914, the CIA 1962, the CIA 1968 and the IAA 1969 and introduced a unitary regime regulating the conditions for entry and residence of both non-nationals and Commonwealth citizens. It was the first immigration legislation equating certain Commonwealth citizens to foreigners in terms of their right freely to enter the UK. Commonwealth citizens still retained their status as British subjects, but their immigration rights were further restricted by the introduction of the concept of 'patriality'. Only those with British parents or grandparents and those who had been 'ordinary residents' for the last five years before the entry into force of the act had the 'right of abode' and thus were granted indefinite leave to enter and remain.[54] This measure disproportionately affected non-white Commonwealth citizens who were less likely to be descendants of British-born relatives (Cohen 1994: 49; Hansen 2000: 195). Indeed, recent disclosure of secret cabinet minutes shows that the idea of 'patriality' was aimed at concealing a discriminatory ban against non-white Commonwealth immigration. As Home Secretary Reginald Maudling put it:

The number of aliens who want to settle here is relatively few, and for this reason – because they come from a cultural background generally fairly akin to our own – it is not difficult to assimilate them. But of those wishing to come here to work from the Commonwealth, particularly the new Commonwealth, the vast majority would want to settle permanently and by reason both of this factor and of the fact that they come generally from a different cultural background, the task of assimilation – as experience so bitterly shows – is all but impossible. If we put the Commonwealth citizen on the same basis as what at present is the practice for aliens, and abolish the quota which presently applies only to Commonwealth citizens, the result would be a great increase in coloured immigration.

(quoted in Travis 2002b: n.p.)

The decision to dispossess most Commonwealth citizens of their rights even further sharply contrasted with the provisions entitling Europeans freely to enter and work in the UK, following the signing of the Treaty of Rome in 1973. The restrictions imposed on Commonwealth nationals, at the time when the rights of many citizens of Europe to settle in the UK were recognized, represented one of the main controversial aspects of the new legislation (Joppke 2005: 100), and it remains a polemic aspect of Britain's foreign policy: its drift apart from the Dominions and turn towards Europe. The IA 1971 also made more apparent the problems of curtailing rights to a category of citizens without reforming nationality laws. Immigration and nationality laws were decoupled only in 1981 when Parliament passed the British Nationality Act (BNA 1981). This act created a single British citizenship, eliminated the concept of British subject, and recognized the right of abode only for British citizens (those born from British parents or grandparents, or naturalized).[55] From then on, only British citizens enjoyed all the rights granted to citizens. By contrast, non-British citizens were deprived of these rights and therefore subject to immigration laws.

Along with extending the grounds for deportation of aliens and non-patrial Commonwealth citizens[56] and restricting appeals against certain deportation decisions[57] (De Smith 1972: 3), the IA 1971 reproduced the provisions of repealed legislation on 'immigration crimes'. They included illegal entry,[58] assisting illegal entry and harbouring a person who illegally entered the UK or overstayed,[59] obstructing the normal administration of immigration controls under the act,[60] and offences committed by captains, owners or agents of ships or aircrafts and managers of ports who breached their obligations under the act.[61] The offence of assisting or facilitating was meant to be applied against people smugglers who until then were proceeded against under the general offence of conspiracy to contravene the law. Further, it was intended to cover a wide range of conduct, not limited to aiding the evasion of immigration controls, but also any act intended to further illegal entry – as for example, providing a job or a place to stay.[62] With the exception of the offence of facilitation, Parliament did not address provisions incorporating criminal offences in detail, again because they were considered 'necessary ancillaries' of a system to control population flows. In fact, the introduction of these offences was unanimously welcomed by the members of both Houses.

While the IA 1971 incorporated an important number of immigration offences, little is known about their actual use. Statistics prior to 1980 do not compile data on the prosecution and conviction of people for offences under immigration acts. From 1973, control of immigration statistics compiled data on the number of people who were detected entering the country illegally and how they were dealt with; however, there is no mention of criminal charges brought against them (Home Office 1979: Table 15). Data from 1979 until 1983 show that the number of people prosecuted – and even more so convicted – for these offences was very low. Except for the offences of overstaying and the failure to observe the conditions attached to a leave, the number of prosecutions for other offences was far below 100 (Home Office 1985: Table 21). During the debates on Police (Drugs and Illegal Immigration),[63] the Minister of State for the Home Office, Mark Carlisle, explained in the House of Commons that between the passage of the CIA 1968 – that is, 1 March 1968 – and 31 December 1972, only 74 cases of 'illegal immigration offences' involving 307 illegal immigrants were brought before the courts.[64] Likewise, three senior immigration barristers practising at that time referred to prosecutions of such offences as very rare. Instead, people accused of illegal entry or breaching the conditions of a leave were simply removed or deported without being prosecuted.[65] One of these practitioners, a retired barrister at Garden Court North Chambers, told me that the attitude of the judiciary was also very different when any such cases reached the courtroom:

> In the 1970s there were very few prosecutions . . . I remember I represented someone working in breach or overstaying, or a student who is not supposed to work but who was working, and magistrates would very often just let the person off.
>
> (Respondent 6, 20/04/2010)

The IA 1971 set up a system which modelled – and to some extent conditioned – the way in which immigration laws are enforced today. Even though immigration offences are much older and have been inherent to the construction of British immigration controls since their early foundations in the nineteenth and early twentieth centuries, the IA 1971 institutionalized a system of controls, systematizing and expanding immigration powers, and served as the basis for recent legislation in the field. Particularly, it created a system in which criminal sanctions are attached to most breaches of immigration rules. Even though most of the offences introduced were underused, it provided the tools for future enforcement. In fact, one year after the IA 1971 was passed, a new branch of the Metropolitan Police specializing in immigration issues was established – the Illegal Immigration Intelligence Unit (IIIU).[66] Its primary function was related to information gathering and exchange about 'known or suspected offenders' (Home Office 1972). The IA 1971 extended police powers in immigration procedures – particularly, the power of arrest without warrant – and the involvement of the police in these proceedings was amplified after the adoption of the act (Gordon 1985: 24).

At that time, there was no special force responsible for the inland enforcement of immigration regulations so the police were entirely in charge of that role. The police were not particularly pleased to be granted these prerogatives over migration controls because of the impact that such responsibility might have on the already poor relations with ethnic communities. Violent encounters between the police and non-white youth, the harassment experienced by the latter due to selective policing of ethnic communities, and a shared perception of disbelief made the relations between them tense and difficult. This tension was apparent when, during the parliamentary debates on the bill for the IA 1971, the inclusion of a requirement by Commonwealth citizens to register with the police was discussed.[67] Even if requirements for reporting to the police had been established for aliens early on, the extension of the measure to Commonwealth citizens was criticized by some MPs because it would give the police further control over immigrants' lives and was not welcomed by the force. The reluctance of the police to perform immigration controls was one of the motives for creating a special border force – the Border and Immigration Agency (BIA) – in April 2007 (Weber and Bowling 2004: 204).[68]

The IA 1971 completed a shift in the status of (non-patrial) Commonwealth citizens that had started with the 1962 and 1968 legislation. This trilogy of laws operated a 'manipulation of categories and rights of citizenship' (Gilroy 1982: 145) that resulted in the creation of second-class British subjects equated to aliens. In so doing, it generated a whole new population of individuals subject to the state's sovereign powers of exclusion. The IA 1971 also introduced a substantial number of immigration offences and extended immigration powers, thus marking the beginning of a period of increasing reliance on criminal law powers in immigration enforcement.

The (re)discovery of the criminal law for immigration enforcement: the asylum crisis and the 'fight' against illegal immigration

> *[O]ne does not tear up passports and documents if one has nothing to hide.*[69]

Margaret Thatcher's Premiership (1979–1990) furthered a period of restrictionist policies aimed at cutting down both primary and secondary immigration. With these policies, Thatcher intended to attract voters of the National Front – a right-wing party advocating further restrictions to immigration – which at that moment was gaining electoral appeal with some Conservative Party[70] voters (Layton-Henry 1994: 286; Spencer 1997: 147). While there was little legislative activity on immigration during the first years of Thatcher's Premiership, the government enacted a number of immigration rules through secondary legislation.[71] Whereas primary legislation only deals in general terms with the matter, it is in the 'half-world of executive closure' of immigration rules where the specifics of the procedure are shaped (Joppke 1999: 115). Moreover, legislation already in place was more strictly enforced: peak removals of illegal entries of both foreigners and Commonwealth citizens were reported for 1979, 1980 and 1981; and deportation orders served were also higher after 1979 (Cohen 1994: 51, 61, 2006: 81; Bloch and Schuster 2005: 496).

Alongside changes in secondary legislation, during the Thatcher government the Immigration Act 1988 (IA 1988) was passed to tackle the problem of visa overstayers. This act introduced restrictive measures against those who breach their conditions of leave. With the slogan of 'firm but fair', the government justified these new measures as a 'realistic' approach, judged on the basis of the immigration rates and the anxiety of the public about them (Holmes 1991: 5). This act made it a continuing criminal offence to exceed the time limitation of the leave, or overstay,[72] thus loosening the time-limits for prosecution. Section 6 states that this offence is committed 'on the day when [the person] first knows that the time limited by his leave has expired and continues to commit it throughout any period during which he is in the United Kingdom thereafter'. The act also restricted the right of appeal against deportation orders in cases of breach of limited leave,[73] which made them more strictly enforceable. The impact that this last clause has had in the use of section 24(1)(b) (breach of limited leave or overstaying) is particularly interesting. Before the new provisions on deportation came into force, overstaying used to be the most frequently enforced immigration offence (Macdonald 2010: Chapter 14) as the numbers of prosecutions and convictions for this offence were relatively high compared to those for other immigration offences.[74] With the restrictions on appeal rights on deportation orders against overstayers, the prosecution of this offence became rare. As shown in Figure 2.4, from 1980 to the early 1990s there was a progressive and sustained drop in the number of prosecutions in magistrates' courts.

The amendment to deportation provisions has had an important effect in the way criminal provisions inside immigration laws are used to deal with suspected

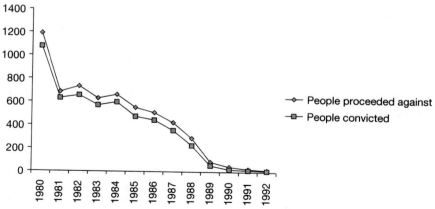

Figure 2.4 Overstaying trends at magistrates' courts (1980–1992)
Source: Home Office (1985, 1990, 1995)

immigration offenders. This amendment made it easier for authorities to remove immigration offenders, rendering the use of criminal punishment against them redundant, unnecessary or inconvenient. The impact that these reforms had on the way that overstayers are dealt with demonstrates how closely interconnected the two regimes – administrative and criminal – are, and how criminal punishment acquires specific functions in the context of immigration management. Because criminal punishment is one of a number of alternatives that public officials have at hand to deal with immigration offenders, it is used only when it serves immigration objectives and where a calculation of costs and benefits involved make it a reasonable option. As I will explain in Chapter 4, a similar rationale underpins the criminal prosecution of immigrants who cannot be removed from the country.

Until the mid-1980s, a major concern for the government was to manage decolonization in terms of the population movements generated by social, economic and political changes in both Britain and its former colonies. From then on, attention turned to the growing number of people claiming asylum and undocumented migrants. Previously, during the post-war period, there were few refugees – mainly Hungarians, Chileans and Russian dissidents – so it was not a noticeable phenomenon.[75] However, civil wars and political turmoil in South Asia, Africa and, later on, Eastern Europe produced a large 'stock' of people claiming asylum in many Western countries, including Britain. In the UK, this inaugurated a period of 'asylum hype' and the beginning of a period lasting two decades that was characterized by an obsession of the tabloid media with 'bogus refugees'. This put enormous pressure on the government and resulted in draconian measures on asylum seekers.

The Sri Lankan conflict, which intensified in 1983, was the precursor of the 'asylum crisis'. Because of the large number of asylum petitions, a visa for nationals of that country was introduced in 1985. In the following years, visa requirements were extended to nationals of other Commonwealth countries (Bangladesh, Ghana, India, Nigeria and Pakistan) considered to be main 'producers' of asylum seekers.[76] The imposition of visas places an important obstacle for people fleeing persecution because they often do not have the time and the resources to apply for a visa. In addition, asylum seekers are fearful about resorting to official authorities as applying for a travel document or a visa may alert them of their intention to leave the country. To enforce the visa regime, the government introduced measures to ensure that passengers do not arrive in Britain with improper or no documentation, thus preventing people with no right to enter from leaving their own countries.

The first specific legislation on carriers' liability – the Immigration (Carrier Liability) Act 1987 (I(CL)A 1987) – established a duty on carriers which transport people (ships and aircrafts) to check passengers' travel documents and visas, imposing fines of up to £1,000 for any breach. As early as 1905, the AA 1905 obliged the masters of ships to comply with regulations on the entry of foreigners to the country and their return to the ports of embarkation; failure to comply with those norms made them liable to fines.[77] These were strict liability offences and so ship masters were criminally liable even if there was no fault on their part.[78] Later on, the offence of facilitation introduced in the IA 1971[79] penalized any person '*knowingly* concerned in making or carrying out arrangements for securing or facilitating the entry into the United Kingdom of anyone whom he knows or has reasonable cause for believing to be an illegal entrant'. This offence applied to carriers transporting undocumented immigrants. However, because it required proof of the fault element (knowledge or reasonable cause to believe), it was difficult to enforce. The civil penalty regime introduced by the I(CL)A 1987 facilitated the enforcement of the obligations on carriers, thus virtually turning airline employees into first-line immigration officials (Pham 2008). By the time this piece of legislation was passed, the imposition of civil sanctions on reckless carriers was a policy measure already mandated at the European Union (EU) level by the Convention Implementing the Schengen Agreement of 14 June 1985.[80]

Both visa requirements and carrier liability severely restricted the possibility for people escaping persecution in their home countries to travel with valid passports and visas to Britain, and made the resort to 'agents' who provide the required (false) documentation the only alternative (Dunstan 1998: 209; Macdonald 2010: Chapter 14).[81] The introduction of these measures shows the underlying distrust by the British government of asylum claimants, believed to be economic migrants or 'bogus' asylum seekers, rather than genuine refugees, who would be discouraged from migrating to the UK and would choose a different destination (Cohen 1994: 81). In fact, the enactment of the I(CL)A 1987 was a response to the arrival at Heathrow airport of 68 Tamils from Sri Lanka in February of that year. The decision by the courts rejecting claims for asylum in most of these cases was used by the government to argue that the refugee route was being abused by economic migrants: '[T]he one loophole that has been exploited . . . is the claim to refugee status . . . [M]any of these unfortunate people are seeking to leave their own country for economic reasons and not strictly for reasons of oppression.'[82] It is not surprising then that government policies towards asylum seekers were driven by the rhetoric and methods deployed to control (illegal) immigration (Joppke 1999: 129).

The post-Cold War years brought an increase in the number of applications for asylum from citizens of former Communist countries.[83] This was the context in which the two further acts specifically directed at asylum seekers were passed in 1993 and 1996: the Asylum and Immigration Appeals Act 1993 (AIAA 1993) and the Asylum and Immigration Act 1996 (AIA 1996).[84] They were fundamentally aimed at reducing bottlenecks in processing applications in a system increasingly overwhelmed by the volume of work (Flynn 2005). They did so by limiting opportunities to appeal and restricting housing allowances for applicants. They also increased penalties for certain offences and the powers of immigration officers to arrest and search without warrant.

These acts also expanded the catalogue of immigration crimes. The AIAA 1993 made it an offence to conceal or provide information to induce an immigration official to believe that someone is or is not an asylum seeker or a dependant.[85] The AIA 1996 introduced the offence of obtaining leave to enter or remain by deception,[86] which has been applied against failed asylum seekers who aimed to seek asylum once again under a different identity (Macdonald 2010: Chapter 14). Nevertheless, it has not been systematically used.[87] Finally, the offence of facilitation of illegal entrants was amended to include those assisting an asylum seeker or someone seeking to obtain a leave by deception.[88] This amendment was subject to a heated debate in Parliament, particularly regarding the criminalization of assisting asylum seekers. It was aimed at filling a gap in the legislation as evidenced by the courts in *R v Naillie*. In this case, the House of Lords examined the question as to whether assisting a person who arrived without a valid passport and subsequently claimed asylum was covered by the offence of assisting an illegal entry, under section 25(1), IA 1971. The Lords concluded that that offence did not cover the case of facilitators where the person assisted is an asylum seeker.[89] While the offence of assisting an asylum seeker was directed at targeting racketeering groups, despite the assurance given by the government, there was a widespread concern about that provision being applied against lawyers advising people about their asylum cases, not-for-profit organizations, churches, airline staff, etc. This offence resulted in a number of successful prosecutions until the mid-2000s after which prosecution and conviction rates dropped.[90]

These new offences targeted abuses in the quest for asylum and those helping asylum seekers. Paradoxically, even though by this time, the catalogue of immigration-related offences was expanding, immigrants and asylum seekers trying to enter or leave the country with false documents were charged with offences in non-immigration statutes (Hales 1996; Dunstan 1998). From 1994 on, a growing number of people were caught in British airports – mainly Heathrow – using false documents and were charged, imprisoned and convicted for the use of a false instrument under section 3 of the Forgery and Counterfeiting Act 1981 (FCA 1981), or for attempting to obtain services by deception under section 1 of the Criminal Attempts Act 1981 (CAA 1981).[91] In 1993, there were 53 arrests under these sections. In the subsequent two years, arrest numbers increased to 126 for 1994 and 376 for 1995. The rise in the enforcement of fraud-based offences was a reaction to the growing number of asylum claimants resorting to smugglers and false documents to enter the country. It also reflects a change in the response by the government to migrants and asylum seekers using false documents. The British government started to use the criminal law in these cases to punish those who sought to bypass immigration controls and to deter others prepared to follow the same route. The use of criminal law to control immigration has severely affected asylum seekers and is one of the most problematic aspects of the criminalization of immigration, as it has reduced the level of protection offered in Britain[92] and throughout Europe (Black 2003: 42; Council of Europe 2010: 20).

The AIA 1996 also introduced for the first time a criminal offence of employing illegal workers.[93] Working without entitlement had been a crime since 1971.[94] The introduction of this offence marked a shift in the legal framework against illegal labour which from then on was directed also at the demand side of the equation.[95] Illegal employment of foreigners has been a constant feature of certain businesses – such as restaurants and hotels – in metropolises like London. These businesses largely depended on foreign workers with no right to work because they were illegal entrants, visa holders with no permission to work, or simply overstayers. In a recently released record of a cabinet meeting held in May 1971, it was recognized that the hotel and catering industries largely and 'unduly' relied on foreigners who were 'prepared to accept low wage rates and inferior standards of living'.[96] This 'black economy' was largely overlooked by the government not only because it served economic needs, but also because it was not considered a serious problem. Hiring adult illegal workers was certainly not considered a criminal matter and so the offence of illegal working was seldom enforced (Jordan and Düvell 2002: 171). The government attempted to address this situation, identified as a major pull factor of illegal immigration to the country, by making employers hiring illegal workers criminally liable. As a strict liability offence, it did not require knowledge or recklessness on the part of the employer about the lack of entitlement to work of the foreign employee. The absence of a fault element in the offence was supposed to facilitate prosecutions; however, there were no prosecutions under this provision until 1997. It was not until 2006 that new legislation was introduced to deal with illegal employment, in the light of the poor outcomes following the AIA 1996.

The tightening of both external and internal controls in Britain coincided with a period of increasing openness within the EU and closure to non-European immigration, particularly after the adoption of the Schengen Convention and its incorporation into EU law by the Treaty of Amsterdam in 1997.[97] Even if Britain did not completely lift its external frontiers – in fact, it did not relinquish its power to control passengers coming from Schengen states – the adoption of an array of 'compensatory measures' to strengthen external borders in continental Europe was an opportunity to tighten up external controls on ports of entry (its traditional strategy) while introducing inland ones (Anderson *et al.* 1995; Morris 1998: 954; Kaye 1999). The UK's 'legal tradition' of relying on the criminal law to enforce immigration rules has in turn influenced the recent drive towards criminalization at the European level, in part encouraged and even mandated by EU rules (Council of Europe 2010). The explicit support from European institutions of a system based on the criminalization of immigration breaches is an important factor in the continuation and expansion of such a system and in the ruling out of any alternative option.[98]

Conclusion

The contemporary contours of the British system of immigration controls have been largely shaped by the struggle to strip British privileges from Commonwealth citizens during the dismantling of the Empire. Immigration and race have been crucial themes in the history of forging Britain's 'frontiers of identity' and the drawing of the line between those who belong and those who do not. Not surprisingly, then, immigration debates bring to the fore not only the relationship of British society with 'its outsiders', but also how such interaction contributes to create and recreate the community within (Cesarani 1993). A quick look at this debate throughout the last century shows continuities in the portrayal of foreigners as disruptive of vernacular customs; producers of unemployment, housing overcrowding and crime; and more recently, abusive of the immigration and welfare systems.[99]

It also shows the existence of an immigration enforcement system that has appealed to the criminal law since early legislation, even before a comprehensive framework and institutional organization had been put into place to police the borders – or the shores. As I have demonstrated above, immigration offences are older than sometimes thought. The first pieces of legislation passed during the late eighteenth and nineteenth centuries to regulate foreigners' entry to and residence in the country contained many of these offences. Indeed, criminal sanctions – such as imprisonment, hard labour and transportation for life – were a chief immigration enforcement mechanism and constituted important parts in the early foundations of the system of immigration controls. This coincides with what Juliet Stumpf (2009) tells us about the American context where immigration offences were widespread in eighteenth-century legislation, albeit seldom used, and criminal sanctions appeared in federal statutes before deportation. Although it is not clear whether immigration offences are older than deportation as enforcement tools in the British legal system, this brief review of early immigration legislation shows that since the 1790s, foreigners in breach of these rules were liable upon conviction both to criminal punishment – which included banishment – and expulsion from the country.

Perhaps because of this 'legal tradition' – as the Attorney General clearly put it in the parliamentary debate on the Commonwealth Immigrants Bill 1962 – criminal sanctions have been considered a constitutive part of the immigration control system and have not been subject to strict scrutiny over their need, proportionality or convenience.[100] Criminal sanctions attached to immigration rules have barely been applied to immigration offenders, as evidenced by the few charged with these crimes. Except for overstayers until the mid-1980s, foreigners in breach of immigration rules have been largely dealt with through the exercise of administrative powers of deportation and removal. The system of immigration controls barely relied on such powers until the mid-1990s when the appeal to criminal law started to become more frequent.

Because the British immigration system drew on the model of criminal punishment, developments in both areas of law are closely related. In order to understand immigration 'management', it is necessary to look at the role that criminal law plays in it, particularly the intended and unintended consequences of criminalization in and beyond the criminal justice process. Conversely, the convergence of criminal and administrative regimes broadened possibilities for decision making and made immigration policy imperatives a key element in the administration of discretion. This focus will guide the analysis of contemporary policies and practices in the field of immigration which follows in the rest of this book.

3   The Labour years

Contemporary contours of immigration policy and enforcement from 1997 to 2010

In this chapter, I examine the recent history of immigration legislation in Britain during the New Labour tenure from 1997 to 2010. While this is a long period, its consideration as a whole is important to identify changes and continuities in immigration policy making. As this chapter will show, while policy objectives and targeted groups changed during Labour's years, broad ideas about how the immigration system should work and how both British people and foreigners subject to controls should perceive such a system were relatively stable.

I identify three main features characterizing this period. First, there was a significant expansion of immigration legislation including the growth of the catalogue of immigration crimes. Second, there was an enhanced and more systematic enforcement of such crimes and a greater reliance on the criminal justice system. The criminal law was increasingly deployed against undocumented migrants, many of whom were asylum seekers. Third, criminal and immigration enforcement agencies converged following the overhaul of the Border and Immigration Agency (BIA) in 2007 and the creation of a police-like immigration enforcement bureau, the UK Border Agency (UKBA), in 2008. The creation of immigration crimes – and the greater enforcement of them – was part of the government's plan to tighten up an arguably obsolete immigration system and to increase public confidence in it.

Promises (un)fulfilled: New Labour and the immigration debate

While in opposition, the 'New Labour' Party was careful about criticizing Conservative policies, especially on social issues. It adopted a 'twin track approach', publicly opposing Conservative initiatives, but in such a way that it could not be seen as too liberal. Regarding immigration, this meant that the party wanted to avoid being portrayed as lax on immigration controls (Kaye 1999: 28; Gibney 2008: 155). Labour was concerned about the increasing support for the British National Party (BNP)[1] among its electorate (Schuster and Solomos 2004: 280). Labour policy makers were also worried that a 'too' liberal stance would be 'out of touch' with the reality of large sections of the population[2] and at odds with their demands for a firmer intervention by the state. This may explain the fact that, as far as immigration is concerned, the Labour Party's policies resembled its opponent's in many ways (Bloch 2000; Schuster and Solomos 2004).

When New Labour won the general election in 1997, immigration was not a priority for the new government. In fact, it did not even appear in Labour's electoral manifesto. As Sarah Spencer (2007: 341) put it, in relation to immigration policy, Labour 'came to power with no vision, no policy goals, no anticipated "third way"'. Soon after the 1997 elections, however, immigration became a major political issue. At the peak of asylum applications in 1999,[3] and with a steady increase in foreign population flows (particularly since 1997), the issues of asylum, family reunification and labour migration lay at the top of public concerns (Boswell 2005; Home Office 2006a: Figure 1).[4] They also had become the focus of attack by the opposition and the popular press (Düvell 2007; Spencer 2011: 55).

By the late 1990s, the 'immigration issue' – and particularly the abuse of the asylum system – became a major concern. Prime Minister Tony Blair was for some years personally involved in policy making in this area. In Spencer's (2007) account, he pushed targets to increase removals of failed asylum seekers – even over the objections of the Home Secretary, David Blunkett – and succeeded in silencing dissenting voices within the cabinet (see also Gibney 2008). An academic closely involved in the immigration debate during the Blair years explained: 'a lot of the movements to develop the framework to deal with illegal entry was really to do with asylum seekers . . . So, politically asylum is just the huge, huge driver of all of that' (Respondent 16, 1/07/2010). She recalls that the decision to introduce a new bill in Parliament was not made – as it would usually be – by bureaucrats, but was ordered directly by the Home Secretary because of the strong political pressure to bring immigration under control:

> So he would say: 'I'm Home Secretary. I'm under fire from all sides for failing on this. I'm going to do something about it. I've got these administrative problems which really . . . I haven't got any money to solve them, so I'll legislate.'
>
> (Respondent 16, 1/07/2010)

From this moment onwards, the state began to use its powers to detain and remove immigrants more systematically. This included the resort to the criminal law and its agencies to enforce immigration rules.[5] As some scholars (Bloch and Schuster 2005; Bosworth and Guild 2008; Gibney 2008) have shown, both deportation and detention of immigrants were used only sporadically until the 1980s and 1990s, largely because of practical difficulties and legal and moral objections to them. Before 2000, there were only four immigration detention centres. During the 2000s, the government opened five more and redesigned three detention facilities to hold immigrants.[6] The Labour administration significantly expanded the detention estate – particularly to detain 'destitute' and 'failed' asylum seekers (Malloch and Stanley 2005; Bacon 2005; Welch and Schuster 2005a, 2005b). It also increased the UK's capacity to enforce deportation and removal orders from

1999, with 2002 being a peak year for removals (Home Office 2008a: Figure 13; see also Gibney 2008; Anderson *et al.* 2011: 550).

The New Labour administration inaugurated a new way of governance, adopting a 'tough but fair' approach to crime, anti-social behaviour[7] and immigration (Stenson 2001). Particularly in relation to immigration, the underlying rationale was to transform the terms of the debate and create a 'third way' (Young 2003). The objective was to avoid polarized positions held by the Right (that advocated for increasingly tighter controls and disregarded asylum claimants as bogus) and the Left (that condemned those backing immigration controls as racists). In its public rhetoric, New Labour explained people's concerns about large numbers of newcomers as not necessarily racist and recognized the existence of abuses in the system.[8] Successive Home Secretaries advocated stricter but 'fair' scrutiny to filter out the 'deserving' migrants (considered to be refugees, skilled migrants, business travellers, tourists) from the 'undeserving' ones (among whom they numbered bogus asylum claimants, unskilled and poor economic migrants and foreign ex-offenders).[9] In keeping with its new approach, the government deployed a managerial logic to 'administer' immigration flows. Aware of the impossibility of suppressing immigration altogether and convinced about the need for legitimate migration, Labour organized controls to smooth the way of legitimate travellers and restrict unwelcome ones (Amoore 2006; Wilson and Weber 2008; Aas 2011b).

Fairer, faster and firmer

> *The criminal law has a role to play in stamping out abuse of immigration control.*
> (Home Office 1998)

The Labour administration laid out its plans for the reform of the entire immigration system in the White Paper *Fairer, Faster and Firmer* (Home Office 1998) which underpinned and shaped the Immigration and Asylum Act 1999 (IAA 1999). The point of departure for the White Paper was that the current system was inefficient because of its complexity and fragmentation, and because it allowed abuses. It was a magnet for bogus asylum claims, and allowed multiple appeals and the use of procedural tricks to violate immigration laws (Sale 2002; Flynn 2005). The promise of the White Paper to undertake a complete overhaul of the immigration system was reflected in the size of the bill presented to Parliament, characterized as 'by far the biggest piece of legislation in this area ever seen in the UK' (JCWI 1999). The first aim of the bill was to introduce and strengthen a number of measures aimed at deterring asylum seekers from choosing the UK as their final destination[10], and economic migrants from 'abusing' the asylum route.[11] The second was to respond to the general criticism of the inefficiency of the Immigration and Nationality Directorate (IND) in the management of such applications, which caused considerable backlogs,[12] and to adopt a swifter and tougher approach towards those who 'keep playing the system'. Finally, a more general purpose was to restore the public trust in the immigration system.

Among other measures, the IAA 1999 enacted 35 different immigration-related offences – many of them targeting asylum seekers. When introducing the bill in Parliament, the then Home Secretary, Jack Straw, announced that '[e]nforcement must be backed by the criminal law'.[13] Accordingly, this piece of legislation introduced more immigration-related offences than any other in history.[14] It extended the offence of deception by criminalizing those who deceive to circumvent in any way enforcement actions against them[15] (originally, the offence covered only those who used deception to enter or remain in the country).[16] According to the explanatory notes, this extension was intended to deal with 'failed asylum seekers whose claims have involved blatant deceit'. The IAA 1999 also increased the maximum penalty for deception from six months to two years.

Other offences introduced relate to the provision of support for asylum claimants (false representation, dishonest representation, delay or obstruction, and failure of sponsor to maintain).[17] As Ian Macdonald (2010: Chapter 14) observed, many of these criminal offences are modelled on crimes to enforce social security provisions. The act includes another group of offences related to the enforcement of discipline inside removal centres.[18] These offences are equivalent to those existing in regulations for prisons and they are aimed at bringing the rules governing prisons into immigration detention.[19] Even if these provisions considerably increased criminal law powers, the debates in Parliament gave little or no consideration to them. In fact, during the parliamentary debates on the 1999 Bill, there was no substantial scrutiny of the new penal powers.

These new immigration offences were followed by a steady increase in prosecutions and convictions for immigration-related crimes, both in magistrates' and crown courts. This trend picked up in 2000 and 2001, and continued until 2005 and 2006, when the rates started to fall, as illustrated in Figures 3.1 and 3.2, below.

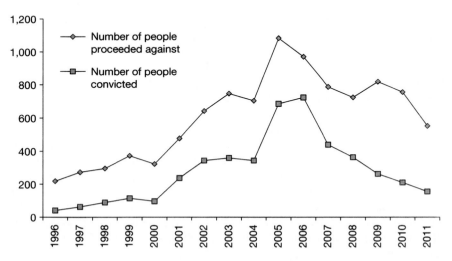

Figure 3.1 Immigration-related cases before the magistrates' courts
Source: Home Office (2010b, 2012)

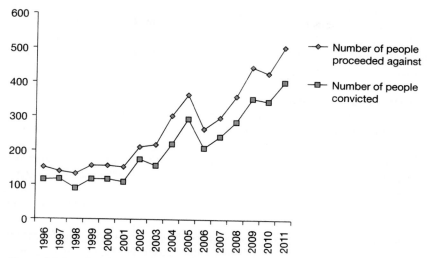

Figure 3.2 Immigration-related cases before crown courts
Source: Home Office (2010b, 2012)

A note of caution is due, though, when considering these numbers. First, between 2004 and 2008 there has been an under-recording of immigration offences in magistrates' courts due to inconsistencies in data. Similarly, since 2005, crown courts' data present other inconsistencies (Home Office 2009a: Table 6.7). Second, many people are charged with related offences of fraud and deception, such as those in the Identity Cards Act 2006 (IDCA 2006). These cases are not included in immigration statistics because the IDCA 2006 is not an immigration act; however, the behaviour incriminated – particularly the possession of a false, an improperly obtained or another's identity document – could well fall under immigration acts (such as the IA 1971).

Along with introducing a number of criminal offences, the IAA 1999 included two provisions which are closely connected to the criminalization of immigration: the creation of civil penalties for carriers and the regulation of the prohibition to impose penalties on refugees under the 1951 Convention Relating to the Status of Refugees (hereafter 'Refugee Convention'). I will address each of them in the next two sub-sections.

Civil penalties: making immigration offenders pay?

The IAA 1999 introduced a civil penalty on carriers responsible for clandestine entrants and on carriers who transport people without proper documentation.[20] This provision extended carrier liability to all forms of transportation of human beings. In response, lorry drivers' organizations argued that the penalty was unnecessary because there was a criminal offence that punished the same conduct – the offence of facilitation under the IA 1971.[21] The government, on the other hand, claimed that due to evidentiary difficulties in proving criminal intention by the facilitator, this offence was hard to enforce. During the parliamentary debate and in response to a question by an MP, the government's representative, Mike O'Brien, explained:

> There can be a criminal prosecution when someone who has the intention of carrying illegal immigrants then carries them . . . One of the difficulties is that lorry drivers can simply say, 'We didn't know they were in the back'. Unless we search the drivers and find the £2,000 per illegal immigrant that is some-times paid to those who bring them in deliberately . . . it is difficult to prove that they were aware that the illegal immigrants were in the back. It is neces-sary to have a system of civil penalties.
>
> (Hansard, HC Deb 22/02/1999, col. 121)

A similar rationale lay behind the enactment of the civil penalty regime for hiring illegal workers. As I explained in Chapter 2, the AIA 1996 introduced a criminal offence of employing a person aged 16 and above subject to immigration control, punishable by summary conviction with a fine of up to £5,000.[22] This was a strict liability offence where proof of *mens rea* was not needed to secure a conviction. Until 1997, though, there was not one prosecution for this offence (Home Office 2001: 95). In 1998, one person was proceeded against and convicted for this offence. In 1999, four defendants were charged and only one of them was con-victed for the same offence (Home Office 2003: 97). While in later years these numbers went up slightly, the prosecution and conviction rates for this offence remained low.[23] Between 1997 and 2006, only 37 people were convicted. The under-enforcement of this offence was due in part to the costs involved in mount-ing criminal prosecutions and the low conviction rates. Moreover, when the defen-dant was found guilty, the fines imposed were so low, far below the maximum limits, that they were insufficient to cover even the prosecution costs (Law Commission 2010: 44). It was also due to a lack of concerted political will and consistent enforcement to stop illegal working, a lax regime of exemptions for employers (Ryan 2006: 37), and the difficulties in changing the social perception of illegal employment as 'wrong but not so wrong' (Ruhs and Anderson 2010).[24]

In view of these poor outcomes and concerns about illegal working as a pull factor for illegal immigration, in 2006, the government introduced reforms to this legal framework. It explicitly recognized that a strict liability offence, which puts all employers at the same level regardless of knowledge, was not an adequate tool to address the allegedly widespread problem of illegal working (Home Office 2005b). Further, advocacy groups complained that a strict liability offence for illegal employment was disproportionately severe and potentially damaging to race relations (e.g. IAS 1999). The Immigration, Asylum and Nationality Act 2006 (IANA 2006) repealed section 8 of the AIA 1996 and introduced an offence for *knowingly* employing adults subject to immigration control, along with a civil penalty regime which currently carries a maximum penalty of £10,000 for each illegal worker employed. This dual system of sanctions aimed at 'increasing the risk and speed of receiving a penalty for non-compliance, proportionate to the level of non-compliant behaviour' (Home Office 2005b), by differentiating between, on the one hand, careless employers who hire foreign workers without undertaking a proper check of their documents and entitlement to work or where intention of criminal wrongdoing cannot be proved; and on the other, those who knowingly employ foreigners without authorization to work.

Under the new system, most cases fall into the first category where wrongdoers would be subject to fines and cases decided in quicker and less cumbersome proceedings, freeing up courts' time to consider more serious and complex cases of illegal employment. Thus the two regimes created a 'hierarchy of wrongdoing' by diverting low-level misconduct from the courts and reserving criminal law for the most serious offenders. As expected, the number of employers fined under the civil penalty regime has increased since its introduction,[25] whereas the prosecution numbers remain low.[26] The average fine imposed was £5,000, higher than those imposed by the courts under the AIA 1996, and the costs involved in proceedings were much lower than those for a criminal prosecution (Law Commission 2010: 45). While a substantial portion of cases of illegal hiring of foreign workers – by mainly British citizens[27] – have been diverted from the criminal justice system, the situation of non-British workers is drastically different. Working without entitlement or entering the country without proper documentation are still crimes very much enforced in practice.[28]

The decriminalization of most cases of illegal employment and the stricter enforcement of employers' sanctions have been detrimental to migrant workers. A study by Martin Ruhs and Bridget Anderson (2010: 206) suggested that the stringent enforcement of this framework during the past few years has had a harsher impact on workers than on employers (see also Ryan 2006: 55). This is because employers caught with undocumented workers on their work sites have incentives to report them or to cooperate with investigations against them. The former may have their fines reduced if they report 'any suspicions about [their] employees' entitlement to work' or when they 'co-operate . . . with the Border and Immigration Agency in any investigation, or in any consequent operation to detect and detain illegal migrant workers within [their] workforce' (Home Office 2008c: 15). Evidence indicates that businesses in certain sectors, such as cleaning companies, may be aware that their employees have no right to work in the UK. If their employees complain about their labour conditions, the companies have few qualms about reporting them to the authorities. Though the companies, officially, are at risk of prosecution, the precariousness of their employees is far greater (Anderson 2007, 2010b; De Giorgi 2010, 2011: 116). In his statement before Parliament during debates on the UK Borders Bill 2007, Jack Dromey, a trade union leader, quoted the case of a cleaning company where 200 employees were subject to compulsory redundancy. While the dispute was resolved in favour of the workers, 24 hours later they received a letter requesting a number of documents and warning that failure to provide those documents would result in them being sacked.[29]

This stricter enforcement has also increased the criminalization of workers for document fraud. The intensified pressure on employers to ensure that their employees are entitled to work contributed to a rise in the use of fraudulent documents to access work and resulted in an increased rate of prosecutions against employees for forgery (Ryan 2006: 33). When employees are caught using forged documents, they are more likely to be prosecuted than their employers are to be fined, as the latter are penalized only if the falsity of the document is 'reasonably apparent' – that is, apparent for an average person without the aid of technological devices (Home Office 2008c: 11). In this regard, a high-ranking official in the Criminality and Detention Group at the UKBA told me that when an employee is caught with a false document, the practice is to prosecute the worker, and not to fine or prosecute the employer (Respondent 5, 16/09/2010).

The new civil penalty regime increased the pressure on the supply of labour – the immigrant. This conclusion is consistent with the general objective of employers' sanctions which is to control illegal immigration rather than to punish employers' wrongdoing. When there has been any discussion or scrutiny of the extension of criminal law powers for immigration enforcement during parliamentary debates, they have been focused on offences which penalized those who aid or harbour illegal immigrants, not on offences which punished immigrants directly. The use of criminal law against the latter has not been generally subject to criticism. The debate has rather concentrated on the legitimacy and proportionality of criminal or civil liability of 'third parties' in order to pursue immigration control objectives.[30] As in other regulatory spheres, parliamentarians have historically been concerned about striking the right balance between firm border controls and the economic interests of third parties affected. For example, during the debates on the Aliens Bill 1905, Lord Tweedmouth asserted that:

> [The provision regarding shipowners] was a great hardship on them that they should have to bear the expense of taking aliens who were refused admission into this country back to the place from which they came. That was still more intensified by the fact that not only were the shipowners so obliged to take back alien immigrants as defined by the Bill, but they had also to take back at their own expense cabin passengers.
>
> (Hansard, HL Deb 3/08/1905, A2 6)

The introduction of civil penalty regimes for carriers and employers – and the diversion of low-scale wrongdoing from the criminal justice system – are consistent with the recent over-criminalization of a variety of conducts. As criminal law scholars (Ashworth 2000; Ashworth and Zedner 2008; Duff *et al.* 2007) pointed out, along with the addition of a large number of offences in many fields, in recent years there has been a trend to repress conduct without subjecting the offender to a criminal trial. In the case of civil penalties, the main reason for their 'mass production and "consumption"' (Hildebrandt 2009: 64) is their effectiveness to deal with the problem of illegal immigration: they are cheaper and more effective as a deterrent than criminal proceedings.

Prosecuting asylum seekers and the limits of the sovereign state

Although under the convention subscribing states must give sanctuary to any refugee who seeks asylum . . . they are by no means bound to facilitate his arrival. Rather they strive increasingly to prevent it.[31]

The IAA 1999 introduced section 31 which regulates Britain's international obligations under the 1951 Refugee Convention,[32] particularly in relation to article 31. Under this article, contracting states to the Refugee Convention 'shall not impose penalties, on account of their illegal entry or presence, on refugees', providing certain conditions are met.[33] The main aim of this provision is purely instrumental: to prevent refugees from going underground once they arrive at a 'safe haven' and to encourage them to regularize their status. It intends both to protect refugees and aid the receiving country by reducing the incentives of refugees to become 'illegals' (Hathaway 2005: 388). Britain, as a contracting party to the Refugee Convention, was bound by article 31 since its entry into force. However, until the IAA 1999, that provision was not incorporated into domestic law and was poorly observed in practice (Bye 1999).

Until 1994, the arrival of people into Britain or en route to another country without proper documents was largely dealt with through immigration powers. People were either refused entry and sent back to their port of embarkation, or held in detention while their claims were assessed (Hales 1996: 2). From 1994, however, the immigration service started to refer these cases to the police and the Crown Prosecution Service (CPS). This change in policy increased the detention and criminal prosecution of asylum claimants, particularly, for the use of a false instrument under the FCA 1981 and for attempting to obtain services by deception under the CAA 1981 (Dunstan 1998). Criminal lawyers rarely invoked article 31 of the Refugee Convention and advised their clients to plead guilty. Upon conviction by magistrates' courts, asylum seekers were typically sentenced to between six and nine months of imprisonment (Bye 1999). Many of them had their asylum applications considered and, if successful, they were recognized as refugees only after serving their criminal sentence.

The 'Adimi' case is an example in point. An Algerian asylum seeker, Mr Chouki Adimi was charged with the offence of using a false instrument soon after arriving at Heathrow airport and claiming asylum. Adimi's defence counsel interposed article 31 as a defence, but it was dismissed by the magistrates. Even after he was granted refugee status, the Crown refused to discontinue his prosecution. On appeal, Simon Brown LJ called attention to the limited knowledge and practical application of the convention provision:

So far as the police and CPS are concerned, no consideration had ever been given to the immunity provided by art 31. Until Mr Adimi's counsel took the point in the magistrates' court, no one involved in the criminal justice system ever addressed their mind to the problem.

(*R v Uxbridge Magistrates' Court, Ex parte Adimi; R v Crown Prosecution Service, Ex parte Sorani; R v Secretary of State for the Home Department, Ex parte Kaziu* [1999] INLR 490 [at 526])

Lord Justice Brown offered a generous interpretation of article 31, asserting that not only refugees, but 'presumptive refugees', who claim asylum in good faith, were covered by this provision. He also argued that refugees should have 'some element of choice' on where to claim asylum and consequently stated that a short stopover en route to the preferred country should not deprive the claimant of international protection.

To the problem of how properly to incorporate article 31 into domestic law, Lord Justices Brown and Newman favoured a 'Secretary of State' solution in which the executive would decide on both the asylum claim and the immunity of the applicant, and where prosecution would be brought only in 'the clearest of cases and where the offence itself appears manifestly unrelated to a genuine quest for asylum'. This solution would not require any legislative amendment. Similar proposals were put forward by a member of the House of Lords and the applicants in 'Adimi' which sought to prevent the initiation of a criminal proceeding when there was evidence that the accused was a potential refugee, or to suspend those proceedings until the executive decides on the asylum claim.[34] The government, though, disregarded these proposals because they would have insufficient deterrent effect and lead to abuses.[35] In response to the 'Adimi' judgment, the legislature introduced section 31 in the IAA 1999. This provision creates a defence which is based on article 31 of the Refugee Convention, but restricts the scope of the latter in two fundamental ways.

First, section 31 adds two further requirements not included in article 31: it requires that the person 'make the claim for asylum as soon as was reasonably practicable after his arrival in the United Kingdom',[36] and it precludes protection when the journey to the UK included a stopover in another country, unless the person 'could not reasonably have expected to be given protection under the Refugee Convention in that country'.[37] It also specifies the offences which shall be covered by the defence,[38] which are largely restricted to fraud-type offences.[39]

Second, the fact that section 31 was made a defence[40] – rather than a ban on or suspension of prosecution – means in practice that prosecutions can be brought against asylum seekers before their status is verified (Harvey 2000: 185). In this regard, the Asylum Policy Instructions (APIs), which regulate the government's policy on asylum and guide caseworkers' decisions, make it clear that the CPS has the ultimate decision on whether to prosecute or not, and the role of the immigration service is restricted to advising prosecutors about the potential application of section 31.[41] The domestic regulation is problematic not only because the mere opening of criminal proceedings may be considered punitive, but also – and most importantly – because the ultimate decision on the matter relies on criminal justice actors who often have insufficient information about the refugee case and limited knowledge of immigration and asylum laws.

The ultimate goal of the protection in article 31 is to avoid prosecution. As Guy Goodwin-Gill (2001: 9), a leading authority in refugee law, explains, 'If Article 31 is to be effectively implemented, clear legislative or administrative action is required to ensure that such proceedings are not begun and that no penalties are in fact imposed.' What happens in practice, though, is that even if there is a pre-screening of the asylum claim by immigration officials, this check is superficial. Usually, immigration officials consider that people who have not come directly to Britain are not covered by the defence. Such assessment has considerable weight in the criminal case and a potential defence under section 31 is often not adequately discussed in court. As a consequence, a considerable number of asylum seekers are convicted of document fraud offences (Bye 1999; Darlington 2006).[42] While not against the wording of section 31, this practice seems in conflict with the government's APIs which state that:

> [I]t would normally be appropriate to await the Secretary of State's decision on the asylum claim before proceeding with a prosecution (and then only if it was considered to be in the public interest to do so), **unless** the person falls outside the scope of the defence for another reason.[43]

Despite the assurance given by the Attorney General that these cases will not reach court and, if they do, will be covered by section 31,[44] prosecutions and convictions of asylum seekers for document offences regularly occur.

The restrictive regulation of article 31 by British law – and its interpretation by the courts[45] – is one of the examples of the progressive 'resiling' from obligations under refugee law by Western countries noted by Catherine Dauvergne (2008: 51). Without walking away from the Refugee Convention, Britain has successfully limited the impact of article 31, thereby retaining control over the administration of punishment and amnesties. In addition to domestic restrictions, refugee law is itself limited in scope (Dauvergne 2004). Because it aims at offering subsidiary protection, only a circumscribed group of people who comply with a number of requirements can invoke it. States are not obliged to offer protection to asylum seekers before they reach their borders. For these reasons, measures intended to prevent asylum seekers from arriving in Britain have not been considered in breach of the Refugee Convention.[46] Further, the scope of certain requirements – such as 'coming directly' – is still subject to different interpretations and state practices are not necessarily bound by the most generous ones (Juss 2005). Finally, asylum determination is complex. Caseworkers and judges make these decisions with limited information and a number of cultural and communication barriers which leave many refugees without state protection (Bohmer and Shuman 2008; Thomas 2011: 48). So in addition to the restrictive nature of international protection and the various, conflicting interpretations of refugee law, states frequently choose to restrict international norms even further.

The indefinite overhaul of the immigration system

The policy objectives set down in the 1998 White Paper continued to drive government policy in its second term (Home Office 2002). However, particularly after the early 2000s, there was a slight modification in strategy from 'control' to 'managed migration' in relation to economic migrants, even though it was short-lived (Clayton 2012: 45). Due to shortages in certain sectors of the labour market, the government opened up some avenues for skilled and unskilled labour migration.[47] The launch of programmes for low-skilled workers was justified as a legal channel for migrants who would otherwise resort to illegal means (Spencer 2007: 350). At the same time, tougher measures were introduced to tackle illegal immigration. The Nationality, Immigration and Asylum Act 2002 (NIAA 2002) and the White Paper that anticipated it, *Secure Borders, Safe Haven* (Home Office 2002) linked unlawful immigration to different forms of organized crime and fraud, where foreigners are involved as perpetrators or victims (Kostakopoulou 2006; Somerville 2007: 44). The White Paper explicitly sought to:

> [C]lose the gaps for illegal entry, illegal working and abuse of the system. Irregular migration undermines the integrity of the system. It profits traffickers, smugglers and unscrupulous employers, damages legitimate business, makes illegal migrant workers vulnerable to exploitation and social exclusion, and may be costly through lost revenue from taxation and National Insurance contributions.
>
> (Home Office 2002: 16)

As it is sometimes the case with public policy making, the new emphasis on organized crime in immigration policy was in part elicited by the tragedy which led, in June 2000, to the deaths of 58 Chinese migrants trying to enter the UK clandestinely through Dover in the back of a lorry. The driver, a Dutch national who was later convicted of manslaughter and conspiracy to facilitate illegal immigration,[48] was found to be part of an organized smuggling operation to bring illegal migrants to the UK and to have negligently caused the death by suffocation of the immigrants by closing the air vent. A report by the Home Affairs Committee in 2001 placed organized crime as one of the main reasons for the rise in asylum applications and quoted the tragedy at Dover as an example of the wide involvement of organized gangs in the business of bringing illegal immigrants to the country (House of Commons 2001: paragraph 25).

The offences incorporated by the NIAA 2002 were either new offences or amendments to those already contained in the IA 1971 (particularly in section 25 of IA 1971) which were widened in the NIAA 2002 to encompass a broader range of conducts. Most of these are 'crimes of solidarity' (Fekete and Webber 2009) or 'organized immigration crimes': assisting unlawful immigration to a Member state by a non-EU citizen inside or outside the UK,[49] helping an asylum seeker to enter the UK 'knowingly and for gain',[50] assisting entry to the UK in breach of a deportation or exclusion order,[51] and trafficking in prostitution inside or outside the UK.[52]

The focus on smuggling was very much at the centre of EU policy making at the time. In November 2002, the Council of Europe approved a directive defining the 'facilitation of unauthorised entry, transit and residence' and a decision providing for minimum penalties for such an offence.[53] Precisely, section 25 of the IA 1971 was modified to comply with the EU directive. However, the new section 25 is broader than the directive in two important aspects. First, while the latter refers to 'intentionally' assisting, the former imposes liability on those who have 'reasonable cause for believing' that their acts facilitate the breach of immigration law, thus accepting negligence liability. Second, the directive mandates the imposition of penalties when the facilitation is done for gain. Instead, in the domestic regulation, the requirement of gain is omitted.

The gain requirement was inserted, instead, in section 25A (which made it an offence to help an asylum seeker to enter the UK). While the Refugee Convention does not preclude penalization of organizations helping asylum seekers,[54] it is evident that punishing those who aid refugees to flee from persecution negatively affects the ability of the latter to seek protection (Hathaway 2005: 403). Due to the need for false or forfeited (adulterated) documents, the resort to 'agents' is for many the only option to escape persecution. While the law punishes those who help asylum seekers to enter the UK only if they do so 'knowingly and for gain', and exempts from penalty organizations that assist asylum seekers without charging for their services,[55] in practice, some 'humanitarian smugglers' are caught by the penal system (Weber and Grewcock 2012). For example, in a court file I examined for this study at Isleworth Crown Court, both the mother and her eldest son were charged with the offence of assisting unlawful immigration for facilitating the entry of her youngest son to the country. The son assisted claimed asylum upon arrival to the UK.[56] He was charged with the offence of obtaining leave to enter the UK by deception – he was accused of using his brother's passport. To the charge of assisting unlawful immigration, his mother pleaded guilty and was convicted to an eight-month suspended sentence and his eldest brother was found not guilty (Isleworth Crown Court, Court file, Case 57). At the same court, 14 out of 58 defendants charged with assisting unlawful immigration had allegedly facilitated the entry of someone who subsequently claimed asylum. In 7 of these 14 cases, the person assisted was a relative of the defendant.

This pattern can be explained by the fact that the offence of assisting unlawful immigration is being used against 'commercial' and 'humanitarian' smugglers, and evidence of 'humanitarian instinct' is usually taken into account for the purpose of mitigation, but not immunity.[57] Those who facilitate the arrival of asylum seekers regarded as illegal entrants are usually charged with the assisting offence which, unlike the offence of helping an asylum seeker, does not require proof of gain. As noted by immigration barrister Frances Webber (2008: 9), immunity is only given to people who assist asylum claimants to reach the port without resorting to deception or other illegal means – for example, using false passports.[58]

English courts have rejected arguments grounded on the Refugee Convention against conviction for this offence precisely because the person being helped used deception. In the case of *R v Alps*, the defendant, Mr Alps, was charged with assisting the entry of his nephew into the UK by passing off a passport as belonging to his nephew. His nephew claimed asylum, but because he tried to enter the country with someone else's document he was deemed an 'illegal entrant'. According to the Court of Appeal, the fact that his nephew claimed asylum did not exempt the defendant from penalty for attempting to bring his nephew to the country by deception. Thus, it concluded that Mr Alps was rightly charged with the offence of assisting – rather than with the offence of helping – and that he was not covered under the protection of article 31 of the Refugee Convention because he facilitated the entry into the country of someone whom he knew or had reasonable cause to believe to be an illegal entrant.[59]

The NIAA 2002 also introduced offences of failing to disclose information by private individuals or institutions;[60] relating to false or altered registration cards;[61] of possessing immigration stamps or replicas;[62] and of returning to the UK after leaving under arrangements made by the Secretary of State.[63] In total, it added 20 further immigration offences, making it the act that introduced more immigration offences than any other in history, apart from the IAA 1999 and the IA 1971. It also expanded police powers of immigration officers[64] and made further provisions regarding the liability of carriers.[65]

Just two years after the NIAA 2002 was enacted, the government introduced a new immigration and asylum bill in Parliament. The Asylum and Immigration (Treatment of Claimants, etc.) Act 2004 (AI(TC)A 2004) sought to reform a still congested system by cutting down appeals and speeding up proceedings. It introduced a number of provisions directed at tackling the main obstacles to a 'seamless' asylum and immigration process: the concealment of identity and the lack of cooperation with immigration authorities.[66] The act criminalized these behaviours in two separate offences which I address in the following sub-sections.

No papers, no excuses: entering the country without a passport

Even though the House of Lords during the hearing in *R v Naillie* (in 1993) ridiculed the suggestion that a duty to submit a passport upon arrival may give rise to a criminal offence for its non-production (Macdonald 2010: Chapter 14), the AI(TC)A 2004 made the failure to produce a passport a crime in 2004.[67] This is currently one of the most frequently used immigration-related offences (Brennan 2006: 158). The increase of 54 per cent of immigration-related cases heard at magistrates' courts from 2004 to 2005 was largely due to the introduction of this offence – 475 persons were charged with this crime in 2005 which represents 44 per cent of total proceedings (Home Office 2006a: 25). For subsequent years, the rate of prosecutions remained high in comparison to other immigration offences.[68] Still, these rates are quite low if they are considered in relation to the number of undocumented migrants caught and the number of people claiming asylum.[69]

The new clause punishes those who deliberately destroy or dispose of their passport between embarkation and claiming asylum. According to the government, the provision would not be applied against those who have never had a passport or did not destroy their documents – false or genuine ones. The main objective was to stop people from concealing their identities, nationalities and the routes they travelled, in order to make a proper asylum determination and to remove those who are not eligible for entry.[70] This offence is connected to the provisions introduced by the AI(TC)A 2004 on the credibility of an asylum claimant. They state that the deciding authority should take into account as damaging to the claimant's credibility the 'failure without reasonable explanation to produce a passport on request to an immigration officer or to the Secretary of State' and 'the destruction, alteration or disposal, in each case without reasonable explanation, of a passport'.[71]

The offence of 'no document' has its own statutory defences: to have a 'reasonable excuse' for not being in possession of a passport; to produce a false document and prove that this has been used for all purposes in connection to the journey to the UK; or to prove that the person has travelled without any immigration document.[72] The government was explicit in not extending the defence under section 31 of the IAA 1999 to this offence, and so were the courts.[73] By making section 31 not applicable, the government was clear that it would not grant immunity to those disposing of or destroying their travel documents:

> We do not think that a person should be automatically protected against prosecution or conviction for such behaviour when they are a refugee who can show that they meet the other requirements of Section 31. In such cases, the person will have had a passport when he left the country where he feared persecution. Having left that country, there is no reason why he would need to destroy or dispose of his passport.
>
> (Baroness Scotland of Asthal, Hansard, HL Deb 5/04/2004, col. 1629)

Such a view ignores the fact that most asylum seekers travel with the aid of 'agents' or facilitators who have absolute control over travel arrangements.[74] People are required to follow their instructions which in most cases include the handing back of the passport used to travel. The provision in section 2 recognizes this element of 'duress', when 'in the circumstances of the case it is unreasonable to expect non-compliance with the instructions or advice [given by a person who offers advice about, or facilitates, immigration into the United Kingdom]'.[75] However, reasonable non-compliance has been restrictively interpreted by the courts to cover only extreme cases.[76] The government's position also demonstrates that international obligations against the penalization of asylum claimants can be sacrificed for the sake of immigration imperatives.

A decision by the High Court in *Thet v DPP* mitigated the restrictive scope of the defences under section 2. The court interpreted the defence under section 2(4) (c) regarding the availability of a reasonable excuse as covering those who travel without a 'valid immigration document' from the beginning to the end of the journey, even if the appellant entered with a false passport and subsequently destroyed it, if he can prove that he was unable to obtain a valid document in his country of origin.[77] In that case, Lord Phillips of Worth Matravers stated that the person is likely to disclose the country from which he comes. Therefore the purpose of the legislation would be fulfilled.[78] This interpretation implicitly recognizes that those who have never had a passport would necessarily resort to a false one in order to flee their countries and reach a 'safe haven'. A different interpretation would deprive such defence of any practical application. A later judgement (2007) by the Court of Appeal, however, disregarded this interpretation as illogical. In *R v Mohammed*, Justice Elias reasoned that the conclusion reached in *Thet v DPP* would provide the defence to those who travel with a false document and then dispose of it, whereas the holder of a genuine document in similar circumstances would be deprived of such defence.[79] As a consequence, he concluded that defendants who travelled with a false document are required to submit it upon arrival in order to be covered by the defences in section 2.

Such an ill-drafted provision in section 2 leaves room for variable and conflicting interpretations. In practice, it creates confusion among criminal lawyers who are doubtful of its application in a concrete case and the interpretation that the courts will follow. This together with the fact that it is a strict liability offence – and does not require proof of *mens rea* – may contribute to the high rates of conviction for this offence.[80]

Criminalizing non-cooperation

From 2003, when asylum applications started to go down, the government's priorities shifted. No longer so concerned with stopping arrivals, it began to pay more attention to identifying and removing failed asylum seekers illegally residing in the UK (Home Office 2005c; Somerville 2007: 44). The removal of failed asylum seekers was the underlying objective of the offence of failure to cooperate with deportation or removal procedures without a reasonable excuse,[81] introduced by the AI(TC)A 2004. Cooperation in this context is related to the re-documentation process when the person to be removed is a national of a country with which the UK has no bilateral agreements to return people without passports.[82]

As with the 'no document' offence, the offence of failure to cooperate addresses the obstacle for removal posed by people without documentation. Both are non-compliance offences. They create a duty and then make a criminal offence to fail to comply with it. Such crimes are regulatory in nature – that is, they support a 'regulatory scheme' (in this case, immigration controls) – by enforcing compliance with a (non-penal) requirement, duty or obligation (Ashworth 2000; Law Commission 2010). The mushrooming of these offences is responsible for the expansion of criminal law since the mid-1990s (Ashworth 2009; Duff 2010a). Because of their common characteristics – strict liability, omission liability, and reverse onus of proof – which depart from traditional principles of criminal law, their reproduction is worrisome (Ashworth 2000). The reverse burden of proof in the context of immigration could be considered as part of the strategy to decentralize immigration controls through 'burden-sharing norms' (Lahav 1998). In the same way that the government imposes a 'duty to control' on carriers, local authorities, financial institutions, hotels and employers, it obliges the person subject to investigation to provide evidence which facilitates his or her removal. The relaxation of criminal law principles eases the work of prosecutors. However, according to the government, this offence is supposed to be a 'lever' or deterrent for 'stopping people from being obstructive' and may only be used 'in the most extreme circumstances'.[83] Even though in recent years, the number of prosecutions slightly increased, since its introduction in 2004, enforcement rates are still quite low.[84]

Still, the use of criminal law may prove unsuccessful to force removals. Because of their (lack of) legal standing, undocumented migrants are deprived of any positive incentives to comply voluntarily with state orders, particularly if that state seeks to push them out. Identity stripping (the destruction of identity documents and the refusal to cooperate with re-documentation) are indeed acts of resistance and a clear limit to state coercion (Ellermann 2010). More coercion – through criminal punishment – is unlikely to disrupt this 'cycle of non-compliance' and yield positive outcomes.[85] A barrister specializing in immigration offences put it clearly:

> [T]here is a certain futility because someone says '[L]ook I'm happier spending my time in prison here than being sent to somewhere where I'm gonna get killed'. So they sit in immigration detention, you prosecute for this, then they get to prison for three months or whatever, they come back into immigration detention and you start all over again. What does it actually achieve?
>
> (Respondent 15, 28/04/2010)

A particularly problematic aspect of this offence and its enforcement is the policy of multiple prosecutions to force compliance. It is not only a disproportionate measure, it is also impractical. The case of 'Rostami'[86] clearly illustrates this. Feridon Rostami, an Iranian national whose application for asylum was refused, was prosecuted three times for failing to cooperate. The immigration judges reasoned that in a case where there is no prospect of prompt removal, the detainee should generally be granted bail. Uncooperative persons are instead criminalized, with the consequence of acquiring a criminal record and facing deportation. This, the judge concluded, 'smacks of oppression' and is unlikely to have any practical effect on removal.[87] Mr Rostami's detention of 34 months – administrative and penal – was declared unlawful because it was too lengthy and there was no evidence that removal would take place in a reasonable time.[88]

The resort to the criminal law did not serve as a substitute for the government's administrative powers to remove immigrants. Rather the former supplemented the latter. New Labour not only created an unprecedented number of immigration-related crimes; it also started to use those powers more systematically, as evidenced by the sharp increase in the rate of prosecutions against immigration offenders. Figure 3.3 shows that in addition to the rise in the use of criminal powers against immigration offenders, there was also a sharp increase in removals, particularly from 2004 and 2008. While prosecution and conviction rates remained considerably lower than the number of removals, the use of criminal powers was enhanced during a period of stricter enforcement of immigration rules.

The main source of criminalization of immigrants has been through document offences which particularly target asylum seekers. Strictly speaking, then, it seems more accurate to refer to the criminalization of undocumented migrants (Melossi 2003: 381).

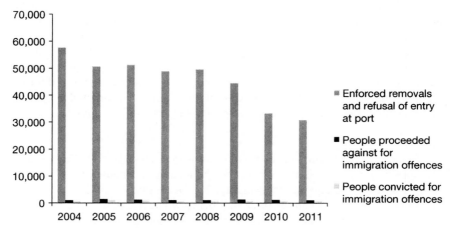

Figure 3.3 Administrative actions versus criminal proceedings
Source: Home Office (2012: Tables rv.01 and pr.01)

The new directions of immigration enforcement: the FNPs crisis and its repercussions

From the mid-2000s onwards, government policy continued to focus on the people illegally remaining in the country after their asylum applications were refused. In addition to the emphasis on the borders – a traditional British immigration strategy – the government expanded the reach of immigration controls to police immigrants within the country (Boswell 2003: 64). Legislation passed during this period did not significantly expand the catalogue of immigration offences.[89] In fact, the main relevant feature of the period starting in 2006 was not the extension of the crime list, but rather changes in enforcement, particularly after the foreign national prisoners' scandal.

In April 2006, it was revealed that over 1,000 foreign national prisoners (FNPs) were released from prison before the IND had considered them for deportation. Her Majesty's Inspectorate of Prisons qualified this as 'an acute symptom of the chronic failure of the two services [immigration and prisons] to develop and implement effective policies and strategies for people who were not seen as a "problem"' (HMIP 2006: 1). The Home Office's mishandling of the matter was quickly exploited by the opposition and the tabloid media. The media focused on those released, describing them as dangerous and threatening individuals who instead of being sent back home were released onto Britain's streets (Toner 2009: 190).[90] In the words of some parliamentarians, the wrongly released prisoners were not only serious criminals; they abused the hospitality offered by the British people.[91] 'Foreigners' and 'criminals' in this context resulted in a toxic combination. The competence of Home Office officials was called into question and prompted the resignation of Home Secretary Charles Clarke. These events had an impact on the whole immigration system, which once again came under the spotlight.

The consequences of this crisis were manifold. Foreign national prisoners became a top priority of the immigration agency after the scandal (Home Office 2006b). They were the first target for removal actions. The government deployed immigration officers in prisons to identify FNPs at an early stage in order to speed up repatriation or deportation after they finished their sentences (Home Office 2006c: 25). As part of the same strategy, it introduced the 'Hubs and Spoke' policy, which segregates FNPs in particular prisons ('hubs'),[92] and the automatic deportation of those sentenced to custody for 12 months or more (Bosworth 2011a).[93] It also affected the detention regimes for FNPs who were now less likely to be allowed into open prisons and more likely to be detained in 'hub' establishments with tighter security arrangements (Singh Bhui 2007). Caseworkers were less likely to grant temporary leave to remain in cases involving FNPs. The Head of Law of an organization supporting asylum seekers told me that these are the cases where caseworkers would 'fight and fight and fight' to try to remove 'people like that' (Respondent 13, 14/06/2010). The political pressure not to release foreigners subject to deportation also led to longer terms of post-sentence administrative detention (London Detainee Support Group 2009: 6).[94]

The impact of the FNP crisis on immigration offenders is obvious. In a context of tougher enforcement of immigration crimes, some[95] of the people falling into the category of FNPs are immigration offenders. Because people convicted for immigration offences are part of the universe of FNPs, the more stringent conditions imposed on the latter since 2006 have had an impact on immigration offenders. The supervising solicitor at Refugee and Migrant Justice (RMJ) explained that this scandal had the effect of extending these unfavourable conditions to immigration offenders and blurred the line between them and people convicted of non-immigration crimes:

[B]ecause in 2006 there was a big push to get rid of foreign national prisoners from the UK, and they are not necessarily people who've committed immigration offences, they are just foreign nationals who have committed crimes, so it could be immigration offences or it could be other crimes. So those sort of tended to kind of merge into one.

(Respondent 10, 8/06/2010)

The impact that this crisis had on immigration offenders shows that criminalizing immigration breaches has not only symbolic effects, but also important practical consequences. Because of criminalization, foreigners with irregular status 'end up being treated by systems which are designed to deal with people who have committed offences'.[96] As the FNP crisis shows, once someone is caught by the criminal justice system, there is little differentiation between 'real' and 'immigration' offenders (Bosworth 2007).

Most importantly, the focus on foreign-national offenders in immigration policy as a result of this crisis had important institutional repercussions. It forced the government to boost the resources of the IND's Criminal Casework Department. It also prompted changes in the enforcement approach and priorities of the department, which was replaced in April 2007 by the BIA and later on, in 2008, by the UKBA. It also provoked a new overhaul of the immigration system aimed at simplifying the legal framework[97] and improving the enforcement of immigration laws. In 2007, Home Secretary John Reid diagnosed that the IND was 'not fit for purpose'. In the government there was a perception that the immigration system was increasingly complex, there was no consistency throughout the organization and that it was failing to face the challenges of mass migration in a globalized world. In the Home Secretary's words, 'we have not been tough enough in enforcing the rules' (Home Office 2007b: 3).

Two documents set up the shape of the new immigration agency – *Enforcing the Rules* (Home Office 2007b) and *Enforcing the Deal* (Home Office 2008b). As the titles of these documents imply, the emphasis was placed on enforcement and particularly immigration enforcement tailored to that of a crime control agency (Weber and Bowling 2004; Bosworth 2007).[98] They defined the abuse of the immigration system as criminal and offered criminal prosecution and punishment as a response for many immigration breaches. Both documents gave great importance to criminal law powers. They announced an addition of prosecution staff in the BIA to increase the rate of prosecutions (Home Office 2007b: 25) and established prosecution targets for immigration crimes at a rate of 1,400 successful prosecutions for 2008 and 2009 (Home Office 2008b: Appendix C; see also Home Office 2009c: 21). Consistent with this approach, immigration officials have progressively gained police-like powers with respect to many immigration offences.[99] This was aimed at decreasing the dependency on the police in the arrest and removal of immigration offenders which is now carried out almost entirely without police intervention. Providing immigration officers with these powers has virtually transformed the agency into an 'immigration police force' (Macdonald 2010: Chapter 14.1; see also Vogel *et al.* 2009: 218).[100] Police officers, who are reluctant to intervene in immigration enforcement operations and consider most of this work as 'rubbish', benefited from this change. It also favoured immigration officers who prefer operational work to casework (Weber and Landman 2002: 12; Weber and Bowling 2004: 205).

The creation of the UKBA in 2008 was part of this overhaul of the immigration system. The agency integrates the work of the BIA, UKvisas and the border-related work of HM Revenue and Customs, both inside and outside the UK (Cabinet Office 2007). The purpose was to develop a more comprehensive and coherent system of controls at the borders and inside the country. As such, the establishment of the UKBA has not brought fundamental changes to immigration enforcement, but rather has consolidated ongoing reforms. Its creation sent a symbolic message of 'a strong force at the borders' with uniformed and better resourced staff. A securitized, unified border force was deemed necessary to face the new threats of terrorism, organized crime and illegal immigration. Irregular immigration was positioned within a 'criminal law-enforcement paradigm' (Spencer 2011: 168)[101] not only because it is alleged that criminal gangs are behind three-quarters of illegal immigration (Webb and Burrows 2009), but also because it is considered as damaging to public services and to fair labour competition (Home Office 2007b,

2010d). A further institutional reform that split the Home Office into two in 2007 contributed to the perception that immigration was aligned institutionally to crime, terrorism and security. Indeed, the new focus of the Home Office would be on matters related to immigration, policing, terrorism and security, leaving probation supervision, prisons and prevention of reoffending to the newly created Ministry of Justice. As Gina Clayton (2012: 44) explains, 'this allocation gave a clear signal about the way that immigration was perceived, and the direction that further institutional change would take'.

As part of the strategy to increase enforcement capacity and strengthen internal controls, the agency regionalized its work into different Local Immigration Teams (LITs) in charge of low-level immigration offences – mainly dealt with by administrative action. It also created Immigration Crime Teams (ICTs) formed of immigration and police officers in charge of more serious crimes. As another feature of the move towards a police-like enforcement agency, in 2010, the UKBA set up the Crime Directorate to tackle organized crime both at the borders and inside the country. Additionally, the immigration agency has increasingly borrowed the tone and rhetoric of the police. References to 'Immigration Crime Partnerships', a 'watch list' for immigration offenders, immigration 'hotspots' or naming an enforcement visit as 'Operation X' (Home Office 2008b) very much resemble terms used by the police.

The new enforcement agenda was translated into a series of measures aimed at differentiating levels of illegality and targeting those who cause the most harm. In policy papers (Home Office 2006b, 2007b, 2008b, 2010d), the agency distinguishes between breaches to immigration laws in terms of their actual or potential 'harm'[102] and tailors different 'interventions' to 'minimize' the harm caused by them. In this vein, a number of actuarial devices have been introduced to prioritize enforcement action against certain conducts. Similar to Feeley and Simon's (1992, 1994) view of criminal justice, decisions in the immigration arena are largely shaped by actuarial instruments (Miller 2003; Weber 2007; Bosworth and Guild 2008: 712; Bosworth 2008). The 'harm' criterion has permeated many facets of UKBA work including the decisions on whom to take action against first,[103] on whether to prosecute (Home Office 2010d), on where to allocate foreign prisoners once their sentences have expired,[104] and on whom to remove first (Home Office 2009a).[105] The introduction of the 'harm matrix' seeks to regulate decision making and guide immigration and police officers in their work. Those who cause the most harm are targeted for prosecution and removal (Home Office 2007b, 2010d). However, I will show in Chapters 4 and 5 that the cases which continue to crowd the criminal courts are what the agency would characterize as 'low-level' offences.

The new approach to immigration enforcement has not resulted in a substantial increase in prosecution and conviction rates for immigration offences; in fact, they started to decline between 2005 and 2006 in the magistrates' courts.[106] Prosecution targets were removed in 2010 because they were not considered an appropriate measure of the agency's performance. As a high-ranking official at UKBA's Policy and Strategic Group told me, '[i]t is quite easy to do lots of variable prosecutions and tick the box against targets', but this does not necessarily have an impact on the strategic objectives of the agency (Respondent 14, 12/08/2010). Even for the most frequently used immigration offences – document-related and deception offences – the Ministry of Justice (MoJ) and the UKBA launched pilots in November 2010 to divert these cases from prosecution through the use of cautions, mainly to facilitate removals and reduce the burden on the criminal justice system and prison estate (Ministry of Justice 2010b; see also Home Office 2010d: 27). Such pilots, however, resulted in few cases being diverted: simple caution was used in only five out of 109 eligible cases.[107]

Conclusion

The Labour years of immigration law (1997–2010) can be characterized as a period of hyper-activity resulting in an over-regulation in many areas of immigration policy concomitant with increasing complexity. As Cathy Gardner (2006: 4) has observed, there is a tendency in recent policy making 'to add to, rather than exercise existing powers'. As a consequence of its enlargement and sophistication, immigration legislation has become increasingly difficult to interpret and enforce. A number of conducts not regulated before or dealt with by administrative law have been criminalized, and those breaching these rules are now subject to criminal sanctions. Currently, 'almost all breaches of immigration and customs law have a criminal sanction attached to them' (Home Office 2010d: 26).

Likewise, immigration officials have been gaining powers similar to those granted to police officers to investigate immigration crimes. This has created a hybrid system in between administrative and criminal law. Internal controls are increasingly important as a large proportion of illegal immigrants come to the country through legal means, but become illegal once in Britain (House of Commons 2006: 25). Alongside the expansion of immigration crimes and their enhanced enforcement, the government has sought to prioritize enforcement actions against the most harmful people and to divert low-level offences away from the criminal justice system (such as illegal employment and minor fraud offences). This has been largely motivated by the lack of deterrence and the high costs of the criminal justice route. Still, most of those caught in the net of criminal justice are undocumented migrants.

Even though more restrictive measures to deal with different faces of the immigration system have been continually introduced, these changes do not seem to leave the British public at ease with the 'immigration problem'.[108] Moreover, the efficiency and fairness of these measures continue to be put into question.[109] The increasing restrictiveness of British immigration laws may be explained in part by the fact that they are directed at 'others'. Immigrants – particularly if they are undocumented – have no voice and little possibility of influencing decisions because illegality forfeits the exercise of civil and political rights, and many are pushed underground. As such, there is an asymmetry in the distribution of benefits and burdens of these policies: the benefits are for 'us', whereas the burdens are for 'others' (Loader 2002: 143; see also Melossi 2000, 2005).

4 The use of criminal law powers against immigration offenders

The decision to prosecute

This chapter and the next describe and analyse the use of criminal law against immigration suspects. They are based on empirical data obtained from interviews with UK Border Agency (UKBA) officials and practitioners and from court cases. An account of the methodology used for collecting and processing empirical material, and a description of the sample, are provided in the Appendix. In this chapter, I analyse the decision to prosecute immigration crimes: what are the criteria followed by authorities and how is this decision made in practice? In Chapter 5, I look at the cases that reach the criminal courts and the criminal process that follows.

Police and immigration officers have several alternatives when dealing with immigration suspects. One of them is to pursue a criminal prosecution. While the use of criminal law powers to enforce immigration controls has increased since the early 2000s, most immigration offences are dealt with administratively. Instead of being prosecuted, a person who has been caught in breach of immigration laws may be subject to an often long administrative proceeding before removal directions are issued. This process may include reporting to immigration authorities, the initiation of an appeal process against removal orders before the Asylum and Immigration Tribunal and the detention of the applicant. Immigration officials have the discretion to grant leave to remain in certain cases; therefore, removal is not necessarily the final outcome of this process (Macdonald 2010: Chapter 16.46).

This chapter seeks to unravel the criteria informing the decision to instigate a criminal prosecution. In the first two sections, I explain the existing system of parallel (criminal and administrative) regulations, the guidelines for the authorities and the role of different enforcement agencies in the prosecution of immigration offences. The third section looks at how the decision to prosecute is made in practice: which cases are candidates for prosecution and based on what considerations? I find that in the absence of strict rules, enforcement officials have wide discretion to choose which system to trigger and they give significant consideration to practical factors, particularly the possibility summarily to remove the immigration suspect. Because of the existence of different regimes to deal with the same issue, the lack of clear guidelines to determine which system to use and the resulting wide margin of discretion for decision makers, it is almost impossible to know in advance which cases will be prosecuted and which ones will not. The final section contrasts the government's priorities in the use of criminal powers with the everyday practice of prosecuting immigration suspects. Evidence from court cases suggests that the matters which more frequently reach the criminal courts are those involving individual offending, particularly cases related to different forms of document fraud and small-scale facilitation. I argue that such contradiction between policy objectives and practices can only be explained in the light of the dual system of parallel criminal and immigration sanctions where criminal law and punishment are instrumental to the exercise of administrative powers.

The hybrid system of immigration and criminal sanctions

The convergence of immigration and criminal laws in recent years has created a system of juxtaposed controls over non-citizens. The increased criminalization of immigration laws has expanded the alternative interventions that enforcement officers can pursue against immigration suspects. The overlapping enforcement mechanisms and strategies include refusal of entry, executive removal, deportation on 'conducive to public good' grounds by the Secretary of State, and criminal prosecution – which may include a recommendation for deportation. Furthermore, these strategies are not mutually exclusive, but can work together, as the principle of double jeopardy – which proscribes multiple prosecutions for the same act – does not apply in immigration proceedings.[1] For those who fall foul of these rules, foreignness may trigger a 'double sentencing' (Wacquant 2005): first, the criminal process for breaching the boundaries of their status; and second, the administrative action of removal from the country.

The existence of an array of mechanisms and the convenience of using administrative removal to deal with 'low level foreign national offenders' explain the under-enforcement of immigration offences. A criminal prosecution and the proceeding that follows are more time-consuming and expensive than an administrative one (Home Office 2010d: 27; 2011a). Further, the removal of the person from the country – rather than his or her punishment – is the ultimate objective of the immigration agency and so it is often the preferred choice.

At this point, it is important to differentiate between deportation and administrative removal. Even though both measures aim at expelling a non-national from the country, they differ in terms of the grounds on which they can be ordered and their consequences. A deportation order has the effect of cancelling an existing leave to remain and may proceed in three circumstances: when the Secretary of State decides that the deportation of a person is 'conducive to the public good'; when a court recommends deportation of a person convicted of a crime punishable with imprisonment; and when a person is convicted of a crime in the UK and sentenced to either a period of imprisonment of at least 12 months or imprisonment of any length of time for a particularly serious offence.[2] This last ground is known as 'automatic deportation' because a recommendation by the court is not required. A deportation order entails the prohibition to return to the UK until it is revoked.

In contrast, administrative removal is an immigration decision which proceeds against a variety of foreigners including those who have been refused entry, illegal entrants, overstayers and those who have breached their conditions of leave, those using deception to remain, former refugees, and crew members remaining unlawfully.[3] Unlike deportees, people who are removed from the UK have in principle no restrictions to return, according to section 5(1) of the IA 1971. However, recent changes in immigration rules established a presumption of rejection of visas for people who have been removed. Therefore, they may have their future applications to enter the UK refused for a specified period of up to ten years.[4] A further difference between the two is the applicable appeal regime. While a deportation order can be subject to appeals on several grounds, appeal rights against removal orders are limited. When allowed, appeals do not suspend removal orders. Other than in exceptional cases, they are generally allowed only once the applicant has left the country (out-of-country appeal). Non-British immigration offenders are liable under both regimes. Even if they are not summarily removed, they can be deported following a criminal sentence.

Rules and rulers in the decision to prosecute

The decision to prosecute has a number of stages, depending on the circumstances of the case. At the port of entry, an immigration officer is generally the first to interview the suspected offender. The case may then be referred to a chief immigration officer for review. When the latter considers that a criminal offence has been committed and there are grounds for a prosecution, the case is subsequently referred to the police. In this regard, it should be remembered that despite the fact that immigration officers have been granted a number of police-like powers, they cannot press criminal charges. Specially trained (or 'designated') immigration officers[5] are bestowed with arrest powers and can arrest suspected offenders without warrant for a wide range of immigration-related crimes. Immigration officers can gather evidence and question the person arrested. They can detain for up to three hours individuals who are liable to arrest by a constable or who are subject to a warrant of arrest. However, they still rely on the police to detain individuals for longer periods and to charge the arrestee with an offence.

Following the assessment by the police, the CPS will then make a final decision on whether to initiate a prosecution or not, and on which charges. A senior CPS policy adviser told me, though, that at the port of entry, immigration authorities – particularly the chief immigration officer – have a major role in deciding whether or not to send the case to the CPS, while there is more involvement of the police in this decision when the offender is encountered inside the country (Respondent 19, 14/06/2010). This process will generally take place within a short period. In major international airports, such as Heathrow, there are special immigration prosecution units on-site which make the decision-making process swifter.

The role of the police

Immigration officers generally work with the police in enforcement operations, even though police participation in these operations is diminishing as some UKBA employees have acquired police-like powers and training to operate independently.[6] While immigration authorities are more likely to detect immigration offenders at the port of entry, the police play an important role in the policing of foreign nationals and the identification of those who are in breach of immigration rules. In many circumstances, the police encounter immigration offenders when they sign on at the police station or during police operations, such as street raids or the investigation of other crimes (Jordan and Düvell 2002: 177). The police have broad powers of stop and search. A police officer may stop someone if he or she has grounds to suspect that the person is carrying drugs, guns or other items to commit a crime or to cause criminal damage. A vehicle can be stopped at any time and the driver asked to show his or her driving licence to the police officer. The vehicle can also be searched. The police may search anyone in a certain area when serious violence has taken place or may take place.[7] These powers are comparatively broader than those of immigration officers, particularly when exercised 'in-country' (as opposed to at the port of entry), where immigration officers can only examine people in public areas to determine their immigration status when they have reasonable suspicion that they are immigration offenders. At the port of entry, in contrast, immigration officials have ample powers.[8]

Given such broad powers and the discretion the police have in dealing with immigration suspects, it is difficult to draw any conclusion as to how the police generally intervene in these cases. While in certain circumstances police officers may open a criminal investigation, in others they may refer the matter to immigration authorities without opening a criminal case. Even though there are no statistics on the use of criminal powers in this context by the police, research suggests that the UKBA is more likely to press criminal charges in case of minor immigration offences than the police (Weber and Bowling 2004: 205; Vogel *et al.* 2009: 222). Still, the police play a crucial role in identifying, detaining and handing over 'immigration wrongdoers' (Jordan and Düvell 2002).

For example, the head of a Local Immigration Team (LIT) near Heathrow airport told me that the police 'bring a lot of work to our attention'. The LITs handle low-level immigration offences and mainly use administrative channels to deal with them as they do not have prosecution-trained officers and cannot pursue a criminal prosecution. He referred to cases in which the police come across foreign nationals with no legal status and hand them over to immigration authorities without pressing charges:

> [I]f the police picks somebody up for simply speeding, for example, or driving without a licence – say a minor offence for example – or they just encounter them – you know, there is somebody in the back of a car, the car has been stopped for speeding and they question the person. [If] the person does not have a right to remain in the UK, the police will have no interest in that.
>
> (Respondent 18, 10/06/2010)

The chief of the LIT explained that in these cases, 'the police will normally not pursue a criminal case . . . because it's a low level crime and it will be expensive to the taxpayers to pursue that as the person is leaving the UK anyway' (Respondent 18, 10/06/2010). Likewise, sometimes judges defer the decision on cases of non-serious crimes involving undocumented foreigners to the immigration service. During a hearing of a case involving a person who entered the country illegally being accused of driving without a licence and without insurance, the District Judge at Uxbridge Magistrates' Court addressed the police officer in the room: 'Can you please communicate with UKBA? If they want to do something, tell them to do it now.' The hearing was then adjourned awaiting the UKBA's decision on whether the accused would be subject to removal proceedings. Such determination may affect the fate of the criminal process for motoring offences. If the person was liable to removal, the latter would probably be discontinued.[9]

A similar account was given by a lawyer specializing in immigration and criminal law at Fisher Meredith Solicitors. He explained to me that, unlike minor 'ordinary' offences – such as petty thefts – where criminal prosecution is the only option, immigration offenders can be dealt with by immigration powers:

> I just think it's a knowledge thing, it puts [it] under the heading of immigration and I think in the head [of the police officer] it's considered separate . . . I just think the bigger picture takes over. That's considered so minor, that there's a much bigger consequence, whereas [in the case of] a minor criminal offence [if] they don't prosecute, nothing really happens. If you commit [an immigration offence] and they don't prosecute it, at least there's someone else to deal with the bigger picture which is their asylum and their removal.
>
> (Respondent 4, 16/07/2010)

A barrister at Doughty Street Chambers referred to the reluctance by some police officers to pursue immigration-related cases – such as document fraud – and mentioned that they do not want to interview 'the petty person who doesn't have a passport'. He also claimed there was a 'tension' between police and immigration officers within prosecution teams: 'so you've got these immigration officers [as part of the prosecution team] . . . [who] are dedicated to the prosecution of these offences and the police . . . [who] are far less interested' (Respondent 15, 28/04/2010). The police have historically been reluctant to engage in immigration matters. As Weber and Bowling (2004: 205) affirm, except when it involves organized criminality, such work is by and large perceived by the force as 'rubbish', 'draining police resources and unlikely to lead to any result in terms of prosecution or crime control'.

While the testimonies quoted above suggest that the police may refer cases of individual immigration offenders to the UKBA, in the absence of 'hard data' it is difficult to be certain about the consistency of police response. Connected to this issue is the question of whether or not the identity of the law enforcement agency – i.e. the police or the UKBA – in the investigation of these crimes has an impact on prosecution rates. The response to this question is again loaded with speculation. In this regard, a senior official at the UKBA's Criminality and

Detention Group conjectured that the expansion of police-like powers for immigration officers may have contributed to the rise in the enforcement of immigration offences in the late 1990s and early 2000s:

> [A]bout 2001 [there] were seconded police officers to this agency who came in and worked alongside to train enforcement officers and it was about then that our enforcement officers got powers of arrest, so before that UKBA or the immigration group couldn't prosecute anyone . . . So that's why you see a sort of a spike [in prosecution rates] then I guess.
>
> (Respondent 5, 16/09/2010)

The expansion of the powers granted to immigration staff in recent years has had an effect on policing practices and the way immigration offences are enforced. It steadily diminished the participation of the police in immigration enforcement and enhanced the role of immigration staff in decision making (Brennan 2006: 195). A senior immigration barrister explained that she noticed some changes during the investigation of such offences since the creation of the immigration border force:

> In the past . . . any prosecution was something that was run by the police. The immigration officers would be in an associated capacity where they might be there for interviewing and asking about the immigration offences. But basically the case was the police officer's case. But now that you have the sort of border agency and you have these functions associated with borders – much more extensive powers . . . – you have immigration people being the dominant people in a lot of these things.
>
> (Respondent 11, 29/04/2010)

It remains unclear, however, whether these institutional changes have had any impact on how immigration offences are handled and, particularly, whether the involvement of forces with different priorities – the police and the UKBA – affects prosecution numbers.

Rules and guidelines for prosecuting immigration offenders

The criteria on when to pursue a criminal case remain largely unclear and vague. The CPS guidance on immigration offences states that 'The fact that a defendant is to be administratively removed by the immigration authority does not, in itself, justify discontinuance [of a prosecution]'.[10] However, a rule that seems to be important in the UKBA manuals is that removal should take precedence over a criminal prosecution, except in cases of 'serious' offences and repeat offenders. The UKBA Enforcement Instructions and Guidance (UKBA EI&G) states that: 'offenders are *not* charged with immigration offences unless serious criminal offences and/or a history of immigration deception are disclosed'.[11] It also mentions that a removal is preferred for a number of reasons:

[I]t is more effective and practicable . . .; it is normally desirable that an offender is removed from the UK as soon as possible; courts are often unwilling to recommend deportation except for serious criminal offences; bail may be granted and the offender may then go to ground.

(UKBA EI&G: Chapter 33.4)

The Immigration Directorate Instructions (IDIs) prescribe that 'overstayers' 'who come to notice when embarking' should not be 'detained for prosecution'.[12] It also states that illegal entrants encountered after they enter the country should be referred to the Enforcement and Compliance caseworking units only if they involve: re-entry in breach of a deportation order; clandestine entry or on forged documents; or deception on arrival as to the person's true intention.[13] In relation to the offence of non-cooperation with removal proceedings, the UKBA issued a detailed guidance on the procedure to follow in these cases.[14] According to it, when the person fails to attend the documentation interview or answer the questions asked during it without a reasonable excuse, 'non-compliance action' should be initiated. In addition, the offender should be removable – that is, when there is a 'reasonable expectation of removal'.[15] So in these cases, the removability of the suspect is a prerequisite for prosecution.

Other guidance, however, remains confidential, such as the instructions from the Immigration Service Enforcement Directorate which cover evasion of control, illegal entry, deportation work, offences against the immigration laws and procedures for investigation (referred to in Macdonald 2010). The Standard Acceptable Criteria (SAC)[16] which define the UKBA's criminal investigation priorities are not publicly available.[17] After stating that low-level offences should preferably be dealt with through administrative means, they mention that strategic UKBA priorities 'such as entry to the UK without a passport, or cases with aggravating features' should be referred to the UKBA crime team. While these criteria prescribe that immigration offences should be considered on the basis of their seriousness, the UKBA's priorities and the 'impact on the integrity of the UK immigration control and its communities', they do not provide detailed, specific guidance on when to employ criminal powers.

According to a senior policy adviser at the CPS, there are other informal guidelines followed in practice by immigration and police officers and prosecutors. She told me that 'low-level offences' – such as the possession of a false passport or other identity document – without aggravated features are often not prosecuted and the person is returned to the port of embarkation. Prosecutors take into account the circumstances surrounding the case when deciding which criminal charges to file in a prosecution. Normally, people caught with a false document on the street – i.e. a raid – are prosecuted under immigration acts, whereas those attempting to use a false document to open a bank account or access work are generally charged with offences under the Forgery and Counterfeiting Act (FCA) 1981 or the IDCA 2006 (Respondent 19, 14/06/2010). Due to the scope of prosecutorial discretion, however, these outcomes are not fixed and vary considerably.

In the absence of clear guidelines, the decision to prosecute is made on a 'case-by-case' basis. According to my interviewees, there are no 'hard and fast lines' to guide the decision in a particular case and this is ultimately based on a pragmatic approach. At the UKBA, both policy and operational staff referred to the lack of rules to determine in advance which cases are candidates for criminal prosecution – except in cases involving trafficking and other forms of serious, organized criminality.

Exercising discretion: the use of prosecution powers in regulatory spheres

The absence of clear parameters and the availability of different mechanisms to deal with immigration offences result in substantial discretion for decision makers. In British law – as in other common law systems – discretion is recognized as inherent to the exercise of police and prosecution powers. Unlike other jurisdictions where a more rigid rule mandates prosecution of each and every breach of criminal provisions ('principle of legality'), the British legal system recognizes that this is just impossible, unwise and unfair because, in practice, discretion is exercised anyway. So enforcement agencies and the CPS are given some margin of discretion in deciding whether to proceed in a particular case. According to the Code for Crown Prosecutors, there are two stages in the decision on whether to prosecute: first, an evaluation of the sufficiency of the evidence; and second, an assessment of whether the prosecution of the case is in the 'public interest'. 'Public interest', however, is a lax and vague concept that grants prosecutorial authorities a certain margin of choice. There are no set criteria on how to interpret this term and decide which cases are candidates for prosecution, even though the 'seriousness' of the offence is generally an important factor (e.g. Ashworth 1987; Fionda and Ashworth 1994; Daw and Solomon 2010).

In immigration enforcement, such margins of discretion are even wider because of the different options to deal with a similar issue and the priorities of the immigration agency. The main concern of the UKBA is not to punish wrongdoing. Rather its primary goals are, first, to enforce compliance with immigration rules, so that controls can be exercised effectively; and second, to exclude and eject people who do not comply with immigration norms. Within this 'compliance approach' which characterizes non-police, regulatory agencies, the UKBA often reserves criminal prosecutions for cases in which other mechanisms are ineffective (Ashworth 2000: 247; Garoupa *et al.* 2011: 242).

Regulatory agencies with enforcement powers generally follow what John Braithwaite and Ian Ayres (1992: 35) called an 'enforcement pyramid'. According to this model, most regulatory action falling at the base of the pyramid is characterized by persuasion to enforce compliance. Criminal sanctions are almost at the top and should remain rare, to be applied only when the individual or corporation proves unresponsive to softer forms of regulation, such as warnings or civil penalties. Research on the enforcement of factory legislation shows that criminal prosecutions are rare in this context, whereas warning notices or formal and informal threats of prosecution are more frequently used (Carson 1970: 392).[18] It is the culmination of an unsuccessful process, usually preceded by numerous attempts to induce compliance (Hawkins 1984, 2002). From an economic perspective, the rationale behind this enforcement strategy is that businesses and corporations are better regulated by non-criminal, negotiated interventions as these are more effective in achieving the ultimate goal of compliance with the law, while keeping enforcement costs down (Ogus 2010).

As such, regulators with enforcement powers – such as the Environmental Agency, the Financial Services Authority or the telecommunications and broadcasting regulator (Ofcom) – have different priorities from those of the Crown Prosecution Service (CPS) and the police: they are concerned with securing compliance rather than punishing wrongdoing. Concomitantly, they have great discretionary powers in the selection of enforcement mechanisms. The enforcement of regulatory offences casts doubt upon the fair and equal treatment of conducts of similar gravity that are dealt with by different enforcement agencies in different ways (Ashworth 2000: 246; see also Lacey 2008: 102). While the crimes of the wealthy and the middle class are dealt with by regulatory agencies which privilege non-criminal justice responses to wrongdoing, the crimes of the poor are dealt with by the police and the CPS for whom the primary form of intervention is through prosecution and punishment (Ashworth and Redmayne 2010: 162). Given this 'bifurcation' in the enforcement of conventional and 'regulatory' crimes, John Braithwaite (2003) proposed an analytical framework that acknowledges the hybridity of punitive and non-punitive regulation and that considers both the 'criminal justice trunk' and the 'business regulatory trunk' as part of the regulatory state.

There are a number of differences between the UKBA and other regulatory agencies. First and foremost, the latter's main targets are economic activities which are legal but are carried out in a dangerous or unsafe way, and the regulatory agency's goal is to induce compliance with legal norms. Second, the regulated subjects are firms which are generally seen as 'partners' with whom the agency seeks to establish a continuous relationship of cooperation and negotiation. There is a certain 'identification' between regulator and regulated (Wells 2005: 24). Instead, the UKBA's prime mandate is to exclude those who are not allowed to enter or stay in the country, thus leaving no room for voluntary compliance. Further, the UKBA's choice of intervention is independent of the subject's conduct or disposition. No such relationship of cooperation exists in the immigration sphere.

Similar to regulatory agencies, though, the UKBA does not regard criminal prosecution as at the top of its enforcement strategy and has discretion on how to pursue a case. Further, its objectives are different from those of the police. The UKBA's guidelines make it clear that in addition to the evidence or threshold test and the public interest test, the UKBA's policy to prosecute should also be considered in the decision to proceed against immigration-related offences. In this regard, they state that '[w]e must ensure that our use of the criminal justice system supports the maintenance of an effective immigration control; furthermore, we must also take into account administrative means of dealing with immigration law breaches'.[19] Hence, the decision to trigger a prosecution is largely determined by instrumental considerations, rather than by questions of retribution and censure. The addition of this instrumental logic underpinning the decision to prosecute expands the scope of options in immigration decision making.

For decision makers, the existence of a parallel system of sanctions that allows administrative or/and criminal penalties

> provides for much more flexibility in responding to criminal offences committed by immigrants than does criminal law alone. Expulsion and deportation thus become repressive measures and a punishment which is added to, or exchanged with, ordinary criminal penalties. Administrative procedures may replace criminal procedures, providing greater administrative convenience and fewer safeguards derived from the rule of law.
>
> (Albrecht 2000: 147)

A number of academics have referred to the exercise of this unregulated, discretionary power in the treatment of non-citizens (Schuck 1984; Juss 1997; Kanstroom 2006). Leanne Weber and Todd Landman (2002) documented that the decision on whether to order detention for asylum applicants is highly unpredictable and greatly depends on 'extra-legal' considerations such as practices, stereotypes and the individual characteristics of decision makers, rather than on official guidelines and rules (see also Jubany-Baucells 2003; Weber 2003). Wendy Chan (2005) showed variations in decisions to deport from Canada non-citizens convicted of crimes. She demonstrated that judicial authorities rely on the personal characteristics of the deportee (gender, ethnicity, links to the country, etc.) as a main consideration for their decisions, while the offence is relatively unimportant. They exercise what she calls 'moral regulation' in immigration by differentiating 'good' from 'bad' immigrants and assessing their possibility of 'moral redemption' and integration to mainstream Canadian society. Similarly, Anna Pratt (2005: 64) in her study of immigration detention and deportation in Canada referred to the influence of the officers' 'professional identity, location and preoccupations' on the decision to detain. She made the point that despite a growing regulation of immigration, discretion in decision making persists because it is considered necessary and desirable to humanize and individualize decisions.

The wide scope of discretion present in the exercise of immigration/criminal law powers contributes to the selective enforcement of immigration laws. In the same situation, a person can be prosecuted and deported, or administratively removed from the country. Because offenders can be dealt with by different regimes and through different interventions, failure to prosecute does not mean that they will go 'scot-free', as is the case in most minor criminal offences. This feature makes the system of immigration and criminal regulations highly unpredictable for immigrants because there is no way of knowing in advance through which regime they are going to be dealt with (Macdonald 2010: Chapter 14.2). Often, the decision to prosecute is based on pragmatic considerations and results in inconsistencies.

Removability and the decision to prosecute: an example of the pragmatic use of the criminal law

The decision to prosecute is based on a number of factors. The most important one is the possibility to remove the offender from the country. When removal is not a feasible option – for instance, because of the lack of genuine identity documents – a prosecution generally follows. In fact, state authorities of the country to which removal is proposed may refuse to admit people without proof of nationality and so removal of undocumented migrants is practically impossible (Macdonald 2010: Chapter 16.65). Defective or non-existent documentation has been identified by the government as a major obstacle to immigration controls (Home Office 1998: Chapter 11). The disguise or concealment of identity by foreigners – by using a false identity or by not revealing one's real identity – jeopardizes the state's 'rational bureaucratic administration' over its population and particularly hinders its capacity to identify and sort a 'society of strangers' in global conditions (Lyon 2009: 36).

The lack of genuine documentary identification brings enormous practical problems to governments – especially in asylum cases (Bohmer and Shuman 2008). As explained in Chapter 3, the prohibition on imposing penalties on refugees in the Refugee Convention is mainly aimed at preventing them from going underground and making them 'legible' for the hosting state. As an academic expert in refugee law put it:

> If you've got an asylum seeker who has no papers and nothing on them whatsoever, how do you deal with them? How can you establish their identity with confidence? How can you know which country they come from with confidence?
>
> (Respondent 7, 12/05/2010)

In addition, asylum seekers cannot be removed while their applications are being examined and until their appeal rights are exhausted.

Faced with practical difficulties in carrying out administrative removals, immigration officials often choose to prosecute. It is not surprising then that the most frequently used immigration offences are those that penalize the lack of documents and the possession of forged ones. In fact, the impossibility of removing undocumented migrants from the country was a driving force for the introduction of the offence of no document and non-cooperation in removal proceedings, under sections 2 and 35 of the AI(TC)A 2004 respectively.[20] In a case involving a person who refused to comply with the re-documentation process, the intervening prosecutor made it clear that this negative response posed serious difficulties for immigration authorities:

> These [three] convictions [for the offence of non-cooperation] show a propensity to commit the same and similar offences . . . It is clear that he has refused thrice before and on the third refusal he was charged . . . In effect *he*

> *is playing the system as without co-operation the government have no way of*
> *removing him* as they cannot confirm which country to remove him to or have
> documents applied for which would facilitate the same.
>
> (Uxbridge Magistrates' Court, court file, Case 143, italics added)

While foreigners arriving into Britain without a passport or with a false one are
usually returned, those who cannot be returned end up being prosecuted. As a
retired immigration barrister told me:

> If the person isn't an asylum seeker and if the person is just trying . . . to come
> [in] as a visitor or trying to come in [on] an EU passport which is put through
> the machine and is fraudulent, then the most likely outcome is that the person
> will simply be refused leave to enter and will be gone on the next flight. [He]
> won't even be detained or be detained for hours or less.
>
> (Respondent 6, 20/04/2010)

Similarly, a UKBA official at the Criminality and Detention Group explained that
the first response is to remove. Prosecution is used against those foreigners who are
not 'readily removable' because their identity is unknown and because they claim
asylum:

> If we deal with false documents . . . if we can't remove them immediately we
> probably will prosecute those and they go to prison for that. Anyone trying
> to enter the country with false documents our first thing we will try to do is
> just return [them] straight back to the country they came from . . . Sometimes
> of course . . . they claim asylum so you've got false documents, claim asylum,
> so we have to admit them to do that process and we'll probably prosecute at
> that stage anyway, we'll prosecute this.
>
> (Respondent 5, 16/09/2010)

The impossibility to remove or to remove within a reasonable time also constitutes
a legal obstacle for holding someone in immigration detention.[21] The use of
criminal law in these cases justifies the subject's detention during the identification
process – especially if there is a claim for asylum being considered. In this regard,
the same UKBA official told me that:

> [I]f [immigration officers] can't remove the person, we've got difficulties to
> detain them because we find we couldn't remove them in a reasonable period
> of time, we might seek to prosecute because that gives us more hold on the
> person and buys us the time we need . . . [I]t will be a pragmatic decision
> based on the particular case.
>
> (Respondent 5, 16/09/2010)

A criminal procedure is then conceived as an alternative to the administrative
proceeding leading to removal, when the latter cannot take place because of legal

and practical obstacles. The criminal law in the immigration context plays a pragmatic role: it is deployed when the primary sanction against immigration offenders is fruitless or ineffective. Its aim is purely utilitarian, to bypass the obstacles for removal. A criminal sanction makes possible the detention – imprisonment – of a person when immigration law mandates release. As my interviewee from the UKBA clearly put it, a criminal proceeding 'buys' immigration officials time to prepare expulsion while keeping the person subject to it behind bars. As such, it 'aids' immigration law and constitutes another means of immigration enforcement. The interchangeable nature of administrative and criminal sanctions reveals a non-moral, non-principled regulatory use of the latter which clashes with liberal principles of criminal law (Ashworth 2000). Criminal punishment does not have a differentiated function, but rather is an extension of or an alternative to immigration/administrative proceedings. Criminal punishment is then used as an ancillary sanction. The government representative, Mike O'Brien, in the parliamentary debate on the Immigration and Asylum Bill 1999 clearly explained this rationale to his peers in the House of Commons:

> We know that most people who obtain their entry by deception are not prosecuted. That will continue to be the case because they will be removed from the UK quickly. It is difficult to see why we should prosecute if simple removal from the UK will deal with the issue . . . There are some people who, because of the way in which they behave, make their removal extremely difficult, but have nevertheless set out systematically to deceive and breach our immigration control. In those cases we need such effective and tough legislation that will deal with people who deliberately set out to break our laws.
>
> (Hansard, HC Deb 20/04/1999, col. 712)[22]

Conversely, when removal is possible, immigration offences are generally not enforced. In these cases, the use of criminal law is generally considered inappropriate and unnecessary. For example, overstaying and illegal entry are seldom proceeded against as evidenced by the low rates of prosecutions since 2005.[23] Overstaying used to be the most common prosecutable offence, but since 1988, when overstayers had their right of appeal against deportation orders restricted and were subject to summary removal,[24] this offence has barely been used.[25] They are generally not charged and the enforcement action against them is removal, unless they are involved in other offences – such as working using false documents. In the case of illegal entry, its under-enforcement is mainly to do with evidentiary difficulties. This offence requires proof of *mens rea*. That is, it requires that a person *knowingly* entered the UK without the leave of an immigration officer or in breach of a deportation order.[26] It is different from the status of 'illegal entrant' which does not require intention or knowledge. The latter includes people who are not aware they were in breach of an immigration rule or who have obtained a leave by the deception of a third party. Even though illegal entrants cannot be prosecuted, they can be summarily removed and this is the option generally pursued in cases of illegal entry.[27]

The functioning of the hybrid immigration–criminal law system resonates with what David Sklansky (2012: 161) has aptly termed 'ad hoc instrumentalism'. 'Ad hoc instrumentalism' refers to 'a manner of thinking about law and legal institutions that downplays concerns about consistency and places little stock in formal legal categories, but instead sees legal rules and legal procedures simply as a set of interchangeable tools'. From this instrumental perspective, the selection of 'enforcement tools' is determined by their effectiveness to achieve a desired goal. Thus, 'whether behavior should be treated as criminal, for example, depends on whether criminal procedures and sanctions will best accomplish the government's objective, not on any abstract considerations of fit or appropriateness'. This 'manner of thinking' is 'ad hoc' because the decision to use the criminal law is decided on a case-by-case basis, thus unsystematically, opportunistically and based on convenience.

Such a pragmatic conception of criminal law is not unique to immigration enforcement. Indeed, regulationist scholars have long distinguished two modes of reasoning within law: on the one hand, law as instrumental, forward-looking, policy-oriented and concerned with efficiency; and on the other hand, law as backward-looking, principled, characterized by a rule-based doctrinal reasoning, and concerned with coherency (Parker *et al.* 2004). Regulatory law, Julia Black (2002: 33) maintained, presents an 'instrumentalist view of law, which in turn poses [a] different set of questions about the legal system (those of effectiveness rather than coherency)'.

From a normative perspective, this instrumentalist appeal to criminal regulation in immigration law – as in other regulatory contexts – severely undermines the principles that should guide its legitimate use. The criminal law, as a distinctive mode of regulation, should be reserved to censure serious wrongs. Criminalization, in other words, should be justified on grounds of principle, not on its effectiveness for achieving a particular outcome (Duff 2010a: 302; Ashworth and Zedner 2012).

Why me? The impact of nationality, resources and local practices in the use of criminal law powers

Because pragmatic reasons weigh heavily on the decision to prosecute, factors which have little to do with the charge itself are of paramount importance. Nationality, for instance, appears to be an important consideration in the decision whether to pursue a criminal action. A senior official at the UKBA's Crime Directorate told me that there is a great difference between a case of false document involving a Brazilian and one against a Zimbabwean: in the first case, the outcome will probably be removal, whereas a prosecution will be the most likely result for the second case. So he recognized that the same offence might be treated differently according to the country of origin of the defendant and whether or not he or she is readily removable (Respondent 20, 28/04/2011).[28] While this practice might amount to discrimination and be in breach of race relations legislation, it seems to be fairly general. In fact, those who are more frequently prosecuted for immigration offences come from countries with which Britain has no bilateral agreements to return people without documents, such as Somalia, Iran and Sri Lanka.[29]

Other more mundane reasons, such as the availability of resources, may also influence the outcome of a case. The official at the Crime Directorate recognized that the resources available – particularly trained staff – to carry out an enforcement operation may define how to approach it. Two similar cases of sham marriage may end up in a criminal investigation or in a removal procedure depending on the number of officers free in the Immigration Crime Team (ICT) at a particular time. Even if pursuing sham marriages is a priority for the agency, he told me that they cannot take on some of these cases because of shortage of personnel. So they call the LIT to deal with them when the ICT is overstretched. Because immigration officials in LITs are not 'prosecution-trained', they can only carry out executive actions. In other cases, they will just deploy a uniformed immigration officer standing outside the registry to persuade the parties and thus prevent the marriage from taking place. He stated that 'people are dealt [with] differently because of lack of resources' (Respondent 20, 28/04/2011).

An example of the impact of enforcement capability on this decision can be found in the practice of prosecuting non-cooperation under section 35(3) of AI(TC)A 2004. It seems that the decision to prosecute this offence varies according to jurisdiction. While nationally the number of prosecutions for this offence is quite low,[30] it tends to be higher in certain areas. Two practitioners told me that this crime is prosecuted in Dover, Kent, because Dover Police have the resources and are willing to pursue these cases. One of them mentioned that in Kent 'there is what appears to be a sort of understanding' between immigration officials, the Kent Constabulary and the CPS to prosecute them.[31] This was confirmed by a UKBA official who told me that the Canterbury prison is a 'hub' with a number of immigration officials deployed there to check those who are liable to deportation and/or removal; and he suggested that the existence of these arrangements may explain the higher rates of prosecutions for this offence in that jurisdiction (Respondent 20, 28/04/2011).

The identity of the decision maker may also influence the way in which a particular case is handled. A UKBA in-country enforcement official referred to different practices by different immigration teams: 'what actually ends up being prosecuted will depend on who is there to do it on the ground'. He referred to the immigration team at Gatwick airport and its approach to document offences:

I know Gatwick [airport] in terms of people using false documents. [The immigration team] very much focus on – or they had a period when they very much focused on – people who were leaving Britain rather than people who were coming into Britain. So if somebody was discovered with false documents trying to enter Britain it was . . . more likely that they [would] just be removed and not prosecuted because the logic there was that those people [who were leaving Britain with false documents] have higher links to the UK and to crime in the UK and that was just the way they were trying to prioritize.
(Respondent 3, 18/05/2010)

The existence of 'cycles' or 'periods' in which particular offences are more likely to be prosecuted because of certain policy priorities was also referred to by other interviewees. The Head of Law of a non-governmental organization that provides legal support to asylum seekers mentioned that 'there do seem to be some sorts of offences which do tend to go through periods of prosecutions'; for example, document offences where the person is in transit in the UK to seek asylum elsewhere (Respondent 13, 14/06/2010). The supervising solicitor at RMJ also talked about 'cycles' in which certain offences seem to be particularly targeted as an 'influencing factor' in the decision to pursue a criminal case. She further explained how difficult it is to predict the outcome in a particular case: 'I don't [know] whether it varies regionally . . . It's really hard to say because I have clients from all different countries who've been prosecuted and clients from all different countries who haven't been prosecuted in very similar circumstances' (Respondent 10, 8/06/2010).

This variation in prosecution patterns once again reveals the pragmatic and arbitrary use of criminal law powers for immigration enforcement. What ends up being prosecuted very much depends on the UKBA's priorities at a particular moment and whether or not criminal law is useful or effective in achieving them. The lack of clear guidelines and the availability of different mechanisms result in inconsistencies and lack of coherence in the treatment of immigration offenders. A snapshot of cases published on the UKBA website shows this variation in decision making. For example, a Ukrainian man who arrived at Bristol airport and attempted to use a forged Estonian passport was arrested and removed without being prosecuted;[32] however, a number of cases of forged or false passports do routinely reach the criminal courts. In a case involving four people caught working illegally, two of them were put in immigration detention, one was released on immigration bail and the fourth was detained on suspicion of 'ID card offences'. Presumably, this last person was caught using a forged identity document for securing employment. In another case, six workers were found working illegally; one of them was caught using a fake British passport. All of the six were considered for removal, including the person using a false document who was not prosecuted.[33] Inconsistency is one of the main reasons mentioned in the Standard Acceptable Criteria (SAC) for adopting guidance on cases for investigation. It is also a motive for the creation of a Crime Directorate within the UKBA whose aim is 'to provide a more cohesive, consistent and effective approach to tackling organized criminal networks'.[34]

Criminalization as a policy goal?

The examination of decision making in cases involving immigration offenders reveals the contingency of crime and of immigration crimes in particular – that is, the labelling of an action as a crime depends on a number of factors independent of the legal definition. A similar conduct may be treated as an administrative or a criminal matter depending on the nationality of the offender, the identity and training of the intervening officer or team, the availability of resources, the policy directions at a particular time, etc. These are factors that have little or no relation to the criminal charge, but are important in the decision on whether or not to proceed against a crime. This is an example of how social practices and its 'actors' play a major role in the definition of the 'frontiers of criminalization' (Lacey 1995).

The use of discretion in practice reveals a very unpredictable and unplanned use of the criminal justice route. Just as there are no clear guidelines about whom and when to prosecute, equally there is no specific goal of subjecting more immigrants to criminal punishment. Rather than a planned, strategically designed policy of criminalization, the practice of prosecution of immigration crimes against non-nationals reveals a more mundane, erratic and inconsistent exercise of (criminal law) powers. The use of criminal law against immigration offenders is not only subject to prosecutorial discretion – namely, the application of the 'public interest' threshold. It also largely depends on its suitability for the purpose of immigration controls for a particular team or jurisdiction. This in turn explains the disparity and lack of patterns noticed in the practice of prosecuting immigration suspects.

These inconsistencies seem to be the result of an unsystematic and haphazard use of power as much as a reflection of a system designed to ensure maximum flexibility and a wider range of alternatives to deal with non-citizens. It is hard to think of a similar regime applicable to nationals whereby they can be subject to parallel systems of (coercive or punitive) state intervention (criminal, civil, administrative) on the basis of the same conduct and with no certainty about which system of sanctions will be triggered in a particular case.[35] The differential legal regimes applicable to foreigners and nationals ultimately reveal the importance of the citizenship status *vis-à-vis* the universality of human rights (Aas 2011a). In fact, the lack of legal limits and the broad margin of discretion and flexibility in the exercise of state powers have been – and still are – features of immigration law (Schuck 1984).[36] Rather than placing non-citizens on a par with citizens, the criminalization of immigration laws increases the possibilities of state interventions against (non-national) immigration suspects. Even though citizens may be proceeded against for immigration offences, only one system is activated to deal with them. Most importantly, they are not subject to deportation and removal.

The harm matrix and the prosecution of serious immigration offences

> *There is a mismatch between those against whom the Government intend to take enforcement action – those regarded as the most nefarious – and those against whom action is actually taken. I can understand why action is taken against them. They are the easiest to pick up and deal with.*[37]

Up to this point, I have analysed the prosecution of low-level immigration offences. However, in recent policy documents, the government has emphasized that criminal law should be used against the most serious offences, particularly those involving organized criminality. As discussed in Chapter 3, the government has given priority to offences that cause most harm, particularly terrorism, drug and human trafficking, organized criminality, facilitation and knowingly employing illegal workers (Home Office 2007b, 2008b, 2010d). People involved in these serious offences are likely candidates for prosecution (Home Office 2007b: 23). The categorization of immigration crimes according to the harm they cause is based on the 'harm matrix' which breaks down offences into three main categories (Home Office 2006b: 14; 2010d: 46):

- Category A (high) includes serious criminal offences such as terrorist activity, murder, rape, people and drug trafficking, violent crime and child abuse.
- Category B (medium) includes offences such as illegal working, dishonest claims for asylum support and identity fraud.
- Category C (low) groups minor immigration offences, such as those resulting in a drain on public funds and anti-social behaviour.

According to the harm matrix, prosecutions should be reserved for serious offences, while low-level offences are supposed to be dealt with by caution and removal (Home Office 2010d).

The concept of 'harm' in immigration enforcement has been institutionalized by its inclusion in the immigration agency's Public Service Agreement (PSA) which makes as one of its four strategic objectives 'ensuring and enforcing compliance with UK immigration laws, removing the most harmful people first and denying the privileges of the UK to those here illegally' (HM Government 2009: 3; see also Home Office 2006b: 23; Home Office 2007c: 7). It has also been introduced as a parameter to measure the impact of the agency's work, particularly in relation to immigration offences and the work of the recently created Crime Directorate (Home Office 2010c). The concept of 'harm' gained currency following the FNP scandal in April 2006 which prompted the institutional overhaul of the IND. One of the repercussions of this crisis was the melding of penal and immigration policies.[38] At the time of the IND review, the language of risk and harm was already prevalent in crime-control policies. The use of actuarial instruments to predict risk and to manage offenders is common in sentencing, bail and post-conviction decisions. Risk assessments are undertaken on all convicted defendants entering the criminal justice system based on their background and offences, and the risk they pose to society when (and if) they are released. These assessments have consequences for the length of the sentence, the conditions while in prison, and decisions on parole and post-sentence treatment (Home Office 2006c: 12).

These criteria have infiltrated immigration decision making on how to manage FNPs effectively after their criminal sentences expire, and spilled over to the other phases of immigration enforcement. Harm is defined as 'all the potential negative consequences of illegal migration' (Home Office 2007b: 10). By tackling those who cause the most harm, a number of public protection objectives are achieved, including removing the incentives for illegal immigration; protecting public services and private businesses from immigration fraud; and protecting the immigrant him/herself. In fact, as it is articulated in policy papers, the crackdown on organized immigration crimes is aimed at protecting, among others, the 'victim' of it from being exploited by smugglers, traffickers and unscrupulous employers (e.g. Home Office 2002: 76; Home Office 2007b: 12; see also Goodey 2003).

The emphasis on preventing harm attempts to reconcile the task of enforcing the law – i.e. keeping people out or expelling them – with the goal of protecting and doing good (Black 2003: 39). Doing 'good' is an appealing goal, particularly in the context of immigration controls. Unlike crime control, which has its 'positive side' – protecting the public and individuals from crime – immigration enforcement lacks this aspect and is seen by many as illegitimate and ethically problematic. The prerogatives of the state to limit the access of certain people to its territory and to exercise its controls over them – by imposing conditions on their residence, detaining and excluding – are subject to contestation not only from some academics and activists,[39] but also from those who are in charge of enforcing these measures (Gibney 1988; Hayter 2003; Carens 2003). When she interviewed immigration staff working in removal centres, Bosworth (2011b) reported a certain ambivalence of such personnel about their job. Some of them were not sure if they were doing the 'right' thing.[40] Probably because of the controversial nature of its work, in recent years the agency has made some efforts to publicize itself and adopt 'customer friendly' strategies.[41] The criminalization of immigration breaches is also a contentious matter.[42] Because immigration offences are generally trivial and victimless crimes, creating a 'counterpart' to them, a victim, is politically and rhetorically persuasive.

In this regard, the recent appeal to the concept of harm in British immigration policy strives to legitimize this policy. As such, the idea of harm is used for the validation of this policy rather than as a limiting principle for the state's coercion, as first envisaged by political philosophers and liberal theorists such as John Stuart Mill and H. L. A Hart. In his famous treatise *On Liberty*, Mill ([1859] 1978: 9) put it simply: 'the only purpose for which power can be rightfully exercised over any member of a civilized community, against his will, is to prevent harm to others'. According to Bernard Harcourt (1999), in the last two decades, states have increasingly appealed to the rhetoric of harm to frame and legitimate their policies on prostitution, pornography, drugs, public drinking, loitering, homosexuality, etc. The state regulations of these conducts have been justified not on moral grounds, but on the basis of the potential harm that they pose to individuals. Harcourt argued that the pervasiveness of harm has made it meaningless as a means to set limits on the use of criminal law (Harcourt 1999: 113; see also Ramsay 2010).

In turn, Bridget Anderson (2012) observed that the appeal to harm within immigration policy was originally taken from the context of trafficking and then slipped into mainstream immigration enforcement. She notes that:

It was the arrival on the scene of the [victim of trafficking] that marked the emergence of the prevention of 'harm' as a concern of immigration policy. Harm is associated with the body, with shared human physical (and related mental) fragility, with suffering bodies, and in policy terms, with public health, drugs, commercial sex and other activities that are deemed risky.

(Anderson 2012: 1247)

Enhanced immigration controls are justified in terms of public protection and particularly the protection of the individual subject to them. However, Anderson (2012) pointed to a problematic aspect of the 'harm reduction agenda', which is the role that the state has in producing and reproducing harm by imposing barriers for legal migration and creating the grounds for illegality and thus exploitation. The state is then captured in a contradictory position when charged with the task of protecting those whom it aims to exclude (Weber and Grewcock 2012).

This tension is reflected in the practice of prosecuting illegal immigrants and the criminalization of immigration offences. The former are generally not seen as victims to be protected, but as perpetrators to be punished and expelled. This conflict is particularly evident in the enforcement of immigration control in workplaces. As I argued in Chapter 3, these controls are primarily aimed at catching and punishing the worker rather than punishing the employer. A consultation paper on illegal employment makes such a rationale clear. It first focuses on the employer:

> Employers who employ illegal migrant workers may do so because they want to avoid providing minimum standards, such as the National Minimum Wage and paid holidays. This is harmful to the workers involved and enables unscrupulous employers to gain an unfair advantage over legitimate competitors.

(Home Office 2008c: 4)

It then goes on to discuss the main aim of enforcement visits:

> The Agency adapts resources where appropriate to carry out specific operations that will yield the greatest results, with the aim of removing the most harmful people from the UK first. Any person found to be working illegally is liable to prosecution and/or removal from the UK.

(Home Office 2008c: 11)

In this context, immigrants are the target of immigration enforcement, not those who take advantage of their illegality and 'victimize' them. The apparent tension between, on the one hand, enforcing immigration controls by not allowing people in and pushing them out of the country, and, on the other hand, protecting them from their traffickers and smugglers is also present in the actual practice of immigration enforcement. The latter seems to contradict the UKBA's priorities.[43] In the following two sub-sections, I analyse the gap between the UKBA's policy and priorities and the actual prosecution of trafficking in human beings and facilitation of unlawful immigration.

Trafficking in human beings

While British legislation has criminalized trafficking for sexual and labour exploitation[44] and has made it a policy priority to disrupt trafficking networks, the rate of successful prosecutions for this offence is still extremely low. There were only two convictions for trafficking for forced labour in 2009 and three convictions for conspiracy to traffic for forced labour in 2010.[45] Low prosecution rates can be partly explained by the fact that trafficking – like organized crime in general – requires a great deal of intelligence work and is very resource-intensive. Trafficking networks are highly sophisticated, well-resourced and resilient, with great capacity to avoid detection. In addition, there are evidentiary difficulties (Gallagher and Karlebach 2011: 3). The required intention is apparently difficult to prove and so, as the senior official of the UKBA's Policy and Strategy Group told me, traffickers are usually charged with facilitation 'because it is just more likely to secure a conviction'. Especially if it is detected at the port of entry, trafficking – he told me – is 'almost impossible to prove' (Respondent 14, 12/08/2010). On the other hand, trafficking victims often retain some level of control or agency, so they do not quite fit into the narrow definition of 'ideal victim' which is often applied by social workers and the police (Hoyle *et al.* 2011). Further, they are difficult to identify and usually reluctant to cooperate in the procedures against their traffickers. All these factors raise important practical and legal difficulties for the successful prosecution of these crimes. Still, some authors have argued that the goal of penalizing human-trade organizations, which are often heavily involved in different sectors of the informal economy – particularly, the business of bringing cheap labour to central countries – and are therefore important economic actors, clashes against economic interests to reduce the costs and wages of services and manufacturing (e.g. Ruggiero 1997; Salt and Stein 1997; see also Anderson and O'Connell Davidson 2003; Anderson 2007).

In many instances, the balance is struck on the 'weak end' of this process, so that individuals trafficked or smuggled into the UK are caught and in some instances criminalized for immigration offences. Even though there are no statistics, recent research on victims of trafficking suggests that they are sometimes proceeded against for document fraud when caught trying to exit the country to escape from their traffickers, or working illegally (Hales and Gelsthorpe 2011; see also Gonzalez 2002; Stephen-Smith 2008; Hoyle *et al.* 2011: 325).[46] Precisely because of these cases, in 2007, the CPS issued two sets of guidance to prevent the prosecution of victims of trafficking for immigration offences.[47] One such case was uncovered by the Court of Appeal. The defendant pleaded guilty to the charge of possession of a false document with intent and was sentenced to eight months' imprisonment. This decision was appealed on the grounds that Ms O's lawyer failed to object to the prosecution of his client on the ground that she had been trafficked for sexual exploitation. While the defendant had disclosed the fact that she was a trafficking victim, her solicitor disregarded this information and advised her to plead guilty. Neither did the prosecutor withdraw or discontinue the case against Ms O. After quashing the conviction, Laws LJ emphatically stated:

> There was no fair trial. We hope that such a shameful set of circumstances never occurs again. Prosecutors must be aware of the protocols which, although not in the text books are enshrined in their Code. Defence lawyers must respond by making enquiries, if there is before them credible material showing that they have a client who might have been the victim of trafficking.
>
> (*R v O* [2008] EWCA Crim 2835 [at 26])

Similarly, in a recent judgment by the High Court, it was revealed that a Moldovan woman who was a victim of trafficking was arrested and accused of possessing a false passport in 2003. She was convicted, sentenced to three months in prison and was sent back to Moldova where she was caught once again by her trafficker and was re-trafficked into the UK. In 2007, she was arrested again and detained in Oakington Removal Centre. After being identified as a trafficking victim by the Poppy Project, she was granted refugee status. She sued the Home Office and was awarded damages for the failure of the department to protect her and for sending her back to Moldova despite evidence that she was at risk of being found by her trafficker, who was still at large.[48]

The small number of prosecutions against traffickers and the criminalization of their victims suggest that there may be a mismatch between the official rhetoric and the actual practice of prosecuting trafficking offences. Such divergence calls into question recent anti-trafficking policies aimed at targeting traffickers and protecting the rights of those who are trafficked. In this regard, the document *Human Trafficking: The Government's Strategy* (Home Office 2011c: Chapter 5) makes it clear that immigration powers (denial of visas, identification of forged passports, refusal of entry, etc.) are to be deployed to prevent the entry to the country not only of traffickers, but also of their victims. The idea behind this enforcement strategy is that traffickers bring their victims through illegal means and thus the same controls deployed against illegal immigration should be effective in disrupting trafficking organizations. This assumption is, however, not based on evidence. Research shows that many trafficking victims enter the country legally (Ruggiero 1997: 236; Buckland 2008: 45). Most importantly, making immigration controls one of the main enforcement tools to deal with human trafficking may increase – and not decrease – the vulnerability of victims to abuse and exploitation (Lee 2005; Anderson 2010a).

Stringent enforcement of immigration laws contributes to blurring the distinction between trafficking victims, smuggled people, refugees and undocumented economic migrants because immigration restrictions force people to turn to smugglers and traffickers to escape poverty, imprisonment or death, or to seek betterment for themselves and their families. Tougher border controls induce enforcement officers and decision makers to adopt a narrow view about those who deserve to be protected. By making such controls central in the crusade against traffickers, the government 'meets [its] goals of restricting immigration while failing in its mandate to protect' (Buckland 2008: 79). As in the case of asylum seekers, the government is fearful that the allegation of being trafficked can be used 'as a source of abuse' (Home Office 2007b: 23). Thus, people who have been trafficked or smuggled run the risk of being treated as immigration transgressors as 'questions of "victimhood" merge with questions of legality' (Goodey 2003: 420; see also Anderson 2010a: 70). Dauvergne (2008: 79) observes that the recent crackdown on trafficking in many Western liberal democratic states is driven by immigration controls rather than human rights (see also Kostakopoulou 2006).[49] Within this context, immigration controls – and the punitive powers attached to them – are more likely to be deployed against the immigrant rather than those who 'service' or do commerce with them.

Facilitation of unlawful immigration

The official rhetoric which announced tougher actions against the most harmful offenders is also contradicted by the practice of detection and prosecution of smuggling organizations – one of the main UKBA targets. Surprisingly, this gap is apparent in the same policy papers and media reports which publicize enforcement operations against organized criminal groups. For example, one of these documents announces actions against facilitators; however, it only reported the detection of 18 people in a tanker who were later on handed to French authorities (Home Office 2010d: 11). Nothing is said about their smugglers and whether they were identified and prosecuted for this operation. In a snapshot of UKBA's enforcement operations based on information on the agency's website,[50] I identified 15 cases: 11 cases of illegal working, two of passport fraud and two of sham marriage. In only two of them (the sham marriage cases), is there evidence of criminal prosecution for facilitation against those directly involved in the marriage. The rest of the cases were dealt with through removal or prosecution for document fraud. These data show that while official rhetoric about immigration offenders generally addresses those who commit the most serious offences, it is the petty crime of illegal immigrants – and not of those who profit from them – on which legislative activity and enforcement operations concentrate.

When prosecutions are brought against smugglers, the small, family-based smuggling organization is generally caught. Facilitation (or technically, assisting unlawful immigration to a Member state)[51] is one of the most frequent immigration offences before the magistrates' court and the most important one at the crown court.[52] According to the review of court files performed for this study, 16 per cent of immigration-related cases that reached Uxbridge Magistrates' Court between January 2008 and December 2009 were 'facilitation' cases. This is an offence which is punished with a maximum of 14 years' imprisonment. So these cases are generally not suitable for a summary trial and are committed to the crown courts. In all but one of the cases reviewed, the decisions were not available because they were decided by the crown court. In the only case decided at the magistrates' court, the defendant pleaded guilty and was sentenced to six months' imprisonment. The magistrates stated in their decision that 'Credit [for the guilty plea] is not sending

[the] matter to the Crown Court' (Uxbridge Magistrates Court, court file, Case 40). At Isleworth Crown Court – where these cases are committed – the rate is even higher: 55 per cent of those accused of immigration offences were charged with assisting unlawful immigration.

Unlike other immigration-crime cases, facilitation cases generally require some measure of investigative work, so case-files are rich in information about the accused and the circumstance of the offence, as well as the procedures followed and the decision taken by enforcement agencies. Most of the accused had residence in the UK[53] and thus were granted bail. Many of them were naturalized British citizens. In the cases before Isleworth Crown Court, at least 17 out of 58 defendants were naturalized British nationals, one was British-born and one had indefinite leave to remain. Nineteen per cent of those charged with this offence had been granted refugee status in the past.

The cases reviewed were small-scale facilitation. From the information in court files, I could not find any evidence of large-scale organized criminality connected to the accused. Organized networks are generally characterized by the involvement of a large number of people who are part of a hierarchical structure, with a clear division of labour and which provides different 'services' to its 'clients' – such as entry, accommodation, employment, etc. None of these characteristics were found in the cases reviewed. Generally, the defendant assisted the person with travel arrangements before and during the journey, such as providing documents, booking the ticket, contacting the travel agent and airline – especially when the person assisted did not speak English – and assisting the passenger during flight connections. At the magistrates' court, in only two cases was there evidence that a second person was involved in the crime (in both cases, they were husband and wife); in the rest of them, only one person was charged with the offence. At the crown court, in five cases there was more than one person charged with this offence: in three of them, the alleged facilitators were family members assisting another member.

In many of these cases, the defendant was charged with assisting a family member (brother, mother, wife, children and other relatives). At the magistrates' court, in 25 per cent of facilitation cases, the accused and the person assisted were members of the same family; this rate was even higher at the crown court where 45 per cent of defendants were accused of assisting family members. In one of the cases reviewed, the defendant, a man from Somalia who had been granted refugee status in the UK, was charged with facilitating the unlawful entry of his wife and his two children. Previously, he had applied for visas on their behalf on family reunification grounds which were refused. His family never had passports, arrived at the airport without documents and claimed asylum. He was found not guilty of this offence (Isleworth Crown Court, court file, Case 70). In another case involving two friends who assisted the sister of one of them to enter the UK and to claim asylum, the lawyer asked the judge for a mitigated sentence because the offence was 'done for humanitarian reasons'. He explained: 'This case is about humanitarian issues, not criminal. This case does not fit in the structure. This was about saving one's life.' The person assisted was granted refugee status. Her brother is a naturalized British citizen originally from Somalia. Both defendants were convicted for the offence of facilitation and sentenced to 15 and nine months in prison, respectively (Isleworth Crown Court, court file, Case 77).

The fact that the selected courts for this study have jurisdiction over a major port of entry (Heathrow airport) may explain why the cases analysed involve individual or small-scale facilitation. Crimes spotted at ports of entry tend to share these characteristics as detection is the product of reactive policing, rather than proactive intelligence work. A pattern identified in the cases reviewed is that people accused of facilitation are caught by police or immigration officers because the person whom they helped was detected as well – using a false document or being without one. One of the main sources of evidence against these people is the testimony of the person assisted who describe them (their clothes, their physical appearance, etc.)[54] and so they can be later identified through CCTV footage inside the airport. Enquiries about their flight booking are also usually made to link smugglers with their clients or victims. In other cases, people are identified during the boarding process abroad by airline staff and overseas immigration officers. People caught at the port can be part of a criminal chain, but this is not uncovered unless further investigative work is carried out. In the files that I reviewed, though, there was no evidence of the involvement of larger smuggling organizations.

These findings resonate with work by Sarah Webb and John Burrows (2009) on prisoners convicted of smuggling and trafficking offences. In relation to smuggling organizations, the authors reported that most of the interviewees refer to medium- to small-scale organizations such as businesses formed by a particular ethnic community based in the UK to engage in facilitating the entry of further members of that community: 'The common requirements for [these community-based organizations] would be to have a facilitator (or range of facilitators) based in the originating country who would be responsible for the commencement of the process' (Webb and Burrows 2009: 21). In other cases, facilitation is organized from outside the country with little foundation in the UK: 'Smaller smuggling organizations would focus on bringing in (extended) family members and close associates. Directed via a contact in Europe, the UK contact would be required to collect the immigrant(s) at the point of entry and provide temporary accommodation' (Webb and Burrows 2009: 21).

A similar pattern is described by Leanne Weber and Michael Grewcock (2012) in their analysis of the actions recently taken by the Australian government to tackle the smuggling of asylum seekers into the country. They pointed to the fact that, contrary to the official policy, many of those prosecuted are fishermen or farmers, and not international criminal networks.

Making sense of prosecutorial practices in immigration-related cases

While the 'harm matrix' mandates the use of criminal law powers against those who cause most harm, low-level offences continue to be the most common matters reaching the criminal courts.[55] Over 60 per cent of immigration defendants at Uxbridge Magistrates' Court are charged with the offence of arriving without documents. Many more are charged with the offences of possession of a false identity document with intent or without reasonable excuse under the IDCA 2006.[56] Moreover, while facilitation cases are one of the most important categories of immigration crimes in the courts, most of them involve individual criminality with low levels of organization. According to sentencing guidelines and the characteristics of the cases reviewed, those accused of this offence are unlikely to be at the higher end of the sentencing range because of the absence of aggravating features.[57]

How can this apparent contradiction between policy and practice be explained? One obvious reason is that governments are not monolithic entities, and in many instances, the policy design is contradicted by its implementation (Ruhs and Anderson 2010: 199). While general policies mandate the use of criminal law powers against serious offenders, other rules encourage different outcomes. The establishment of prosecution targets is a case in point. It is practically simpler and easier for enforcement staff to identify individual offenders without proper documentation and to charge them with a criminal offence, than to investigate criminal networks. It is also easier to obtain a conviction in these cases. As such, prosecution targets promote this policy outcome. Similarly, due to scarce resources, some immigration teams end up prosecuting document offences instead of pursuing more complex cases, as a senior official at the Crime Directorate explained. Because the number of staff in some ICTs is so low – in some cases, only up to three officers – they cannot pursue organized crime cases: 'they can spend their whole career in one of these cases' so 'they just do low level crime' such as fraud-based offences (Respondent 20, 28/04/2011).

There are also contradictions between different policies and regulations. The SAC number the 'entry to the UK without document', a low-level offence, as one of the UKBA's strategic priorities. Therefore, cases of entry without document 'should be referred to and adopted by the UKBA crime team'. The same document, though, states that low-level offences should be dealt with administratively 'wherever possible'.[58] On the other hand, the official at the Crime Directorate described the prosecution of undocumented migrants or those using forged documents as an undesirable enforcement outcome. He referred to this work as 'old stuff' and explained to me that many immigration and police officers have been trained to pursue these offences in the past. There still are units at Manchester, Gatwick and Heathrow airports to deal with cases of passport fraud. He highlighted the need to relocate and train these officers in the UKBA's new national intelligence model and 'crime control strategy' to tackle organized criminality (Respondent 20, 28/04/2011).

Another UKBA official at the Policy and Strategy Group explained the prosecution of low-level offences – particularly, the possession of a false document – as due to the cumulative impact that several prosecutions may have in the prevention of these offences, even though they are not considered serious ones. He indicated that after the entry into force of the IDCA 2006, the number of undocumented arrivals 'plummeted': 'So, yes, you are prosecuting people for offences that [aren't] very serious. But the wider impact was reduction in this sort of behaviour so there was a valid reason for doing that' (Respondent 14, 12/08/2010). In this regard, he said that while there are enforcement priorities, the 'reactive element' of policing takes precedence:

> We have clear priorities that we want to address first and it is the role of senior officers to ensure that those priorities are fulfilled through which particular operations we do . . . But there is still a sort of reactive element . . . you still have to respond to it. So you can prioritize particular sort[s] of activities. Those are the areas that you will be proactive in investigating or building your intelligence around. But that doesn't necessarily mean that ultimately [that is] where the majority of your efforts end up because you [are] still going to do something else.
>
> (Respondent 14, 12/08/2010)

The introduction of the concept of 'harm' and the 'harm matrix' sought to make decision making more coherent by establishing priorities and providing an 'indicator' or 'benchmark' against which the agency's performance could be evaluated. So too did 'harm' imprint the idea of protection of the individual and the general public in immigration enforcement and thus it is intended as a source of legitimacy. The problem with this conceptual framework is that not only does the practice seem to contradict the agency's manifest goals of tackling serious immigration crimes, but these goals are also themselves contradictory. It is difficult to tackle illegal immigration and protect illegal immigrants at the same time.

The main purpose of the UKBA is to control irregular flows and eject those without leave, rather than controlling criminality and punishing offenders. Criminal law is one of the means available to achieve such a goal. This is clearly articulated by UKBA officials. After stating that prosecutions should be reserved for serious criminality, high-ranking officials at UKBA justify the use of it for low-level offences when there is a 'value' in it, either because it 'buys' time for operating expulsion or several prosecutions decrease the number of arrivals of undocumented immigrants. While the official at the Crime Directorate thought that the prosecution of document fraud did not fit the 'new model' and was 'old stuff', the reason he gave for not criminally pursuing document offences 'as a policy' was because 'we realized that it was not having any impact on driving down illegal immigration' (Respondent 20, 28/04/2011). The targeting of 'big fishes' with criminal prosecutions is thought to have a greater effect on the reduction of illegal immigration.[59] But the criminal law is still kept for low-level crimes to tackle particular problems of removability.

Conclusion

The examination of immigration-offence cases demonstrates how contingent the concepts of 'crime' and 'criminality' are (Lacey 1995; Zedner 2004: 39; Wells 2005: 23; Naffine 2009). The idea of 'crime' in general is not immutable as it is subject to a continuous definitional process. Formal criminalization is but one part of it. Enforcement agencies, the judiciary and the public all contribute to the definition of something as 'criminal'. The importance of this definitional process is particularly acute in the case of immigration crimes. From the outset, the label of these offences as 'true' crimes is contentious (Dauvergne 2008: 16). Likewise, their disparate and inconsistent enforcement raises questions about the precise contours of crime. The consideration of a particular conduct as an immigration offence largely depends on policing practices; the actors involved in the decision; the circumstances of the case; the value or utility of a criminal 'intervention'; the availability of resources; and the identity of the 'wrongdoer'. Consequently, similar conducts may be dealt with in completely different ways.

While policy papers and the embrace of a pseudo-scientific category of harm and the instrument to measure it (the harm matrix) give an idea of a perfectly articulated, measured and calculated control programme, the practice of immigration enforcement – and particularly the use of criminal law powers – looks messier and contradicts policy objectives. Even though the government aims to use criminal powers against organized criminality, empirical evidence shows that low-level immigration suspects end up being prosecuted and convicted by the courts. In many cases, they are victims of the 'big fishes' whom the official programmes aim to target. This contradiction between goals and outcomes is not just a problem in the implementation of the former. Most importantly, it reveals how problematic it is to reconcile retribution and punishment with immigration imperatives. Ultimately, what is at stake in the substantial criminalization of immigration violations is not so much punishing wrongdoing – by immigrants or those who aid, engage in commerce with or exploit them – but deterring and expelling unauthorized migrants. Criminal law expands the frontiers of immigration controls where the latter trips over its own limits.

5   Practices of punishment

Immigration defendants before the criminal courts

This chapter examines cases that reach the criminal justice system. It is mainly based on data extracted from case-files at Uxbridge Magistrates' Court and Isleworth Crown Court, and from attending hearings on immigration-offence cases at both venues. As I explained in Chapter 4, being unable to produce a passport is one of the most frequently prosecuted immigration offences. Thus, a large percentage of immigration-related cases handled by criminal courts involve this offence. Once prosecutors decide to pursue a case involving immigration crimes, the normal criminal proceeding follows. In principle, there is no distinction between an immigration-related case and other cases. However, because immigration-related offences bring together two different legal branches – immigration law and criminal law – during the criminal process, some aspects of immigration law and the immigration case of the defendant may emerge in the criminal case.

A clear example of this 'legal overlapping' occurs when the person accused claims asylum. In that case, certain international and domestic norms of refugee law – particularly the prohibition to impose penalties[1] – ought to be considered during the criminal process against this person. Many of the defendants charged with immigration offences are asylum claimants. Because they cannot be removed while their claims are being assessed, they are generally prosecuted.[2] Likewise, the immigration status of the accused may influence other aspects of the criminal process. It is usually taken into account in the decision to grant bail and at the sentencing stage. In cases where the penalty is below the 12-month threshold for automatic deportation, the judiciary is expected to decide on whether to issue a recommendation for deportation against the person convicted.

In this chapter, I concentrate on foreign national defendants who are charged with immigration offences for breaching their immigration status. First, I review the general features of the proceedings in these cases and assess them in the light of the everyday dynamics and practices of the criminal justice system more generally. I then analyse how lawyers and prosecutors handle these criminal cases. I focus specifically on whether and how the immigration case is considered when mounting a criminal prosecution and a defence. These cases are overwhelmingly settled through guilty pleas. In the third section, I explain the factors that might influence this outcome. Finally, I examine judicial decisions in these cases. I look at the weight that the immigration status of the defendant has in the likelihood of him or her being remanded in custody during criminal proceedings and punished with imprisonment for these offences.

The make-up of the criminal process

Research done on lower criminal courts has uncovered the gap between legal theory and the everyday work of these courts. Criminal law theory is predominantly built on core or paradigmatic crimes, such as murder and rape (Naffine 2009; Dubber 2010a: 199). So too, academic debates usually start from the assumption that the ordinary form of criminal adjudication is through a criminal trial (Ashworth and Zedner 2008). In practice, though, the usual clients of the criminal courts are accused of less serious offences and are subject to a minimalist procedure. Ashworth and Zedner have noted that in recent years there has been a diversification of the procedural channels to deal with non-serious offending which has contributed to 'the removal of lesser offences from the hallowed bastions of the criminal trial to the instrumental channels of civil and administrative law' (Ashworth and Zedner 2008: 39). They identified a range of developments in this direction, including the greater incentives to plead guilty and the use of diversion. Underpinning the increasing use of these channels to deal with offenders is a cost-effective analysis; based on this, the criminal trial is considered a luxury and should be reserved for serious, contested cases.

These features are an expression of what some authors have described as the 'administrativization' of the criminal justice system or actuarial justice (Feeley and Simon 1992: 185; 1994: 181). As a consequence, the bulk of the cases that reach the criminal courts are dealt with by the 'efficient methods of the administrative state' and the safeguards of the criminal procedure are eroded (Greenspan 1991: 49). By lowering the legal standards and burdens of proof, Malcolm Feeley (2004: 70) argued, actuarial justice alters the ways in which state intrusions into people's rights are legitimized and transform criminal procedure and criminal law into a regulatory activity.

Criminal proceedings are more often than not characterized by the following features:

> [T]here is no contest, no testing of evidence, no calling for witnesses, and no open court trial. At the hearing itself, the prosecution's evidence tends to be dealt with perfunctorily, and . . . cases are disposed of in a matter of minutes.
> (Baldwin 2007: 246)

In this version, justice is made through repetition and is the result of a superficial enquiry about the facts and the law. Feeley (1979) has vividly depicted the work of the lower courts where judges are bored with the routine of passing format-like sentences, prosecutors become dulled by their monotonous work, and defence lawyers are disaffected and depressed by the fact that in many cases their work resembles more that of a social worker than of a legal professional. This leads them to treat their clients carelessly. Defendants rely on their lawyers and in so doing are excluded from the decision-making process. In most instances, decisions are made prior to a public hearing. So the courts are not deliberative bodies. Instead, 'the courtroom encounter [is] a ritual in which the judge *ratifie[s]* a decision made earlier' (Feeley 1979: 11, italics in original; see also Ashworth 1988: 112). In contrast to the grandiose and intellectually stimulating popular images of criminal trials, the routine work of the courts seems more 'dull, commonplace, ordinary and after a while downright tedious' (Bottoms and McClean 1976: 226). While sophisticated legal arguments are thoroughly debated on appeal, the cases that reach that stage are the minority. Instead, administrative needs to manage case loads and solve cases swiftly drive the daily work of lower criminal courts (Feeley 1979: 5; Baldwin 2007: 246). The result is the mass production of judicial decisions in an assembly-like fashion.

The features reviewed above characterize the handling of immigration-related cases by the lower courts. There are a number of common aspects in the court cases involving immigration defendants. Prosecutors briefly summarize the facts of the case. In their statements, they usually employ similar stock phrases, arguments and words for different cases. Defence lawyers make few remarks, usually limited to explaining the circumstances in which the person arrived in the country. They often urge the court to 'sentence today' and ask it to 'take credit' of the defendant's 'early guilty plea' and 'cooperation with the authorities'. When immigration matters are mentioned, they are generally presented as mitigating factors.

After the lawyers' interventions, the magistrates or judges pass sentence. They barely ask questions and usually use ready-made, formatted phrases which they repeat in cases with similar characteristics. The particular circumstances of the cases and its mitigating or aggravating factors are used to fix the tariff. Probably because judicial decisions look so similar, clerks transcribe them in court files using abbreviations. For example, one of the expressions used by the magistrates with some frequency to justify a custodial sentence is that 'no other method is appropriate'. This phrase is recorded by clerks with the acronym 'NOMA'. Another of these expressions which appears very often in decisions refusing bail is 'no fixed address', transcribed as 'NFA'.

The cases are taken through the various stages of the criminal process speedily. These procedures take place in a short period of time, usually no more than ten minutes. Court files are generally very thin. In particular, files at the magistrates' court involving people charged with the offence of no document comprise no more than a couple of pages, if any. These cases do not require intelligence work and are dealt with by the court generally within the same day. So the defendant is caught in the airport, questioned by immigration authorities and the police, and charged with the offence. The same day or the day after, the case is sent to the court and decided straightaway if the accused pleads guilty. Within a couple of days of arriving in the UK, the person can be serving the sentence in a prison.

Issues concerning the legality, proportionality and necessity of the resort to the criminal law in immigration-related cases remain uncontested and these cases are by and large considered as unproblematic. To some extent, a legalistic approach that dominates the everyday work of the lower courts contributes to the mechanical and uncritical application of the law: if a particular conduct constitutes a crime, then it should be punished. As a manifestation of this reasoning, a lawyer who was representing a person charged with the offence of arriving in the country without a passport, whom I approached after the hearing, bluntly described these cases: 'It is straightforward: you don't have a passport, you destroyed it; that in this country is a crime.' These are generally cases in which an application of asylum is pending, and so where complex issues about facts and laws are likely to arise. Even if there is no asylum application at stake, in many of them, defendants may have defences available and so they may be immune to punishment. However, in the vast majority of cases these defences remain unexamined. When they are, examination of these matters is generally superficial.

A similar pattern of processing immigration-related cases by criminal courts has been observed in the United States – particularly in Southern jurisdictions such as Texas, New Mexico and Arizona – where *en masse* hearings are held daily and up to 80 defendants plead guilty to the charges at any one time (Lydgate 2010: 4). In this regard, Ingrid Eagly (2010: 1316) observed that 'immigration crime produces more guilty pleas at a faster rate than all other federal crime'. As a consequence, she argued, procedural issues or the exercise of law enforcement powers are not challenged.

Hence, not only is the criminalization of immigration laws becoming globalized,[3] but also the specific legal strategies to deal with 'immigration wrongdoers' are being borrowed by one country from the other. The impressive appeal to guilty pleas, the extremely short hearings and the cursory examination of evidence and arguments by criminal justice actors should make one think that the presence of these features in immigration-related cases is not coincidental (Legomsky 2007; Stumpf 2011: 1729). The stricter enforcement of immigration-based crimes in both the United States and the UK since the mid-1990s has resulted in an increase of immigration cases reaching the criminal courts which can only effectively be processed by their massive diversion from the criminal trial (Ashworth and Zedner 2008).

Offences and defences: the decision about impunity

Immigration officers are in charge of the initial decision as to whether any defence applies to people accused of immigration offences at the port of entry. When at this stage immigration staff consider that no defence is available, the case is referred for examination to the police and the Crown Prosecution Service (CPS). Generally, though, this initial decision has great weight on subsequent assessments and hence it is critical. The prosecution is required to undertake an examination based on the evidentiary test and the public interest test. Once the prosecutor determines that both conditions are fulfilled, a criminal case is opened.

The pre-criminal process stage

When a person is encountered without documents or with false ones and claims asylum, immigration authorities are the first to make a decision as to whether or not an offence has been committed. This is a pre-screening process where an immigration officer makes an assessment on the credibility of the person. A prosecutor at Uxbridge Magistrates' Court told me that immigration officials test the credibility of the applicant in the first interview and, based on the person's responses, they decide whether to refer the case to the CPS.[4] In practical terms, questions of credibility lead to a series of factual questions. If, for instance, a Chinese national claims that she was persecuted in her own country because she is Catholic, the immigration officer will question her about the Catholic religion, the name of the Pope, etc. In many cases, though, the defence under section 31 of IAA 1999 is disregarded when the applicant has travelled via another 'safe' country.[5] For instance, in one of the cases reviewed, the failure to make an application for asylum in one of the countries through which the defendant travelled before arriving to the UK was considered by the Crown as damaging to his credibility and hindered the application of the defence under section 31:

> It is considered that you failed to take advantage of a reasonable opportunity to make an asylum or human rights claim while in [a] safe country [Turkey or Italy]. Your failure to do so has damaged your credibility under section 8 of the [A]sylum and [I]mmigration (T[reatment of] C[laimants, etc.]) [A]ct 2004.
> (Isleworth Crown Court, court file, Case 30)[6]

People accused of the offence of no documents under section 2 of the AI(TC)A 2004 are not covered by section 31 even if they claim asylum. So in order to be immune from sanctions, they must prove that any of the defences in section 2(4) apply to them.[7] According to guidance from the Immigration and Nationality Directorate (IND), once immigration authorities encounter a person without a document, they are required to ask brief questions to establish whether an offence under section 2 has been committed and if it is 'considered likely that the person does not have a defence'. This is called the 'initial designated administrative procedure' which precedes the usual screening process. If the immigration officer does not consider that the person has a defence, he or she should refer the case to the chief immigration officer who will discuss it with the police and the prosecutor.[8] As a justification for his decision in one of the case-files reviewed, the chief immigration officer argued that:

> [The accused] had stated to [the] IO [immigration officer] . . . that he had his own national passport and that the agent used his original Sri Lankan passport and a forged Sri Lankan passport to travel to the UK. [The defendant] stated that he handed his original passport to the agent in Sri Lanka about two months ago and was told by [the] agent that everything would be arranged. He did not at any point state that he had been threatened by the agent or that

he was under duress. After considering all of the information provided I am of the opinion that this was not a reasonable defence and that [this person] had therefore committed an offence under section (2) of the [AI(TC)A 2004].

(Uxbridge Magistrates' Court, court file, Case 80)

The interview as reproduced in the file, though, showed the existence of threats that may have given rise to the statutory defence.[9] When the immigration officer questioned the accused about 'what would have happened if you did not follow his [the agent's] instructions?', he replied: 'He would have dropped me in a known place.' The officer went on to ask: 'Why did you listen to [the] agent?' This person said: 'I was frightened, if I didn't listen to him he would have left me somewhere else' (Uxbridge Magistrates' Court, court file, Case 80). Such responses were not investigated further, the defence under section 2 was disregarded and a prosecution was initiated against this person.

The assessment by immigration officers is deemed as preliminary and so it is to be reviewed by the police and the CPS. Generally, though, this initial decision is subsequently ratified. Once the case reaches the court, the availability of these defences often goes unexamined as criminal lawyers seldom raise them and frequently advise their clients to plead guilty.

Criminal lawyers and prosecutors handling immigration offenders: uncertainty, negligence and inconsistencies

> *A lot of people have gone through the system and they don't even know they don't know and they are meant to know . . . You've got a lawyer expecting to do the job properly, and if they don't you suffer.*[10]

Even though the offence of no document is one of the most frequent immigration offences in the criminal courts and despite the fact that many of those accused of immigration crimes claim asylum, defences such as those in section 31, IAA 1999 and section 2, AI(TC)A 2004 are barely raised. Of 232 defendants charged with immigration offences at the Uxbridge Magistrates' Court, 159 were charged with section 2 – as the principal offence (that is, 68 per cent of the defendants). In 41 out of 159 cases, it was mentioned that the defendant claimed or intended to claim asylum.[11] The overwhelming majority pleaded guilty to the charge based on this offence and were convicted for their illegal entry before their claims were examined: 155[12] out of 159 defendants were convicted for this offence. Likewise, the vast majority of the defendants charged with this offence at Isleworth Crown Court claimed or intended to claim asylum: 14 out of 16 defendants filed an asylum petition. Among them, however, the rate of guilty plea was much lower: only seven defendants pleaded guilty to the charge; the rest of them (nine) pleaded not guilty – four of them were found guilty, while five were found not guilty.

The small number of contested cases is surprising, given that in cases where the defence under section 31 is at stake, the accused bears only an evidential burden of adducing 'sufficient evidence' in support of his or her refugee claim. For this, the defendant merely needs to show the real or serious possibility of being persecuted if s/he is sent back to the country of origin. In turn, the prosecution bears the burden of proving 'to the usual standard' that the defendant is not a refugee.[13] In other words, the defendant does not have to satisfy the jury that s/he *is* a refugee, but only that s/he *may be*, because if the defendant tenders evidence of such a defence, the prosecutor has not proven the charge 'beyond reasonable doubt'.

In only three cases that I reviewed was this defence interposed. In two of them, though, it was probably wrongly raised as the defendants were charged with the no document offence. One possible reason for this outcome is that my sample was dominated by cases involving the offence of no document, for which the defence under section 31 does not apply.

Still, vague allegations about 'human rights issues' or 'being a genuine refugee' were raised in very few cases. In the court files that I reviewed at Isleworth Crown Court, various defences were mentioned in ten out of 99 cases. Eight of them were cases of being unable to produce a passport, and the remaining two were cases, respectively, of assisting unlawful immigration and deception. In five of these ten cases, the defendants were acquitted; in four, the defendants were found guilty; and the remaining one was sent back to the magistrates' court. At Uxbridge Magistrates' Court, defences were mentioned only in 7 out of 229 cases. In all of them the defendants were charged with the offence of no document. In two of the seven cases, the defendants were acquitted; in three, the defendants were found guilty; and in the two others, the cases were committed to the crown court. Three of these cases were connected as they involved a brother and two sisters from Uganda. Apparently they had applied for a visa to visit their mother in the UK, but their applications were rejected. The 'agent' they used to travel to the UK suggested that they claim asylum, but they decided not to. Their lawyer argued that the two sisters had been compelled to destroy their passports and that during the journey they were under the absolute control of the 'agent' and their brother. The cases of the two sisters went to trial and they were acquitted, whereas the brother pleaded guilty and was convicted to 16 weeks' imprisonment (Uxbridge Magistrates' Court, court file, Cases 4, 5 and 6).

In the rare instances in which defences were raised, defendants still often ended up pleading guilty. Unfortunately, however, the files did not provide information on the reasons for not pursuing these defences. For example, in one of these cases, the lawyer said that the defendant, a Sri Lankan Tamil woman, 'had a reasonable defence', but she still pleaded guilty and was convicted to three months in prison (Uxbridge Magistrates' Court, court file, Case 93). In another case, the lawyer of the defendant, a Sri Lankan Tamil man, stated in court that article 31 of the Refugee Convention was applicable to him. The defendant had travelled to the UK via Argentina and claimed asylum upon arrival. He then changed his plea from not guilty to guilty and was convicted to four months' imprisonment (Isleworth Crown Court, court file, Case 84). Presumably, the fact that this person made a stopover in a 'safe country' and was accused of arriving without a passport had disqualified him for this defence.

In some other cases, the legal representatives expressed doubts that they could successfully run a defence and so advised their clients to plead guilty. This, for instance, applied in the case involving an Iranian woman who claimed asylum in the UK. All her family claimed asylum as well. The main ground for her claim was that she had had an affair with another man while married. She divorced her husband and since then she had suffered persecution in Iran. Her lawyer told the court that her circumstances 'might not amount to reasonable excuse' and requested a post-sentence report which supported the community disposal of the defendant. However, she pleaded guilty and was sentenced to eight weeks' imprisonment (Uxbridge Magistrates' Court, court file, Case 69). In another case, the defence lawyer asked the court for an adjournment because he was not sure if he should advise the defendant to plead guilty or not; he told the court that he 'need[ed] to investigate case law'. Later on, the defendant pleaded guilty and was sentenced to 12 weeks' imprisonment. The accused, an Iranian man, had travelled through Turkey and other countries. He was helped in his journey by an 'agent' who asked him to destroy his passport once he arrived in the UK where he claimed asylum (Uxbridge Magistrates' Court, court file, Case 27).

In a few cases, lawyers did pursue these defences. For those cases before the magistrates' court, some requested a committal to the crown court. The lawyer of a Sri Lankan Tamil woman argued in court that she was a 'genuine asylum seeker', but she was not believed, and that article 31 applied to her. Therefore, he requested that the case be sent to Isleworth Crown Court (Uxbridge Magistrates' Court, court file, Case 65). A similar strategy was followed in the case of an Iranian woman who claimed asylum. Her lawyer argued that she had a defence and asked for a committal to the crown court (Uxbridge Magistrates' Court, court file, Case 223). In another case at the crown court which was committed from the magistrates' court for sentence, the lawyer asked for the guilty plea to be vacated. The counsel realized that the defendant had a defence to the charge and argued that he was wrongly advised at the magistrates' court. He also said that 'problems with the interpreter on the last occasion made it difficult to deal with it then'. The defendant, an Iranian whose first asylum claim was refused, was charged with deception for allegedly giving details of another person when he made a fresh asylum application. He claimed that he never had a passport and he used a false one (Isleworth Crown Court, court file, Case 7). In one further case, the solicitor announced his intention to request that the plea be reopened because there were 'human rights issues' in the case which might question the correctness of the 'very high tariff' of the sanction imposed. His client, a Middle-Eastern man, had been convicted to a six-month prison sentence for being unable to produce a passport. In this instance, the solicitor's argument was not about impunity, but about mitigation (Uxbridge Magistrates' Court, court file, Case 227). Because these cases could not be followed up subsequently, it is difficult to assess how successful these strategies had been.

These cases demonstrate the negligibly low rates at which defences are pursued in favour of people accused of immigration offences. Among legal practitioners there seem to be doubts about the scope of these provisions and uncertainty on their applicability to the particular defendant. Many lawyers deem it too risky to run these defences. In a number of files that I reviewed, people charged with the offence of no document said that they had never held a passport; some of them offered other identification which might confirm their identity and nationality. For instance, a Zimbabwean woman alleged that she had never had a passport and used a false one to check-in on the flight to the UK. Apparently, she followed her 'agent's' directions and she disposed of the false document before arriving into the UK. She produced her national identity document and birth certificate to immigration authorities. This situation might have fallen under the defence of section 2(4) (c) of AI(TC)A 2004, as interpreted by the High Court in the case of *Thet v DPP*.[14] Yet the chief immigration officer charged her with the no document offence because she disposed of the passport that she had used to travel. When examining the case for prosecution, the intervening prosecutor concluded that 'the fact that she never held a passport is not a reasonable excuse' (Uxbridge Magistrates' Court, court file, Case 142). In court, she pleaded guilty and was sentenced to a period of two months in prison. In contrast, in a case involving a Kuwaiti Bedouin, the barrister raised the defence under section 2 because the defendant had never had a passport. The prosecution agreed that she had a reasonable excuse because she was stateless and nomadic, and thus could not return to her country because of internal problems. She was found not guilty for the offence of no document (Isleworth Crown Court, court file, Case 54). Similar seemingly conflicting decisions were noticed in relation to Somalis charged with the offence of no document. Although in one case, the prosecutor said that Somalis are not 'normally' prosecuted for this offence before withdrawing the charges against the defendant (Uxbridge Magistrates' Court, court file, Case 7), in another case involving a Somali woman, the prosecution under section 2 was initiated. This person pleaded guilty and was convicted to an eight-month prison sentence (Uxbridge Magistrates' Court, court file, Case 134). These inconsistencies in prosecution practices may also influence the decision by the defence lawyer not to run the risk of pursuing a defence. Further, section 2 is ill-drafted, confusing and allows multiple interpretations. Hence a defence based on it may be difficult to put forward.

Other lawyers do not even know of the existence of such defences. Criminal law practitioners sometimes ignore immigration law and the many communicating channels between the two disciplines.[15] Despite the increased convergence of immigration and criminal laws through legislative changes and in practice, there are still rigid disciplinary divisions between the two. The training of criminal lawyers seldom includes immigration as a subject. Neither do criminal law textbooks incorporate it as a separate section.[16] As a result, asylum claimants are still being prosecuted and convicted for entering the country illegally.[17] When I asked a criminal solicitor, defending a person (Mr Hussain) who arrived at Heathrow without travel documents and subsequently claimed asylum before Uxbridge Magistrates' Court, whether he was planning to interpose the defence based on article 31 of the Refugee Convention, he replied that 'that is an immigration issue related to the asylum claim. It's not a criminal defence. I'm a criminal lawyer; I don't know anything about immigration'.

In most of these cases, the lack of knowledge goes unnoticed, unless it is detected on appeal. In one such instance, it was uncovered that the defendant had a defence for the charge of entering the country without a passport which he disclosed in the written document in which he pleaded guilty. The Court of Appeal stated that such defence was apparent in the written document. Therefore, the plea should not have been accepted and the defendant should not have been convicted.[18] However, the cases that reach the higher courts are a small minority. Most of the people who are prosecuted for immigration offences are offered a quick and superficial examination of their cases in a criminal procedure which looks more like a bureaucratic and repetitive administrative proceeding than a genuine exercise of justice. In other words, criminal proceedings in these cases seem to be more about administration than about justice.

When the immigration case does have an impact on the criminal case: exceptions and mitigations

In some instances, the immigration or asylum case is important for the criminal case. First, when the defendant is granted refugee status or humanitarian protection before the criminal case is decided, the person is more likely to be acquitted. Second, the immigration or asylum case is usually mentioned for mitigation purposes, and so it might have some weight on the reduction of the penalty. An asylum claim does not prevent the opening of a criminal proceeding against the applicant. More often than not magistrates and judges pass their sentence before the asylum claim is decided. Therefore, in some cases, people are prosecuted and convicted for immigration crimes, and after serving their sentences they are granted refugee status. A barrister specializing in immigration offences explained that he often observes this sequence where the criminal sentence precedes the asylum determination:

> [W]hat we do see is that someone is arrested with a passport, false passport, they plead guilty. Afterwards they say '[L]ook, I am a refugee'. By the time they say they are refugees they weren't properly represented, they served time in prison, they came out, they made an application for asylum and a deportation order is issued. And they have to defend that on asylum grounds and their asylum application becomes the resistant to the deportation order and at the end of it, the court says '[W]ell, we are not going to deport him because he is a refugee.'
>
> (Respondent 15, 28/04/2010)

In some rare cases, however, the determination on the asylum claim is made before the criminal case is settled. In some files at the crown court, when the claimant is granted refugee status before the criminal judgment, the prosecution is frequently discontinued and the accused is declared not guilty and exonerated. This was the case for an Iranian man who was charged with arriving without a passport. The Crown stated that because the defendant was granted refugee status, it was decided not to proceed with the case (Isleworth Crown Court, court file, Case 56). In another case, a Palestinian man claimed that he had been captured and tortured by the Israelis. His asylum application was successful, and so the prosecutor stated that there was 'no realistic prospect of conviction and no public interest [in the prosecution]' (Isleworth Crown Court , court file, Case 63). In both cases, the defendants were acquitted.

In the case of 'M and Others',[19] the Court of Appeal implicitly admitted that the asylum determination is critical for the criminal case. In that case, the applicants challenged their convictions following their unconditional guilty plea to the offence under section 25(1) of the IDCA 2006 (possession of a false identity document with intention). They submitted that their guilty plea was a nullity – and should be so declared – because their legal representatives failed to advise them about the availability of the defence under section 31 of the IAA 1999. In three of the cases,[20] the solicitors recognized that they did not mention to their clients the availability of this defence, either because they were not aware of the defence, or because they thought it was unavailable to the defendant. In two of the cases,[21] they considered that the defence was unavailable or 'difficult to run' due to the defendants not 'coming directly' to the UK. The Court of Appeal allowed the appeal in three cases and quashed the convictions of three of the four appellants because they were wrongly advised to plead guilty. Because the defendants had a good prospect of successful defence under section 31 and they were not advised about it, these three convictions were declared 'unsafe'. In order to decide whether the convictions were unsafe, the court analysed the prospect of a successful defence under section 31 for each of the cases. The court not only examined the requirements in section 31; it also gave significant weight to the decision by immigration authorities. In fact, the only appeal that was dismissed related to an asylum claimant whose application was refused.[22]

A conclusion that can be drawn from these cases is that if the decision on the criminal case relies on the determination of the asylum claim, the former can only be decided when the latter is solved. Even though this reasoning may benefit those who are granted refugee status or some other kind of international protection before the final criminal judgment, the most likely outcome is that the criminal case is decided prior to the asylum one because the asylum adjudication process is usually longer than a criminal proceeding for immigration offences, and because few of those convicted for these offences file an appeal. This decision pattern reflects a system of immigration and criminal sanctions primarily aimed at deterring those who seek to abuse the asylum route. Within this system, the conviction of successful asylum applicants is conceived as a necessary or 'collateral effect'. Further, it shows that the fate of the prosecution and the criminal proceeding largely rests on decisions made elsewhere.

A second, more subtle avenue through which immigration considerations filtrate into the criminal process is in the defence's plea for mitigation. Criminal judges insist that the immigration and the criminal cases should be dealt with separately.[23] For instance, in one of the cases heard, after passing sentence, the judge referred to the defendant's asylum application as the 'background' of the case which is 'for the immigration authorities to consider when the moment comes' (Isleworth Crown Court, hearing, Case 10).[24] Yet in practice, the matters related to the asylum claim are sometimes brought into the criminal proceeding. As I show, immigration-offences cases are overwhelmingly settled through guilty pleas and in some of them, the defence lawyer 'uses' the asylum claim to beg for a mitigated sentence.

In a case involving an Iranian national who was charged with the no document offence and who claimed asylum upon arrival, his solicitor argued for a mitigated sentence on his behalf. While the defence was clearly based on the circumstances in which Mr Babakhani escaped from Iran due to political persecution by the government, his solicitor stated that the asylum application 'will be considered in due course. This is a criminal matter.' He did not raise any defence, even though he recognized that the defendant had escaped because he risked being killed. The lawyer explained to the bench that the accused had been involved in demonstrations against the results of the last elections and the Iranian authorities had beaten him and wanted him for arrest. He hid in the houses of family members and friends, and his family paid a facilitator to get him out of the country. When he arrived at Heathrow, he destroyed his passport. The solicitor explained his client's conduct in the following terms: '[The defendant] knows it is a difficult road but the alternative was the loss of his life.' He apologetically said, 'the mistake was to destroy the document'. In this case, the magistrates evidently took into consideration the 'asylum background' in fixing the length of the prison sentence. After stating that the case presented 'very difficult circumstances' and that 'we are dealing with the criminal side of this', the magistrates considered in their decision the guilty plea and 'the circumstances of the case', and sentenced him to a 'minimum custodial sentence' of two months (Uxbridge Magistrates' Court, hearing, Case 15).

While in the files reviewed there is little information about the arguments put forward by the defence and the motivation for the judges' decisions, the appeals to these mitigating factors may explain the variation in sentencing tariffs.[25] In the magistrates' court, the penalties imposed on those accused of the offence of no document ranged from eight weeks' to six months' imprisonment. Another important consideration in the decision on the length of imprisonment is whether and at what stage of the process the accused pleads guilty to the charges.

Admitting one's guilt or relinquishing rights? Immigration status and the incentives to plead guilty

In the English and Welsh criminal justice system, the rate of cases that are settled through plea bargains and guilty pleas is very high and has increased in recent years, largely due to cost-effectiveness considerations (Ashworth and Zedner 2008: 34). In 2011, 68.4 per cent of the cases examined in magistrates' courts ended up with a guilty plea by the defendant.[26] At the crown courts, the rate was even higher: 72.8 per cent in 2011.[27] These high rates can be explained by the large discounts in penalties of up to one-third if the guilty plea is entered at the 'first reasonable opportunity'. These incentives are aimed at encouraging defendants to plead guilty because it 'avoids the need for a trial . . . shortens the gap between charge and sentence, saves considerable cost, and, in the case of an early plea, saves victims and witnesses from the concern about having to give evidence' (Sentencing Guidelines Council 2007: 4).[28] While criminal justice system data do not distinguish immigration-related crimes from recorded offences, from the examination of court files for this research, I found a considerably higher number of people charged with immigration offences (as compared to other types of offence) who pleaded guilty at the court hearing. In fact, 95 per cent of defendants in immigration-offence cases decided in Uxbridge Magistrates' Court between 2008 and 2009 pleaded guilty.

This rate is significantly lower at Isleworth Crown Court, where there are more contested cases. Of the 90 defendants accused of immigration offences who were sent to trial, only 48 of them (53.3 per cent) pleaded guilty. In these latter cases, the defendant made the decision to plead guilty at a later stage in the process, once the case was 'trial ready' and before the case was heard in trial. This rate does not take into account the cases committed for sentence (16), where the defendant pleaded guilty in all of them.[29] The lower rate of cases settled through guilty pleas may be explained in part by the fact that the cases which reach the crown court are fairly different from those usually decided in the magistrates' court. In the former, most of the immigration-offence cases involved those who aid undocumented migrants, and defendants are generally British nationals or foreigners with strong ties to the country and with good knowledge of English – inferred from the fact that interpreters are used in few of these cases. On the other hand, the cases that are settled at the magistrates' court are those involving undocumented migrants who are caught when trying to enter the country. As I will explain, they are more vulnerable and less prepared to battle a criminal case.

Criminal law scholars have pointed out the risks of an extensive use of plea bargaining. One of the main problems is the 'possibly coercive effects of increased incentives' that could affect the defendant's rights to a fair trial and the presumption of innocence (Ashworth and Zedner 2008: 35). Even in the absence of these incentives, defendants may not make an informed decision. The police, prosecutors, judges and magistrates are increasingly pressured to clear up cases and manage them in a speedy, cost-effective way. An illustration of the pressure by some judges on defendants to plead guilty is provided in the following extract from a case-file involving an Iranian man accused of failing to cooperate with his removal. This person had no lawyer representing him, pleaded not guilty and was convicted to a six-month prison sentence:

[Judge:]	'Are you going to plead guilty?'
[Defendant:]	He says h[e is] not guilty.
[Judge:]	'Were you interviewed by an officer to sign some papers?'
[Defendant:]	[S]ays yes.
[Judge:]	'Did you say you are not going to co-operate?'
[Defendant:]	'Yes'.

[Judge:]	'Given the fact that you were interviewed and you didn't co-operate that would mean that you are guilty and you have no defence to it . . . If the clerk puts the indictment to you will you say you are guilty?'
[Defendant:]	'I have not committed a crime . . .'
[Judge:]	'If you plead guilty – I would give you a lesser sentence and [I will] sentence you to 4 months which you have already served. If you fight the case and are found guilty by the jury I would sentence you to 6 months imprisonment. Now taken all that into account do you wish to say you are guilty of this offence or go on fighting it [?]'

(Isleworth Crown Court, court file, Case 52)

In another case, at the end of a trial in which the defendant was found guilty of passport fraud, the judge addressed him and said: '[Y]ou didn't plead guilty, which is your right, so I can give you no credit for that.'[30] He was convicted to 12 months in prison.

So too, defence lawyers often make a pragmatic decision or 'strategic bargain' based on the costs and benefits involved in 'fighting' the case for both their clients and themselves in order to avoid the difficult and time-consuming task of mounting a defence. Few defendants are able to make a decision on their plea by themselves because they ignore the law and the consequences involved (Duff *et al.* 2007: 11). Then their choice is usually influenced by the purposes of their lawyer and other actors of the criminal justice system. Additionally, those who cannot afford the financial costs of a trial and do not have enough legal knowledge are more likely to accept a plea under pressure (Scott and Stuntz 1992: 1928; Stuntz 2008: 1978).

Foreignness, immigration status and the ability to resist a charge

As the high rates of immigration-related cases that end up with guilty pleas testify, increased incentives and pressures to plead guilty are even more acute in the case of non-citizens charged with immigration offences. Because of language barriers and the lack of knowledge about the rituals and legal formalities of the criminal process, they are particularly ill-suited to 'fight back'. Most of the defendants, particularly in the magistrates' court, needed an interpreter during the hearing and to communicate with their lawyers. The presence of interpreters, however, does not guarantee that the matters discussed are fully understood by the accused (Dery 1996; Cole and Maslow-Armand 1997; Messier 1999: 1402). Even when access to interpreters is granted, the task of translating formal and legal terms from one language into another is full of difficulties.

There is an obvious link between the vulnerability of the people predominantly caught in these types of cases and the high rate of guilty pleas. They are not only foreigners unfamiliar with the vernacular language and culture; they frequently lack financial resources and are traumatized (Brennan 2006: 156; Bosworth 2011c). Many of these people have just arrived in the country. According to what they claim, many have been forced to emigrate because of political persecution in their own countries. Others are seeking to be reunited with their family and had applied for visas which had been refused. Still others are looking for better social and economic conditions. The very fact of being involved in these offences implies an element of 'duress' or 'involuntary mobility' (Carling 2002). As De Giorgi (2010: 158) put it, many are 'crimes of desperation' or 'crimes of survival'. People involved in these offences are not tourists or businesspeople. They are badly informed; many do not even know that their conducts are imprisonable offences in Britain. Some, though, will still 'try their luck' again as they prefer to remain in a British prison than to be deported back to their country. Once caught, they are more likely to be in pre-trial detention than nationals and thus at greater risk of conviction because of the limitations in fighting their cases from prison. They have few possibilities for resisting a criminal charge and even less a removal (Ellermann 2010). It is difficult to think of a more vulnerable situation to be in. The fact that a large proportion of defendants accused of immigration crimes 'waive' their right to trial, to be 'called into account' and held responsible for their actions tells a great deal about their stance *vis-à-vis* the state.

The high rate of guilty pleas among defendants in immigration-offence cases sharply contrasts with the lower rate of cases involving ethnic minorities in England and Wales that are settled in this way. Roger Hood (1992: 123) found that defendants with ethnic minority backgrounds are less likely to plead guilty than white defendants. When they do so, they plead guilty later in the process than do their white counterparts. This pattern of guilty plea among non-white defendants has been explained by their alienation and lack of trust in the criminal justice system, and the perception among ethnic minorities that the criminal justice system and the police are biased against them (Tonry 1997: 17; see also John 2003: 13). Even though defendants of immigration crimes are overwhelmingly non-white,[31] other factors not necessarily related to their ethnic background explain their inclination to plead guilty and to waive their right to trial. As explained above, these factors are related to the condition of foreigners and the situation surrounding the offence. They are often too vulnerable to challenge a criminal charge. Hence, foreignness plays a crucial role in the decision to plead guilty (Messier 1999: 1404).

Hearings in these cases are characterized by the lack of participation of the accused. They generally remained silent throughout in the cases that I witnessed. Their physical presence contrasts sharply with their absence and exclusion from the proceedings. They are spectators in their own case. As with other defendants in custody, they were escorted by security staff, brought to the court and placed in a glass custody box. In the beginning they were asked a few questions by the clerk – such as their names and addresses in the UK – but remained silent during most of the hearing. While criminal defendants in general rely on their legal representatives and do not actively participate during court proceedings, I observed that in cases involving non-immigration defendants, there were some interactions with court staff in order to clarify certain aspects of the case, for example. In immigration-related cases, such exchanges were less common. When questions were asked, they were generally directed to the lawyer and not to the defendant.

Magistrates and judges addressed them directly only to communicate their decision. For many of them, trying to understand what was going on was itself such a big effort, requiring deep concentration, that they made no attempts to intervene.

On one occasion, after the magistrates declined their jurisdiction and decided to send the case to the crown court, the accused (Mr Joseph) wanted to talk to his lawyer, but he was told by the judge that the decision had been made. Mr Joseph, a Nigerian national, was accused of trying to exit the country with a false Nigerian passport. No efforts were made by his lawyer to hear and transmit what he had to say. The hearing was abruptly ended and the defendant was sent back to custody (Uxbridge Magistrates' Court, hearing, Case 4). In the hearing at the crown court, he just intervened when he was asked his name and address. He was also asked about his plea, to which he replied 'guilty'. His barrister told the judge that Mr Joseph had been living in the UK for 16 years. He entered the country illegally and had never regularized his condition. He was trying to embark to Nigeria to meet his British partner, marry her and enter the country legally. The judge imposed a 12-month prison sentence and automatic deportation. There was no reaction from him and he quietly left the room (Isleworth Crown Court, hearing, Case 4). In this context, the silence of the defendants in the courtroom may hide their confusion, uncertainty, impotence and subjugation (Johnson 2011).

The role of the defence lawyer

Defendants in immigration-related cases are generally assisted by legal aid lawyers at magistrates' and crown courts. Because of the lack of financial resources, most of the people accused of immigration offences fulfil the 'means test' and are eligible for legal aid. While in the files at the magistrates' court, this information was generally not available, the ones at the crown court did contain a separate folder on legal representation. Almost all of the accused were represented by legal aid lawyers. In England and Wales, a person accused of a criminal offence needs to appoint a private or publicly funded lawyer so s/he can be represented before the courts.[32] In the latter case, s/he does not have to pay legal costs. In order to be eligible for legal aid, the person must meet certain financial conditions. People who are receiving welfare benefits or are under 18 years old are automatically eligible. The defendant is required to apply for a representation order to get legal aid representation by a solicitor and, if necessary, a barrister. If legal aid is granted, the defendant needs to appoint a lawyer who does legal aid work. Legal aid is run by the Legal Services Commission and offers legal advice from associated solicitors' firms and non-profit organizations. Lawyers have to meet a number of conditions in order to qualify as legal aid solicitors or barristers – such as obtaining a law degree and completing a training contract. Many firms do both legal aid work and private work.[33]

Legal aid lawyers are paid fixed and standard fees regardless of the time spent on each case. A recent reform on legal aid provisions fixed fees for legal aid work at £515 if the client enters a guilty plea at the first appearance; however, these fees are not increased if the case continues (Legal Services Commission 2006: 18; Davidson 2010). These new measures have substantially enlarged the proportion of summary cases settled in this way. Even though fixed fees for attending the police station at Heathrow airport are twice as high as those for attending the police station at Blackpool (respectively, £340.43 and £138.72), many lawyers are unenthusiastic about taking immigration-crime cases. A criminal and immigration solicitor observed that because some private lawyers consider these rates to be very low, they turn down cases of immigration offences which require expertise on both criminal and immigration law (Respondent 4, 16/07/2010).[34]

Other lawyers take these cases without devoting much time to them. The defence counsel of Mr Hussain, accused of arriving into the country without a passport, told me that this was a case of a friend and he did the 'favour' of taking it because his friend was unavailable. He saw his client once, a couple of minutes before the hearing at the magistrates' court and advised him to plead guilty. He did not intervene in the hearing (Uxbridge Magistrates' Court, hearing, Case 1). I followed this case through to the crown court. The attitude of the barrister was no different. Before the hearing started, the usher warned the participants that 'the court was running late' to which Mr Hussain's barrister responded: '[This is] quite short, it is this document case. It should be short.' His intervention in the hearing seemed to be more directed at clarifying certain circumstances of the case for the court – particularly the countries via which Mr Hussain had travelled – than at defending his client. He succinctly explained to the judge: 'I met [the defendant for the] first time in video conference. I don't understand why he is coming from Hong Kong. He is from Iraq and he is not willing to go back.'

In this hearing, it was revealed that Mr Hussain was found wandering around Heathrow without his passport. When he was interviewed by immigration staff, he said he was coming from Taiwan via Thailand. He also claimed that he disposed of his passport in the toilet. Records obtained by the police seemed to show, though, that he had come from New Zealand via Hong Kong. In fact, the main object of the hearing was to find out through which countries the defendant had travelled. The judge asked the lawyer whether the defendant had applied for asylum, to which the lawyer replied, 'Yes'. The determination of the itinerary was important not only to assess whether he could have claimed asylum in another 'safe country' and thus to decide if the claim was admissible, but also to determine if he was lying. Before passing sentence, the judge stated that 'the circumstances around you remained a mystery and your acts prevented the authorities in dealing with you [as you] provided a false account of the facts. You know you were doing something wrong.' These were considered aggravating factors, and so Mr Hussain was convicted to 12 months in prison. Details about the asylum claim were not discussed at all during the hearing and the hearing lasted for only ten minutes (Isleworth Crown Court, hearing, Case 1).

Another factor which may explain the high rates of guilty pleas among immigration defendants is that few defence lawyers know immigration law. The supervising solicitor at RMJ explained to me:

> [P]eople who are prosecuted at that stage almost always haven't had an opportunity to obtain legal advice in respect of their immigration matters.

They are referred to a duty solicitor who advises them in relation to the criminal prosecution and huge numbers of people are advised to plead guilty, so that they will receive a shorter sentence. And so they plead guilty without even knowing that they have a defence to that offence.

(Respondent 10, 8/06/2010)

A senior criminal and immigration barrister agreed with her about the way people accused of immigration offences are generally treated once they are caught by the police and brought to court:

[T]hese are people who aren't in the system. I think that people are incredibly vulnerable when they aren't in the system. And they don't have access to lawyers . . . [They are] taken down to the police station, get the local solicitor doing the police station duty. And they don't know anything about immigration law on the whole. So they are advising these people to plead guilty.

(Respondent 8, 17/05/2010)

In some of the cases reviewed, the defendants/clients expressed unease with their legal representatives. A Sri Lankan Tamil accused of assisting unlawful immigration complained to the court about his lawyer's careless handling of the case and that his lawyer was not a Tamil speaker, and requested a change in his representation. The notes in the file state: 'No representative came to prison to visit him. He wants to change representation because lawyers don't speak Tamil' (Isleworth Crown Court, court file, Case 3). In another case, the defendant complained to the court and asked for another lawyer because 'the first one advised him to plead not guilty and [did] not give [him] proper advice'. The defendant complained that his lawyer 'doesn't care' about his case 'as [he] didn't go to prison to see him', and mentioned that in one of the hearings there was no interpreter. Even though the defendant did not understand what was discussed, his lawyer did not ask the court for an interpreter. Finally, he expressed his preference for a lawyer who 'knows [his] language and knows Afghanistan'. This person was accused of using deception to enter the country by giving details of someone else when he claimed asylum (Isleworth Crown Court, court file, Case 83).

Although tensions between clients and legal representatives are not unique to immigration-crime cases, the fact that legal representatives frequently do not speak the language of the defendants and rely on interpreters constitutes a serious barrier for communication and may exacerbate frictions. Often these cases involve political and social issues about other countries. While these issues are not strictly related to the criminal charge, they are important to understanding the motives and circumstances of the defendant in engaging in the behaviours in question. The lack of minimum knowledge about these issues by the defence counsel may represent a weakness for the defence strategy (Brennan 2006: 154).

Strategic reasons for pleading guilty

While some lawyers are unaware of the availability of defences in favour of their clients, many defence counsels advise clients to plead guilty for strategic reasons, because the likely sentence would be reduced. Factors such as the likelihood of a conviction, the length of the potential sentence, the time spent in pre-trial detention and the legal work involved (especially at public defender fees) are often considered. A critic of plea bargaining powerfully argued that the guilty-plea system 'leads even able, conscientious, and highly motivated attorneys to make decisions that are not really in their clients' interests' (Alschuler 1975: 1180). The President of the Middlesex Law Society explained the practice of plea bargaining in the case of passport offences. He argued that in order to avoid a lengthier sentence,

> most practitioners would advise pleading in the magistrates' court at the earliest opportunity on the purely pragmatic grounds that the court would probably accept jurisdiction, and so the sentence served would only be three months. Whereas it would take at least three months, and probably more, to list a trial in the crown court during which time the defendant would almost certainly be in custody, and would end up serving more time even if found not guilty.
>
> (Darlington 2006: 170)

Such strategic reasoning was apparent in one of the cases I followed for this study. The defendants were an Afghan couple who claimed to have received death threats from the Taliban. One day, members of the Taliban met Mr Khawas when he was leaving the university where he was studying. They said that his wife should stop her activities as a women's rights activist. Otherwise, they would cut off his head and send it to his wife before raping and killing her. Palwasha Zarifi Khawas is an internationally renowned leader who has been vocal in denouncing human rights abuses against women in her country. Faced with such imminent danger, they decided to leave the country immediately. They could not apply for a visa and thus paid an 'agent' to take them out of the country. They travelled through Pakistan, Turkey and Italy. When they reached the UK, they claimed asylum. Upon arrival, they were asked for their passports. They maintained that they had not used their original passports, but false ones, to leave Afghanistan because they did not want to alert the authorities. They also stated that they handed the false passports back to the 'agent' before passing immigration controls. Afterwards, they were charged with the section 2 offence.

Even though the magistrates accepted jurisdiction, their lawyer requested the bench to send the case to the crown court. Apparently, there is a general perception among lawyers that trials at the crown court are fairer than trials at the magistrates' court (Ashworth and Redmayne 2010: 324). In fact, after the hearing, the usher of the court commented on the case to the couple's solicitor. He crudely said: 'Entering without passport? Rubbish!', to which the lawyer replied: 'That's the reason we are going to the crown court.' The solicitor told me that he believed the defendants had a number of defences available and he intended to raise them at Isleworth. Predicting their prosecution, before leaving Afghanistan, the defendants had made scanned copies of their original passports so they could prove their identity and nationality. The solicitor told me that this proof may exempt them from penalties. From his presentation during two hearings and the short conversation I had with him afterwards, I had the impression that he was very committed to this case and had thorough knowledge about the defendants' asylum claims.

The defendants twice applied for bail, yet on both occasions were refused. In the committal hearing, Mrs and Mr Khawas changed their pleas from not guilty to guilty. No reasons were given in court for this change. The lawyer told the court that 'It is with great pain that they plead guilty.' He then requested a mitigated sentence based on the circumstances of the case – mainly, their asylum claim (Uxbridge Magistrates' Court, hearing, Case 5). The decision on the change of plea may have been motivated by the refusal of bail. In order to save them time in custody, the lawyer might have advised his clients to plead guilty as they had to spend the process behind bars, and there was no certainty that they would have been acquitted at the crown court and a risk that they would have received a longer sentence for not pleading guilty.

While this instrumental strategy is thought to benefit the clients, it has a number of negative consequences in cases involving foreigners. Particularly in the case of asylum seekers, a criminal conviction will certainly affect their credibility and have an adverse impact on their asylum claim. It can even disqualify them for international protection (Weber 2003). The supervising solicitor at RMJ told me that criminal convictions against asylum seekers for document offences 'later affects the credibility in the consideration of their immigration case and quite often affixes their ability to get immigration bail if they are detained. It affixes the case quite significantly all the way through' (Respondent 10, 8/06/2010). In fact, a letter from the Home Office accompanying IND guidance to immigration officers of 21 September 2004 states:

> If a person found guilty of an offence under section 2 were sentenced to the maximum 2 years' imprisonment, he could, for the purposes of Article 33(2) of the Refugee Convention, be presumed to have been convicted by a final judgment of a particularly serious crime and to constitute a danger to the community of the UK by virtue of section 72 of the Nationality, Immigration and Asylum Act 2002. However, a presumption that a person constitutes a danger to the community is rebuttable.
>
> (Quoted in ILPA 2011: n.p.)[35]

Immigration bail is restricted for those detainees with a criminal conviction since immigration courts assess them as posing a high risk of absconding and reoffending (London Detainee Support Group 2009: 10). A criminal conviction of more than 12 months triggers automatic deportation[36] and will affect a future application for a visa, permanent residence and citizenship (Zedner 2010: 384). As Bosworth put it, 'a criminal conviction for non-citizens has a far greater and more deleterious ramification for non-nationals than ever before, creating a kind of double jeopardy, wherein purely on the basis of citizenship, punishment will effectively vary' (Bosworth 2011a: 592). These detrimental effects are even more damaging when a conviction might well have been avoided.

Judging whom and how to punish

Although the courts make it emphatically clear that the criminal case is functionally distinct from the immigration case, as Gabriel Chin (2011: 1420) explained, the immigration status of the defendant is 'a pervasively important factor in almost every aspect of a criminal proceeding'. Indeed, judicial decisions on the cases I examined gave significant weight to the immigration status of the defendant and the immigration imperatives which the courts are called to sanction. The defendant's immigration status is particularly important for assessing whether to grant bail. It is also relevant for the determination of the sanction imposed. Criminal courts usually punish with confinement defendants who are non-nationals and have no or weak ties to the country. So too, imprisonment is generally justified by deterrence and the need to reduce unlawful immigration. What is at stake, then, is not so much individual wrongdoing, but the identity of the defendant and the cumulative effects that similar conducts may have on broader policy goals.

While immigration-crime defendants are dealt with according to the same ordinary criminal procedures, these principles have an adverse impact on them. Because they do not have legal residence and are due to be expelled, they are more likely than British defendants to be remanded in custody and punished with imprisonment.

Negotiating freedom: the decision to grant bail

Foreigners, in general – and those with 'no right of abode', in particular – are often refused bail. Some lawyers do not even apply for it because of the low probability of success. Even though there are no statutory regulations excluding defendants without legal immigration status from bail, courts consider that undocumented non-citizens on principle should be refused bail. Magistrates and judges assess that defendants who lack or have weak community ties, and who are without residence in the country, are likely to abscond and consequently pose a procedural risk. If the defendant absconds, the criminal proceeding and the imposition of a penalty in case of conviction may be frustrated. Therefore, people 'without legal status' – undocumented migrants – charged with immigration offences are very likely to be subject to pre-trial detention. An illustration of the weight that nationality has on the decision on bail is the case of Ms Samuels, a woman who pretended to be French and was caught trying to exit the UK with a Spanish passport which related to someone else. Her lawyer did not apply for bail and so the District Judge asked her: 'Why are you not applying for bail? [Your client] is a French citizen . . .'. After some enquiries, it was revealed that the defendant was a Cameroonian national with a different name. The judge refused the application for bail in part due to her immigration status: '[T]here are substantial grounds to believe that, if released, the defendant will fail to surrender because of the seriousness of the offence, the fact that she has other convictions, *her immigration status* and the lack of community ties' (Uxbridge Magistrates' Court, hearing, Case 9; italics added).

In other cases, bail applications are not submitted to the court because the defendant is under immigration detention. The decision on bail during a criminal process is independent from that taken by immigration authorities under immigration powers. Technically, criminal judges can bail the defendant even though s/he is subject to administrative detention. Although the distinction between bail in criminal and immigration procedures seems clear, it is not, however, fully understood in practice. In fact, in one court file that I reviewed, the lawyer did not apply for bail because he said that the defendant was subject to immigration controls (Uxbridge Magistrates' Court, court file, Case 148). In another case, when the clerk asked for representations regarding bail, the prosecutor said that '[B]ail is not an issue here. He is going to be deported anyway.' The accused, Mr Johnson, was charged of assaulting a fellow detainee in a removal centre. He was detained under immigration powers (Uxbridge Magistrates' Court, hearing, Case 13). This confusion may be in part due to the use of an identical term – bail – in criminal and immigration proceedings to refer to the release of the person subject to them. Further, while criminal justice and immigration authorities have different criteria to determine whether to grant bail, they are increasingly dovetailing as public protection and security considerations are becoming paramount for immigration staff and judges (London Detainee Support Group 2009). For this reason, it is unfortunate that the criminal justice system's jargon and terms have permeated the immigration ones (Bosworth 2011c).

Some of the reasons given by the magistrates and district judges for denying bail were:

- the defendant is not a citizen or has no legal status;
- the offence charged shows the ability to move from one country to another, to access and use false documents, and to use sophisticated means of travel;
- the lack of travel documents;
- the defendant is likely to be deported or has been served with a deportation order;
- the defendant is a failed asylum seeker;
- the lack of community ties;
- the seriousness of the offence and the likelihood of a prison sentence; and
- the history of failing to comply with instructions.

These circumstances are considered 'substantial grounds to believe' that the defendant will fail to surrender him/herself and commit further offences on bail. While these circumstances may be deemed as proxy for assessing risk factors, they are assumed without subjecting them to an objective scrutiny. Further, in two of the cases reviewed, the reasons given were very loosely linked to the risk of absconding. In the case of Mrs and Mr Khawas referred to above, the District

Judge considered as one of the grounds for refusal the fact that the defendants 'clearly claim asylum in the UK and not in the first safe port [Italy]' (Uxbridge Magistrates' Court, hearing, Case 5). In another case, one of the grounds for refusing bail by the magistrates was that the defendant 'travelled without passport and [upon arrival to the UK] gave up [the] passport to a 3rd party' (Uxbridge Magistrates' Court , court file, Case 80). These are examples of how substantive considerations – for example, about the availability of a defence – are taken as justification for denying bail, a decision which should be based on procedural considerations.

In some instances, certain facts – such as the use of interpreters – are presented as indicators of lack of community ties and thus argued as grounds for refusing bail. In a hearing at Uxbridge Magistrates' Court in the case against Mr Alensi, charged with facilitating the entry to the country of a group of Kuwaiti nationals, the prosecutor argued against his release in the following terms:

> Facilitation is a very serious offence and should be sent to the crown court. [The people assisted] destroyed their documents in the toilet. *The defendant has links outside the UK and no links in the country. This is evidenced by the fact that he is using an interpreter.* Perhaps he is not even working.
>
> (Uxbridge Magistrates' Court , hearing, Case 2; emphasis added)

Although Mr Alensi was a UK resident, the prosecutor inferred the lack of ties from the need to use an interpreter. This argument was, however, rejected and the accused was granted bail by the magistrates.

While the policy of restricting bail to those who pose a procedural risk may be considered as 'facially neutral', it has a disproportionately adverse impact on a certain group: those without legal residence, settlement or a permanent job (Tonry 1997: 17). The practice of restricting bail for foreigners without links to the country explains the high rates of pre-trial confinement among them and has an impact on the composition of the prison population, particularly in London. While non-nationals represented 12.9 per cent of the prison population in England and Wales in April 2011, in London, this rate was between 25 and 48 per cent – depending on the prison (Hammond 2007; International Centre for Prison Studies 2011). Nicolas Hammond (2007: 815) observed that the over-representation of foreigners in London prisons can be explained in part by the fact that these prisons cover the courts of Heathrow airport which have a large volume of cases involving foreigners accused of drugs and immigration offences. Because of their immigration status, they are more likely to be remanded in custody during the criminal process.[37]

Particularly in the case of immigration offences, certain features – such as the possibility to move from one country to another and the access to false documents – are interpreted by the courts as justifying the need for precautionary measures during the criminal process. In general, defendants behind bars are less likely successfully to battle their cases and more likely to be convicted than defendants who are free (Hagan and Palloni 1998: 376). So the decision on bail may also have an impact on the outcome of the case.

Protecting the borders: immigration imperatives and the decision to punish

When cases are settled through guilty pleas, as Feeley (1979) puts it, the role of the judge is reduced to 'ratifying' the decision which was made earlier by the parties. Still, magistrates and judges decide on the type and tariff of the sanction. Decisions are often justified on a number of factors: deterrence; the cumulative impact that the same type of offences have on the system of immigration controls; the seriousness of the offence; and the immigration status of the defendant.

Deterrence

Individual and general prevention features as one of the main justifications for punishing these offences. In court cases, judges and magistrates repeatedly referred to deterrence as the main aim of punishment. Before passing sentence, a judge at Isleworth Crown Court asked the prosecutor which sentencing principle was to be considered in the case, to which the prosecutor replied 'deterrence'[38] (Isleworth Crown Court, hearing, Case 1). In many of the court files, the justification was that a 'deterrent sentence [is] necessary to protect the integrity of the country's border controls',[39] that the 'prevalence [of the offence] need[s] deterrent sentences',[40] and that the sentence was necessary 'to deter you and others'.[41] In another decision, the magistrates stated that 'the abuse of the travel document system damages border controls of this country. We have a duty to pass a sentence to reflect this and deter others' (Uxbridge Magistrates' Court, court file, Case 35). In a case involving a person who failed to cooperate with the re-documentation process, the magistracy convicted him to eight weeks' imprisonment and emphasized that 'no other sentence [would be possible] to protect the immigration system which you tried to undermine. *Any other sentence would send out the wrong message*' (Uxbridge Magistrates' Court, court file, Case 165, italics added).[42] Both the conviction and the tariff imposed are generally justified by a (negative) preventive purpose: to impede the commission of the same act in the future by the accused or by others. In this regard, deterrence means not only the threat of punishment, but its actual imposition.

The lower courts follow, in this regard, sentencing guidelines and case law. For instance, the leading case for the offence of possession of a false passport, *R v Kolawole*, refers to the need to pass 'deterrent sentences' in order to prevent the occurrence of this crime: 'Due to international events in recent years and the resulting increase in public concern, deterrent sentences at a higher level . . . are justified.'[43] For facilitation, the leading case is *R v Le and Stark* which prescribes a prison sentence for all but minor offences and states that this 'offence is one which generally calls for deterrent sentences'.[44] Similarly, for the offence of no document, the Court of Appeal in *R v Wang* stated:

These offences are prevalent and usually the sentence imposed should be intended to have a deterrent effect on others who may be minded to commit an offence of this kind as part of an attempt to enter the United Kingdom.[45]

While general prevention has historically featured as one of the aims of punishment and is, under current law, one of the purposes of sentencing, its deployment as a primary reason for the imposition of punishment is contested. The justification of a sentence on an individual case in terms of broader policy objectives such as the reduction of crime and the protection of the borders is not only questionable on grounds of principle, because of the violation of the principle of proportionality, autonomy and commensurate desert that may result from it (von Hirsch and Roberts 2004: 643). It is also mistaken on empirical grounds due to the lack of evidence on the impact that judicial decisions have on the levels of offending. Research done in the field of sentencing and deterrence does not provide conclusive evidence linking severity of sanctions to reduction of future offending. Because of the highly selective process of substantive criminalization and the very small percentage of offences that reach the courts, the impact that one decision can have on the achievement of broader public policy goals is – if any – minimal (von Hirsch 1976: 61, 71; Ashworth 1989: 342; Ashworth and Player 2005: 826). There is little evidence on whether these deterrent measures have been successful so far to slow down immigration flows. Because the likely candidates for criminal punishment are generally unaware of these regulations and even if they are, many are prepared to take the risks, the impact may be minimal.

Immigration imperatives

Generally, judges and magistrates argue in their decisions that immigration offences have the effect of undermining the system of immigration and border controls and the integrity of travel documents.[46] That is, punishment is not justified because the prohibited conduct is harmful *per se*, but because of its broader repercussions on the country's border controls. This is a reason for justifying criminalization rather than punishment. Even so, as a reason for criminalization it presents a number of problems.

The criminalization of harmless conducts has been justified by the symbolic power of the criminal law to prevent the repetition of an undesired behaviour. Jeremy Horder (2012: 100) argued in favour of criminalization when non-prohibition would be harmful because 'wrongful harm [will become] more common if the conduct is left free from criminal consequences'. The attraction of this argument rests on the assumed positive impact of the criminal law to prevent undesirable conducts by, among others, modifying social or cultural perceptions about these conducts (Braithwaite 2010: xvi) or shoring up society's 'collective commitments' (Horder 2012: 84). However, it has also the potential to license an excessive expansion of the criminal law (Ashworth and Zedner 2012). While criminal law has a legitimate preventive function, the decision to criminalize should not lie exclusively on its potential dissuasive effect. Instead, it should be reserved to censure serious wrongs.

Immigration criminalization rests precisely on the assumption that even though immigration infractions do not harm others, were immigration infractions not prohibited more people would resort to illegal means to enter or remain in the country, thus disrupting the whole system of immigration controls. Indeed, most of these offences are victimless because they do not aim to protect individual human beings. Another more contentious argument is that unauthorized immigration has a negative impact on the labour market, the welfare system and public services. So, for instance, in a pre-sentence report in a court file, the probation officer justified these offences in the following way: 'While there are no direct victims of the offence, illegal immigration has an impact on the whole of society and the community at large' (Isleworth Crown Court, court file, Case 24). In relation to this second line of argument, evidence about the negative impact of immigration is weak as no systematic study has been conducted in the UK about this issue.

The justification of criminalization based on the first argument – the likelihood that without it, the conduct will become common and thus disrupt the system of immigration controls – has a number of problems. First, there is the empirical question about how to establish with certainty that a particular conduct will become widespread if not criminalized. Given the lack of evidence about the deterrent effect of sentencing decisions, such an assumption can hardly be corroborated. Second, criminal law is not a legitimate means of regulation. The conducts criminalized are harmless, posing neither a risk of harm to individuals nor the general public. The criminalization of immigration breaches seems to serve merely 'bureaucratic convenience' (Horder 2012: 87). The main aim pursued is the efficient running of immigration border controls and the efficient execution of these controls by enforcement officials, a manifestation of what Eugene Kamenka and Alice Tay (1975: 138) called 'bureaucratic administrative regulation'. Even if these are legitimate goals, they should be achieved through other less intrusive and onerous means.

Moreover, these offences presume that the prohibited conduct entails a danger which is not concrete but remote, not actual but potential, and as such cannot be empirically verified. As an ultimate example of this, a sentence by a magistrate mentions that the offence of entering without a passport 'puts the safety of the State in danger' and thus is considered very serious (Uxbridge Magistrates' Court, court file, Case 130). In many other decisions, the threat to national security – i.e. terrorism – appears as recurrent justification for reprimanding these offences. Immigration crimes punish the mere disobedience to the law – a breach to an administrative rule – which is linked by the criminal law to the potential for or risk of harm, not actual harm (Ericson 2007: Chapter 5; Zedner 2009). Appeals to a remote harm license the criminalization of acts and omissions which are otherwise innocuous and harmless, and at most candidates for less intrusive measures.[47]

The seriousness of the offence

In all of the court files that I reviewed, the decision mentioned the 'seriousness' of the offence: the offence is 'so serious', the magistrates argue, that 'no other method is appropriate',[48] a 'custodial sentence is inevitable'[49] and 'no community order would be practicable'.[50] According to magistrates' and judges' arguments, this seriousness mainly lies in the 'prevalence' of these offences, their potential to undermine Britain's system of border controls, thus justifying the need for sentences that 'deter' potential offenders (that is, imprisonment). Section 152(2) of the Criminal Justice Act 2003 (CJA 2003) has limited the use of imprisonment to 'serious' offences that cannot be dealt with through a fine or a community sentence. Since the act was passed, however, the category of serious offences has been expanded by the courts in order to justify the imposition of custodial sentences (von Hirsch and Roberts 2004: 645). According to the Sentencing Guidelines Council, 'The seriousness of an individual case should be judged on its own dimensions of harm and culpability rather than as part of a collective social harm.' However – they state – in 'exceptional local circumstances', a higher sentence may be justified when 'a particular crime is prevalent in [that] area and [the judges] are satisfied that there is a compelling need to treat the offence more seriously than elsewhere' (Sentencing Guidelines Council 2004: 9). The courts interpret this to be applicable to them because Uxbridge Magistrates' Court and Isleworth Crown Court, both with jurisdiction over Heathrow airport, receive a disproportionate number of these types of cases. The prevalence, and thus the seriousness, of the offence justify a custodial sentence.[51]

The consideration of immigration crimes – particularly the arrival into the country without a passport – as 'serious' and grave offences by the judiciary, however, sharply contrasts with the assessment by enforcement and prosecution authorities. As I showed in Chapter 4, these offences are largely deemed to be minor offences and therefore the bulk of them are dealt with through executive removal.

Immigration status

The choice of sanction is also determined by the immigration status of the convicted defendant as those without 'community ties' are not candidates for non-custodial sentences. A pre-sentence report is ordered only for those defendants with residence and legal immigration status in the UK. In this report, alternatives to imprisonment are considered, and, based on it, the court should decide the most appropriate sanction. Because rehabilitation does not come into play in relation to people who are due to be deported,[52] non-custodial penalties are not contemplated for them. Pre-sentence reports were not ordered by the court for the defendants in my sample who appeared and were convicted by the magistrates' courts and imprisonment was imposed on all of them.

The judges at the crown court ordered such a report more frequently – for 27 defendants. Most of them (23 defendants) were charged with the offence of assisting unlawful immigration. Of the 106 defendants charged with immigration offences before the crown court, though, only 10 were given a suspended sentence with other conditions (such as performing unpaid work or being subject to electronic monitoring). In one other case, the defendant was discharged. In all of these cases, the defendant had legal status in the UK – three of them were naturalized British citizens and another had indefinite leave to remain. In one of these cases, a Somali woman was accused of assisting the unlawful entry to the country of her mother, who applied for asylum and was given indefinite leave. The defendant pleaded guilty and her sentence was suspended for 12 months as recommended by the pre-sentence report. When passing sentence, the judge made it clear that the offence was serious: 'Usually this is an immediate custodial sentence'. Subsequently he referred to

> [the] exceptional circumstances in this case . . . There was no commercial gain. [You experienced] pressure from your mother and your family. Second, you have made a credible effort to work hard here in the UK. The Court is not going soft, but there are here unusual circumstances in this case.
>
> (Isleworth Crown Court, court file, Case 15)

Similarly, in a hearing against a Romanian man who in 2006 entered the country by deception – he claimed asylum under a false identity – the judge at the crown court considered in his decision the date of the offence, the fact that he is an EU national entitled to live in Britain and his ties to the country (he has a family and a work permit). He suspended the prison sentence and imposed a number of hours of unpaid work on Mr Dobrin after clearly stating: 'Immigration laws are strict and anyone who breaks them faces [a] custodial sentence' (Isleworth Crown Court, hearing, Case 11).

Presumably the ineligibility of convicted immigration defendants, who are undocumented or have weak ties to the country, to non-custodial sentences is largely related to their prospective deportation from the country. The courts reason that because they are due to be removed, they will be unable to comply with the terms of probation, nor should their sanctions contemplate any rehabilitative aim.[53] Even though there is no statutory norm mandating custodial sentences for these defendants,[54] courts systematically rule out non-custodial sanctions for them. This is another aspect in which the immigration status of the defendant plays to his or her disadvantage.

The judicial decisions reviewed above are difficult to defend from a normative perspective. In the first place, deterrence alone is a weak justification for punishment, particularly in the absence of empirical evidence which can prove the effectiveness of sentencing in reducing the incidence of immigration crimes (Ashworth 2007: 998). Second, the principles of harm and proportionality are compromised by the penalization of conducts that have no direct victims and can be dealt with through less intrusive and burdensome interventions. Finally, the deprivation of liberty that results almost automatically from convictions for these offences is not substantiated by the protection of rights with equal rank.

These offences allegedly protect a risk of undermining immigration controls. While in the public interest, the maintenance of immigration controls – and even more a remote harm to them – is an insufficient justification for criminal punishment, especially if the sanction imposed is imprisonment (Ferrajoli 1989: 477). As a result, the sanctions are disproportionate because they bear no relationship to the blameworthiness of these offences (Husak 2005). The disproportionate nature of the sanction imposed is even more acute when it is coupled with a deportation order.[55]

The resort to general and individual prevention as justification to penalize cases involving immigration offenders – both foreigners and citizens – should be considered against a background of increased social hostility towards illegal immigration and, in particular, 'criminal aliens'. 'Immigration crimes' bring together two of the most politicized topics in recent public discourse and policy-making: illegal immigration and crime (Tonry 1997: 2). In the context of high unemployment, depreciation of wages and budget cuts, an 'exemplary' punishment for those who appeal to deception and fraud to secure entry to the country and employment for themselves and for others is considered as appropriate and deserved.

Conclusion

Formally, immigration crimes are treated in the same way as any other case reaching the criminal justice system. This formal equality may be in itself a cause for concern. Bottoms and McClean (1976: 226) describe the usual business of a magistrates' court as dealing with 'unexciting offences handled in the ordinary routine way by court personnel who had seen it all before many, many times'. Likewise, the practices of punishment in immigration-related cases are made of routines, rituals, repetitions and almost mechanical imposition of custodial sentences. In this regard, the way that immigration-offence cases are dealt with by the criminal justice system looks like a bureaucratic, administrative-like exercise which contributes to standardizing them, erasing the differences between them and the suffering of those accused. Defences based on the immigration status of the accused are seldom raised. Lawyers advise their clients to plead guilty because of ignorance or negligence or for strategic reasons, without considering the broader impact of a criminal conviction on their clients' ability to win their immigration cases. Magistrates and judges clearly differentiate the immigration from the criminal case and expeditiously 'administer' punishment by repeating similar formulas over and over, and calibrating the length of the sentence according to the particularities of the case.

Separating the criminal case from the immigration case makes decision-making less complex and easier as criminal justice actors need only to discuss whether or not a particular statute has been infringed. Likewise, putting aside or obscuring this broader context hinders the possibilities for 'mercy'. Prosecutors and judges make decisions in a social and political climate which favours harsher punishment. Thus, judicial inertia and an uncritical application of criminal powers result in the imposition of tough and exemplary sanctions. At the same time, the mechanical application of the law forecloses the possibilities of resisting this 'punitive systemic tendency' in the form of moderating or even forgoing sanctions (Steiker 2010: 41; see also Lacey 2008; Bosworth and Guild 2008: 709).

In the same vein, no one questions the legality of immigration offences. Decision makers explicitly endorse immigration policy goals and the use of criminal law to attain them. Individual wrongdoing is then considered in the light of the negative repercussions the aggregate of similar conducts might have on government policies to reduce illegal immigration. In practice, the embracing of these policies by judges and magistrates has the effect of extending the exercise of immigration controls onto them. In relation to asylum adjudication by administrative courts, Robert Thomas (2011: 16) observed: 'The decision-making context is ... informed by a strongly authority based relationship between government and foreign nationals.' This feature very much resonates with judicial decisions in immigration-crime cases. Some of the judgments quoted above emphasized the duty of the judiciary to censure harshly any attempt to undermine the state's powers to police its territory. For instance, in the case of Mr Hussain, the judge made it clear that 'High courts consider these offences very seriously. To protect the borders is important in this country' (Isleworth Crown Court, hearing, Case 1). As Eagly (2010: 1351) explained, the criminal process operates in this context as a 'border screening device': 'Not only does [the] criminal process function as a substitute for traditional immigration removal processing, but also its structural design resembles immigration court in many respects.' Criminal courts enforce immigration norms and, to some extent, judge who should be let in and who should not. The mere fact of bringing unauthorized foreigners before a criminal court re-enacts and upholds the state's powers to grant or deny entry.

Bringing immigration issues to the criminal justice venue carries other difficulties. Contrary to the assumption that the criminalization of immigration breaches results in more safeguards for immigrants who otherwise would be subject to less protective administrative proceedings, the practice shows that immigration defendants are not offered the full-fledged criminal procedure, but a simplified version of it. Further, although the courts make it clear that the criminal process is functionally different from the immigration case, in practice, the defendant's immigration status is critical for criminal justice decisions, as foreigners without legal status are rarely granted bail and are likely to be punished with custodial sentences. Non-citizens are hence offered a second-class criminal justice process. In this sense, the observations by Steven Legomsky (2007) about the United States are valid for Britain as well. He pointed to the asymmetric nature of the convergence of immigration and criminal law, in which only some aspects of the latter are imported (those related to criminal enforcement), but not others (procedural rights). Most importantly, criminal punishment does not serve as a substitute for expulsion (Stumpf 2009: 1691). In many of these cases, after serving their sentence, people convicted for immigration offences may be detained under immigration powers, waiting for their deportation.

6 Explaining the role of criminal law in the control of immigration

Soon after starting this project two central aspects became apparent. First, immigration-related offences – such as illegal entry, overstaying, deception, etc. – are barely considered in parliamentary debates and scholarly discussions about the criminalization of immigration. Second, despite their expansion in recent years, these offences are seldom used by authorities. Immigration crimes are considered as necessary corollaries of the immigration control system. Criminal sanctions for immigration breaches have historically been deemed an enforcement mechanism which may be triggered when other sanctions are not effective, and a deterrent. This may explain why there have not been any attempts to justify the enactment of immigration-related offences. The reasons for criminalizing certain conducts, the terms in which offences are drafted, the consequences of making these conducts subject to criminal punishment, and possible alternatives are rarely examined in parliamentary debates. While policy papers have discussed the strategic use of criminal law powers against immigration offenders following the introduction of the 'harm matrix', such accounts have been chiefly motivated by cost and efficiency considerations. So a critical scrutiny of the role of criminal law in immigration enforcement is still needed.

Likewise, in academic circles, the category of 'immigration crimes' is seldom considered. While the criminalization of immigration has attracted a significant degree of scholarly attention (Calavita 2003; Melossi 2003; Wacquant 2006; Bosworth and Guild 2008; De Giorgi 2010; Cecchi 2011), the rise of immigration offences at the core of immigration laws has inspired much less reflection, particularly in Britain.[1] Criminal law literature has not considered immigration law as a branch in which 'over-criminalization' takes place, despite the recent concern of criminal law scholars with this phenomenon.

In this chapter, I will use the recent scholarship on (over-)criminalization (Lacey 2004, 2008, 2009; Ashworth 2008; Ashworth and Zedner 2008; Husak 2008; Duff 2010a) to account for the increased reliance on the criminal law to enforce immigration statutes. I begin by explaining the historical roots of a legal system like the British one that has relied on criminal law for regulatory purposes. I then go on to look at the main factors that have reinforced the criminalization trend in the immigration field. Many countries have started to introduce so-called 'immigration offences' into their legislation. Further, the criminalization of certain immigration violations has been mandated by international and regional bodies – such as the United Nations (UN) and the European Union (EU). These global trends have reinforced the criminalization trend at home – and foreclosed the search for alternative options – in the context of increasing pressures on the Labour administration to bring down the number of immigrants coming to the country and, particularly, to prevent economic migrants from abusing the asylum system.

I argue that it is also important to look at the dynamics of immigration enforcement and the processing of immigration-related cases by the criminal justice system. From this perspective, the criminalization of migration appears to be a mundane, bureaucratic and repetitive exercise of criminal law powers geared by convenience and efficiency in delivering outcomes, rather than aiming to reflect a punitive rationale to censure wrongdoing. Criminal law is one of various enforcement tools to achieve the effective regulation of border and inland controls. Finally, I reflect on the role of criminal law and punishment against immigration wrongdoers. Because the goal is to eject them from the country once they have served their sentence, criminal sanctions against immigrants are emptied of any normative function and are unjustified.

Criminalization the British way

As this book has demonstrated, the inclusion of criminal offences in immigration statutes is not a new phenomenon. Legislation regulating the entry and residence of foreigners in eighteenth-century Britain contained many criminal law provisions. Similarly, criminal offences can be found in contemporary non-criminal legislation, such as competition, corporate, health and safety, and consumer laws. In fact, the trend to criminalize an ever expanding range of conducts is neither new nor confined to immigration legislation. Particularly in countries like Britain and the United States, criminal law has historically served functions seemingly extraneous to its core task of censuring wrongdoing (Lacey 2004; Husak 2008). More recently, the use of criminal law to ensure compliance with societal goals and roles has been identified by some authors as a main factor behind the expansion of criminal law and the redefinition of its boundaries (Ashworth 2000; McSherry *et al.* 2009; Duff *et al.* 2010).

In this regard, Markus Dubber's book *The Police Power* (2005) traces the origins of the power of the state to punish in contemporary societies – particularly the United States. Dubber identifies a particular form of state power which derived from that exercised by a householder over the members of a household in feudal societies. Unlike the political or legal power which is premised on the idea of heteronomy and equality of rights among the members of a political community, police power bestowed wide prerogatives upon the head of the household over its members, who were inferior by definition. Because this authority was directed to maximize the welfare of the household, it was not constrained by principles of justice. The goal of protecting the household against internal and external threats justified almost any means, including the use of force against rebellious members. Following the consolidation of monarchical regimes in Europe, the King exercised the police power. Considered 'the father of his people', the King wielded wide disciplinary powers over the macro-household, the kingdom, in order to maximize its welfare and wellbeing.

Dubber argues that this unconstrained, patriarchal, disciplinary power did not disappear, but rather was entrenched in pre-modern criminal law statutes, particularly in so-called 'police' or 'welfare' offences. These offences were considered necessary for the due regulation and domestic order of the kingdom (see also Foucault 1991; Farmer 1996). The quintessential examples of these were the vagrancy laws which appeared in the criminal laws of many countries in Europe – including Britain (see also Baratta 2002; Melossi 2002). They sanctioned a large range of vaguely defined conducts and minor breaches to the public 'peace' such as begging and vagrancy. Because the aim was to benefit the macro-household, the scope of the police power was infinite: anything and anyone could be policed. Coercion in this context was important to impose obedience, which was in turn vital to ensure the smooth operation of the household (Dubber 2005: 73). According to Dubber:

> [Police or welfare offences] have the same object: threats. They are measured by the same standard: efficiency. They take the same form: regulation. And they protect the same cluster of interests: public welfare (or 'social betterment') and social order, and the authority of the state to maintain them.
>
> (Dubber 2005: 151; see also Dubber 2010a: 208)

Following Dubber's description, it can be argued that immigration law is *par excellence* a site of police power which remains relatively untouched by legal and constitutional constraints. As Simon (1998: 585) claimed, the imprisonment of refugees and 'criminal aliens' under immigration provisions reflects the vestige of a monarchical, unlimited power over non-citizens (see also Schuck 1984). Similarly, some immigration offences – particularly those penalizing non-compliance – share certain characteristics of the police or welfare offences, as spelled out by Dubber: their main object is to deter people from breaching immigration rules in order to ensure the smooth and effective operation of the immigration control system.

Dubber identified 'a residual, slippery, elusive, oppressively amorphous power [of the state] to manage people and things in order to maximise the welfare of a community' (Loader and Zedner 2007: 143). Such power is manifested in the wide and unconstrained scope to criminalize conducts for regulatory purposes which puts criminal law 'on the muddy border between political/legal and police power' (Lacey 2008: 99). When comparing different criminal justice systems, Nicola Lacey (2008: 101) maintained that in countries such as Britain and the United States, where this unrestrained, disciplinary power has been absorbed by or become undifferentiated from the legal power, criminalization drives are less restricted than in continental Europe, where this differentiation is clearer (see also

Hildebrandt 2009).[2] Moreover, Anglo-American legal systems contain few constitutional constraints on the state's criminalization powers (Lacey 2009: 940; see also Whitman 2003). Unlike continental civil law countries which deploy criminal law only to reprimand the most serious wrongs, Anglo-Saxon common law countries, she argued, commonly resort to the criminal law to regulate social life. Under such conditions, criminal law easily becomes a means to implement particular policies. In other words, non-moral, regulatory objectives are imprinted into criminal law, thus blurring the line dividing civil and criminal law (Lacey 2004; see also Steiker 1997; Klein 1999; Sarat *et al.* 2011). Lacey (2012: 31) also argued that, due to the exponential rise of substantive criminal law since the nineteenth century, it has become increasingly difficult to rationalize the scope and function of the criminal law – as opposed to other forms of regulation.

The existence of so-called 'regulatory' or 'welfare offences' (Ramsay 2006) in British legislation is one of the expressions of the wide, regulatory scope of the criminal law (Dubber 2010a: 200; 2011: 22). Many of these offences were introduced in legislation passed during the nineteenth century when, arguably, without the threat of criminal sanctions, it would not have been possible to enforce regulation (Leigh 1982: 12; Farmer 1996). In the context of industrialization and faced with the need to regulate a new set of economic activities – and their repercussions on society – legislation was enacted imposing public duties which were backed up by formal, criminal sanctions to ensure compliance. As Leigh (1982) explained, regulatory offences were not regarded as 'real' criminal offences and the courts considered them as 'less than crimes', regulatory offences or 'quasi-criminal' offences. The main purpose of these offences was to minimize danger to others by dissuading people and businesses from engaging in lawful activities in an unlawful way.

Peter Ramsay (2006) explained that 'regulatory criminal law' – formed of statutory offences which often do not have a fault element and are aimed at distributing the burden of harm or risk of harm – was more common and widespread in the nineteenth and early twentieth centuries than offences based on the subjectivist doctrine – or the paradigm of agency. According to the latter, criminal censure should follow a wrongful action committed with knowledge and intention. In contrast, '[p]unishment for the regulatory public welfare offences is not a question of desert . . . but of deterring specific injuries to conditions which ensure the single civilization promoted by social citizenship' (Ramsay 2006: 50). The different forms of criminal liability (fault or subjective liability; and strict or objective liability) delineated by Ramsay are connected to and define the function of criminal punishment, either as retribution or as deterrent. In justifying these differences, Ramsay explained that the post-war years witnessed an 'ideological balance' between two competing paradigms – the paradigm of agency and the paradigm of welfare. The first asserts the formal equality of all citizens by treating them as responsible subjects; while the second upholds the value of welfare protection and risk avoidance by imposing a positive, social duty on the citizens to refrain from causing harm or creating a risk of harm in their everyday conduct.

Over-criminalization revamped and the politics of immigration

Since the mid-1990s there has been a resurgence in reliance on the criminal law as the government has sought to fix any social problem with 'reactive, populist criminal legislation' (Lacey 2004: 163; see also Duff 2010a). This expansion of the 'frontiers of criminalization' has been linked by criminal law scholars to the use of criminal law for symbolic and instrumental purposes. In particular, Ely Aharonson and Peter Ramsay (2010: 182) argued that the dominance of neoliberalism in social and economic policies has fostered the 'role of criminalization as a mechanism of social ordering'. On similar lines, others have explained that governments, facing criticisms about the limits of state action in relation to certain social and economic issues, use criminal legislation to fix them, or at least to be seen as fixing them (Garland 1996, 2001; Pratt 2006; Simon 2007; Loader 2009). As Jonathan Simon (2007: 14) put it, 'it is crime through which other problems are recognized, defined, and acted upon'. This is so in areas that have become politicized in recent years, such as crime and immigration policies, particularly in Britain (Zedner 1995: 521; Tonry 2004a). As such, these two policy fields have become rich soil, in which 'populist punitiveness' or 'penal populism' has flourished (Tonry 2004b: 138; see also Bottoms 1995: 39; Roberts *et al.* 2003).

Criminal law scholars have branded this phenomenon as 'over-criminalization'[3] (Husak 2008) and 'over-punishment' (Stuntz 2001, 2011; Steiker 2010). In this vein, Antony Duff (2010a) defined over-criminalization as the criminalization of conducts that should not concern the criminal law. He pointed to two trends in this regard: first, the addition of offences in non-criminal legislation – particularly, the criminalization of non-compliance – and, second, the creation of a range of 'ancillary' offences. As such, 'over-criminalization' refers not only to a quantitative phenomenon, but also to the extension of criminal law to realms traditionally regulated by non-criminal legislation or not regulated at all.

In the UK, the 'legal tradition' of overusing or misusing the criminal law to regulate social life in recent years prompted Andrew Ashworth (2000) to qualify English criminal law as a 'lost cause'. Between 1997 and 2006, the New Labour government created more than 3,000 criminal offences. Put another way, during nine years in office, Labour created twice as many offences as its Tory predecessor created in 18 years. Moreover, this has been an upward trend: while in 1998, 160 new offences were created, the number rose to 346 in 2000 and 527 in 2005 (Morris 2006; Pantazis 2008). Most of these offences have been created to ensure compliance with public duties and to support the work of agencies in charge of enforcing such duties (Sparks and Spencer 2002: Chapter 1). There is evidence, however, that many of the offences created by the Labour government are rarely, if ever, used. A recent consultation paper by the Law Commission (2010: 7)[4] found that most 'regulatory' offences – including 'illegal use of migrant workers' – are seldom used. Only 10 per cent of those before magistrates' courts are charged with regulatory offences, while the numbers are much smaller in crown courts, where only 1.5–2 per cent of defendants are charged with these crimes.[5] Such under-enforcement, or 'passive overcriminalization' (Stuntz 1996: 35), means that an increasing number of people subject to these provisions are under 'illusory or empty threats of criminal prosecution' (Law Commission 2010: 8). In fact, it may imply that the creation of new offences conveys little more than a symbolic message that the government is taking care of a particular problem.

The recent increase in criminal offences in immigration legislation is a clear example of regulation through punishment – or the threat of it. While there has been a longstanding practice of criminalizing immigration breaches in British legislation, since the mid-1990s there has been a noticeable change in the intensity of this criminalization. Parliament passed a piece of immigration and asylum legislation, on average, every two years. In total, six acts were passed which created 84 immigration offences. The preceding Conservative administrations introduced five immigration and asylum bills which created only five offences.[6] The period between 1997 and 2009 witnessed the fastest and largest expansion of the catalogue of immigration crimes since 1905, as illustrated by Figure 6.1.

This expansion should be explained not only as part of the general growth of substantive criminal law, but also as related to factors closely linked to immigration politics, law and enforcement practices. In this vein, an academic involved in immigration policy making during this period explained:

> The imperatives to have immigration under control were so strong . . . that even had the criminal justice system been reformed to be decriminalized, I'm not sure if [it] necessarily would have affected IND . . . The politics of immigration control is somewhat separate from the politics elsewhere. But clearly in immigration by creating new criminal offences, they won't go

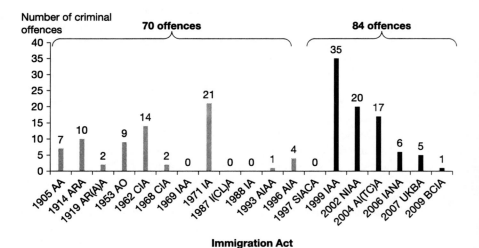

Figure 6.1 Criminal offences introduced in immigration acts

against the flow of what the rest of the government were doing. They were creating criminal offences everywhere.

(Respondent 16, 1/07/2010)

Faced with pressure from the public, the media and the opposition to bring immigration under control (Welch and Schuster 2005a: 408), the government introduced more legislation. As a retired Labour MP interviewed for this research mentioned, legislative hyperactivity has been a trend across government: 'I think it's a tendency in government, if there is a problem think about legislation . . . to look for a legislative answer to what is not essentially a legislative problem . . .' (Respondent 12, 28/05/2010). A number of MPs[7] attacked the government for adding more legislation to an increasingly crowded and complex field, instead of solving administrative problems at the heart of the system's backlog. These critiques were largely ignored as administrative solutions were more difficult and expensive to implement, and they were less glamorous in the eyes of the electorate.

In this context, the government's appeal to criminal sanctions to enforce immigration rules had a 'presentational aspect': to be seen as doing something about immigration law breaking. The Legal Officer at the Immigration Law Practitioners' Association (ILPA) explained that:

[There was] a belief [in the government] that criminalizing in certain areas, introducing offences and greater powers was going to make it more effective in terms of tackling abuse. I think there is also a degree . . . of thinking that . . . it is not just about tackling abuse, it is even more important to be seen to be tackling abuse. So creating immigration offences appeals to a certain body either of the political establishment or the electorate in that it looks at you as getting tougher and the rhetoric around this period has increasingly been about toughness.

(Respondent 17, 29/04/2010)

In immigration – as in other fields – one of the ways to look tough is to create new offences. David Garland (1996: 459; 2001: 131) described this reaction as 'acting out' – a form of denial or evasion by the state which, conscious about the impossibility of or difficulties in solving a particular problem, such as reducing crime, adopts more criminal legislation. Similarly, Ian Loader (2009, 2010a, 2010b) described what he called 'contemporary forms of penal excess' and stated that responses to crime and insecurity in the United States and Europe are characterized by a seemingly insatiable appetite for 'a semblance of security' (Loader 2009: 245–246). In response to people's demand for order, governments in the Western world assume 'a punitive, hyperactive and consumer-appeasing political posture which typically glosses over the complexities of lay sensibilities towards crime in favour of simplistic, risk-averse and electorally satisfying readings of "public opinion"' (Loader 2009: 250). In doing so, instead of seeking to temper those demands, Loader posited that these governments 're-enact' excess.

The British government's response needs to be read in a context of increasing social anxieties about the steady dismantling of the welfare state, the erosion of social security protections and the restructuring of the labour market. The working class was particularly affected by these changes. First, since the late 1970s, the diminishing bargaining power of trade unions undermined their capacity to protect workers. Second, many low-skilled jobs either disappeared as they started to be done by machines or were 'shipped abroad', or were considerably downgraded by the depreciation of wages – in part as a consequence of the influx of economic migrants, particularly from Eastern Europe in the mid-1990s (Ruggiero 1997: 233; Garland 2001: 82; Reiner 2007: 151; De Giorgi 2011).[8] Faced with structural limitations to implementing inclusionary social policies, the Blair administration sought to appease an important fraction of its electorate by promising a halt on immigration and by resorting to draconian measures to tackle the 'unauthorized mobility of this ever more globalized proletariat' (De Giorgi 2010: 151).

Successive governments had set out a trend of using criminal powers to deal with immigration, making it electorally risky for the Labour administration to move in a different direction. As the Legal Officer at ILPA observed: 'What happened is that by starting on that road . . . the government has opened itself up to be . . . pushed further and further in that direction, and in a sense it can't really stop because that looks weak' (Respondent 17, 29/04/2010). The legal tradition of relying on the criminal law to enforce immigration legislation – mainly established in the Immigration Act (IA) 1971, but inherited from much older legislation – shaped later reforms and made it harder for politicians to justify any attempt to change the system in place by, for instance, decriminalizing some offences (Spencer 2011: 165). Such a proposal was perceived as deadly for any government. This was even more so for the Labour administration, expected to be 'soft' on immigration. Even though the Labour government did not decriminalize immigration-related offences, in later policy papers it announced a *de facto* decriminalization of minor immigration offences (Home Office 2007b, 2010d). The statement in a policy document that 'low level' offences will not be criminally pursued is less controversial than passing a law which 'downgrades' certain breaches as administrative rather than criminal (Spencer 2011: 165).

This criminalization drive is also apparent in other countries which have introduced similar offences in their legislation. The fact that this trend has barely been questioned, and in some instances has been instructed by regional and international bodies, has reinforced the criminalization option in Britain and precluded alternative courses. Particularly in Europe, the criminalization of many immigration infractions has been either directly mandated by EU norms or supported by EU institutions.

Globalizing the criminalization of immigration breaches?

The 'crimmigration' trend (Stumpf 2007) is not unique to Britain. Other countries with similar legal traditions have introduced immigration offences into their legislation. In the United States, immigration offences preceded deportation.

Criminal sanctions, including incarceration, fines and hard labour, were the first mechanisms to enforce immigration laws in the late nineteenth century (Stumpf 2009: 1711). From then on, the US Congress has incorporated many immigration offences into federal laws. Since 1929, unlawful entry is a misdemeanour and unlawful re-entry is a felony.[9] Re-entering the United States after being removed, deported or denied admission without authorization by the government is an offence[10] as is failure to depart from the country when this has been ordered[11] (Medina 2011: 95). Illegal employment and sham marriage were made criminal offences in 1986 and 1990, respectively (Medina 1997). Other offences related to immigration status were created in 1996 (such as driving above the speed limit to avoid an immigration checkpoint[12] and failing to cooperate in one's removal).[13] Assisting unlawful immigration and different document fraud offences also formed part of this catalogue (Legomsky 2007: 477; Medina 2011: 100). Recently, some states, such as Arizona, have enacted immigration offences. In June 2012, the Supreme Court struck down these sections of the Arizona law because it considered the creation of immigration offences through state laws as an obstacle for the federal regulatory system. The court clearly stated that, under the Supremacy Clause, the US Congress has exclusive power on immigration and naturalization matters which precludes states from regulating conducts in this field.[14]

Immigration crimes in the United States were barely enforced until the mid-1980s when prosecutions started to go up. Between 1994 and 2000, there was a 34 per cent increase in prosecutions for these offences; and in 2000, they represented 14.5 per cent of all the criminal cases commenced in that year (Demleitner and Sands 2002: 247). This rise is most noticeable in the cases of unlawful employment and document fraud against asylum seekers. Nowadays immigration offences represent half of the federal criminal workload, constituting the largest category of federal criminal prosecutions (Eagly 2010: 1282; Sklansky 2012: 158).

Likewise, Canada and Australia have incorporated a number of immigration offences into their legislation. Besides the criminalization of smuggling and trafficking (Grewcock 2009; Weber and Grewcock 2012), Australia punishes hiring illegal workers with imprisonment and fines. It also criminalizes the harbouring of illegal entrants, the use of false documents and visas, and sham marriage.[15] Other countries in the Asia-Pacific region have followed suit, creating a number of criminal offences to deal with growing migration flows within the region. Nowadays human smuggling, trafficking in human beings and aiding immigration breaches are crimes as are unauthorized arrival and overstaying (Schloenhardt 2008; Sim 2008). Canadian legislation contains a number of criminal offences, including offences related to document fraud, a general clause which punishes contraventions to any provision of the Immigration and Refugee Protection Act 2001, employing an illegal worker and escaping or attempting to escape from immigration detention.[16]

Even though countries with different legal traditions have not yet witnessed a great extension in the criminalization of immigration laws, there is a certain 'legal convergence'[17] in this field, particularly in continental Europe (Lahav 1998;

Albrecht 2000; van Kalmthout *et al.* 2007; D'Appollonia and Reich 2008), a development which has been explained as 'part of the spreading of Anglo-American (legal) culture' (Nelken 2010: 30). Irregular border crossing or irregular stay is a crime in 17 EU Member states – in 14 of them it is punished with imprisonment or/and a fine (FRA Europa 2011: 42). In Germany, irregular entry and residence is an offence under criminal law, albeit seldom used, with imprisonment of up to one year or a fine (Broeders 2010). The German penal code also criminalizes smuggling. Since 2005, Greek legislation imposes criminal sanctions on irregular entry and exit with up to three months' imprisonment and fines.[18] This offence is, however, not generally prosecuted unless the accused is a trafficker or uses false documents (Amnesty International 2010: 18). In 2008, Italy passed legislation criminalizing illegal entry and aiding such entry. Illegal entry is punished with a fine of up to €10,000.[19] Italian law punishes with imprisonment of up to three years those who 'let out an accommodation to a foreign citizen illegally residing in the Italian territory'[20] (Merlino 2009). Foreigners caught illegally in the country contrary to a removal order by the police are liable to imprisonment of up to five years.[21] Being illegally in the country is also an aggravating circumstance for those convicted of an ordinary crime.[22] In France, both illegal entry and residence are criminal offences, as is assisting an unlawful immigrant (Council of Europe 2010: 16). Illegal residence is also a crime in Finland and Cyprus. In the Netherlands, failure to comply with an order to leave the country after being declared 'undesirable' is a crime.[23] This is punished by a prison sentence of up to six months or a fine. A number of European countries, such as Germany, France and the Netherlands have introduced criminal sanctions for illegal employment (Martin and Miller 2000; Junkert and Kreienbrink 2008). Spain, on the other hand, has maintained a system of administrative sanctions for immigration violations and only imposes criminal sanctions in cases of human trafficking and facilitation (Monclús Maso 2009).[24]

While recent examples in some European countries – such as the abolition of the death penalty and the embracing of human rights – point to a moderation in penal policy and a 'resistance to punitiveness' (Snacken 2010), the expansion of offences penalizing immigration wrongdoing reveals a trend in the opposite direction (Lacey 2008: 144). The criminalization of immigration infractions in many European countries is the outcome of domestic dynamics as well as regional and global developments. As unwanted flows of migrants have been portrayed as security, social and economic challenges for rich, Western countries, the artillery to 'pre-empt' movements from poorer regions of the globe and fortify Europe's borders has been expanded (Bigo 2005; Weber 2007; Aas 2011a). Criminal punishment and ejection are the most stringent manifestations of state coercion in liberal democracies (Garland 1996; Bosworth 2008). It is not surprising, then, that in an era of 'social panics' about immigration (De Giorgi 2010: 154), the governments of these countries appeal to criminal law to deter potential migrants and punish those who risk their luck (Melossi 2003). By criminalizing illegal status, nation states send a powerful symbolic message to both would-be immigrants and citizens that they are increasing their grip on immigration flows.

This criminalization trend is also largely influenced by external actors (Green and Grewcock 2002: 95). International organizations, such as the UN, have endorsed and even prescribed the use of criminal sanctions against people smuggling 'when committed intentionally and in order to obtain, directly or indirectly, a financial or other material benefit'[25] and against trafficking in human beings.[26] In Europe, this trend is connected to the process of European integration and the consequent 'Europeanization' of immigration regulation. In fact, the EU has been pushing for penal sanctions in many policy areas (Guild 2003; Guild and Minderhoud 2006; Guild and Geyer 2008). Early on in 1985, the Schengen Convention prescribed the introduction of 'penalties' against unauthorized crossing of external frontiers of the Schengen zone, carriers who transport undocumented migrants and 'any person who, for financial gain, assists or tries to assist an alien to enter or reside within the territory of one of the contracting parties'.[27] According to the 'Carrier Liability Directive' of 2001 which supplements such provisions, penalties should be 'dissuasive, effective and proportionate'.[28]

However, it was not until the 2000s that the EU explicitly mandated criminal sanctions to deal with immigration breaches. This was first stated in 2002 in the 'Directive on Unauthorised Entry, Transit and Residence' which prescribed that Member states should adopt appropriate sanctions against those who facilitate unauthorized entry, transit and residence of 'aliens'. Its associated Framework Decision further established that these sanctions should be 'punishable by effective, proportionate and dissuasive criminal penalties'.[29] Later on in 2009, the 'Directive on Illegal Employment' established that, along with imposing financial penalties, Member states shall ensure that 'knowingly' hiring an illegal worker is a criminal offence when other aggravating features are present.[30]

The European Convention on Action against Trafficking in Human Beings prescribed criminal sanctions for a number of conducts concerning trafficking,[31] as did the Framework Decision 2002/629/JHA.[32] The criminalization of trafficking, though, is distinct in some respects from other immigration offences. First, unlike offences such as illegal entry or passport fraud which are victimless, trafficking offences entail the infliction of harm on individual human beings. The offence aims to protect individuals rather than a collective or abstract entity, like the 'immigration system' or the 'security of the state'. As such, the use of coercion, abduction, fraud, deception or abuse against someone for the purpose of exploitation are constitutive elements of the offence as defined by European Convention and the 'UN Protocol against Trafficking'[33] (Hoyle *et al.* 2011: 316). Second, the use of criminal law in trafficking cases is directed at punishing serious moral wrongs (particularly, egregious forms of exploitation and abuse). In contrast, most immigration offences aid immigration enforcement when other sanctions are insufficient to achieve particular policy or regulatory goals. Trafficking is exempt from some of the principled critiques on immigration-related offences put forward in this book. In fact, the label of trafficking as an immigration offence remains contested (Moss 2011). In this regard, the distinctive features of trafficking offences show the difficulties in grouping together different 'immigration crimes' and analysing them as a homogeneous category.

A number of human rights international organizations have criticized this criminalization trend. The UN Working Group on Arbitrary Detention has stated that 'the criminalization of irregular migration exceeds the legitimate interests of States in protecting its territories and regulating irregular migration flows' (Human Rights Council 2010: paragraph 58). Likewise, the High Commissioner for Human Rights raised objections against the criminalization of immigration violations (OHCHR 2009: 31). The former Council of Europe Commissioner for Human Rights, Thomas Hammarberg, launched a report in which he questioned the compatibility of the use of criminal law to manage immigration with human rights norms (Council of Europe 2010: 38) and insisted that 'immigration offences should remain *administrative* in nature' (Hammarberg 2008, italics in original). Elsewhere, international human rights bodies have scrutinized domestic norms criminalizing immigration status. In a judgment, the Inter-American Court of Human Rights stated that a provision in Panamanian legislation which punished the breach of a deportation order with two-year imprisonment was illegitimate and disproportionate, and hence the sanction imposed on the applicant violated his right to liberty.[34]

In the European regional system, the European Court of Justice (ECJ) examined a preliminary question raised by an Italian court about the compatibility with EU law of the criminal offence of being in the country contrary to a removal order by the police, punished with a term in prison. Mr El Dridi was sentenced to one year of imprisonment for this offence. The ECJ found that sanction to be incompatible with EU law, particularly the 'Removal Directive',[35] because it was disproportionate and violated the gradation of measures established in the directive in the case of non-compliance.[36] While the court did not preclude the use of criminal law powers to enforce removal and the criminalization of immigration breaches more generally, it stated that criminal sanctions should be used as a last resort and only after other less restrictive measures proved ineffective.[37] In turn, the European Court of Human Rights (ECHR) has not yet examined the compatibility of criminal law sanctions to control immigration with human rights norms. The closest it came to considering this matter was in a case brought before the court against Greece. In this case, the applicant, a Turkish asylum seeker, claimed that he was prosecuted for entering Greece illegally and using false documents. This person was ultimately acquitted for these offences. Therefore, the court decided not to examine this aspect of the case.[38]

In a context where the use of the criminal law has been expanded or globalized, scrutiny over the 'frontiers of criminalization' of immigration seems vital. Unfortunately, the impact of human rights norms in state practices in this field – as in others – has been limited (Dauvergne 2008; Husak 2008; Bosworth 2011c).[39] Even if human rights legislation has narrowed sovereign powers towards citizens, very few of these rules can be imposed on states' prerogatives over non-citizens.[40] In particular, the scope for human rights assessment of a state's prerogatives to extend the domain of criminal law against non-nationals for violating their immigration status has been limited. According to the European Court, this is part of the 'undeniable sovereign right to control aliens' entry into and residence in their territory'.[41] The court has insistently established that states cannot label a particular act or omission as civil or administrative, rather than penal, in order to evade the procedural protections of the criminal law.[42] Further, in an *obiter dictum*, the court favoured the creation of criminal offences in the context of anti-terrorism as an alternative to the indefinite detention of terrorist suspects.[43] However, it has said nothing about the scope of a state's powers to turn certain wrongs into criminal offences. As such, this power remains weakly constrained and poorly regulated, at least in Europe.

The other side of criminalization: the banality of everyday criminal law practices

The extent of the global trend towards the criminalization of immigration status and the symbolic appeal to criminal law in the fight against illegal immigration in domestic politics reveal a highly politicized, emotionally charged exclusionary discourse. In this context, the criminalization of immigration breaches is but one facet of what some authors have referred to as the criminalization or securitization of immigration (Welch 2003; Muller 2004; Malloch and Stanley 2005; Huysmans 2006; Brandariz García and Fernández Bessa 2009). There is, however, another side to this phenomenon which is far from the world of high politics and powerful rhetoric, and made up of the everyday practices of criminalization. These are less glamorous and more ordinary exercises of power where decisions are shaped by convenience, pragmatism and efficiency.

In this version of criminalization, immigration offences are merely introduced to provide enforcement officers with additional 'tools' to facilitate their everyday job. In this context, these offences are brought in as 'backups' or 'levers' to enforce compliance, as part of a 'presentational pack' to enhance the role of immigration officers or simply to tackle evidentiary problems. According to this instrumental view of law, as Sklansky (2012: 201) explained, 'all substantive laws and enforcement regimes, criminal and civil, [are deemed] as tools to be employed strategically, as the circumstances demand'. These more mundane reasons behind criminalization were articulated by UK Border Agency (UKBA) policy and enforcement officials. A senior official at the Policy and Strategy Group explained that more offences meant more choices of intervention: 'You can tailor your response to a particular case and you have a great range of deterrent . . . It just helps us to do the job.' He argued that the addition of new offences is inoffensive, even when they are barely, if ever, used:

> Is it harmful to have offences that you either never use or don't use very much? Once you have done the effort of creating, of putting them in the statute book they are not actively harmful even if they are not objectively, desperately useful.
>
> (Respondent 14, 12/08/2010)

Enacting legislation in general, and criminal laws in particular, is relatively easy. It is fairly cheap and does not entail high political costs for the actors involved.

Removing laws is much more difficult for practical and political reasons (Husak 2008: 10). Although some instances of decriminalization demonstrate a 'notable democratic appetite for criminal law reform' as Daryl Brown (2007: 244) argued, often the majoritarian support and bipartisan consensus for expanding criminal liability gravitate in favour of substantive criminal law growth, particularly in the United States and the UK, and in relation to regulatory offences (Garland 2001: 131; Tonry 2004b: 38; Brown 2007: 245; Lacey 2008: 63). Further, William Stuntz (2001) pointed to another practical incentive to expand criminal liability: over-criminalization makes the work of law enforcement agencies easier as they can apply different criminal laws selectively. In the absence of constitutional limits to the production of substantive criminal law, he argued, law makers are inclined to criminalize for pragmatic reasons (Stuntz 1996: 18; 2001). As Husak (2008: 34) nicely put it, this easiness to create criminal offence has turned legislatures into 'offense factories'.

Immigration offences created during the Labour government (1997–2010) were of two types. The first group comprises offences which penalize the failure to comply with a specific duty, which can be termed 'offences of disobedience' (Dubber 2010a: 200). An example in point is the provision of section 35(3) of the AI(TC)A 2004, considered in Chapter 3, which enumerates a number of requirements which may be imposed by the Secretary of State in order to operate the removal of a person and imposes a criminal sanction in response to non-compliance with them. Other examples are offences that punish the failure to attend and give evidence or produce documents before an immigration judge,[44] the failure of a detainee to submit to medical examination,[45] and the failure to supply information requested by the authorities, by employers or financial institutions,[46] and by transportation companies.[47]

The second group is constituted of offences that have specific application in the immigration field and replicate existing offences. This is the case with deception and document fraud. While a number of deception offences were introduced in the Theft Act 1968 and the Theft Act 1978, and later on in the Fraud Act 2006,[48] the IAA 1999 includes a specific offence of deception to deal with asylum applicants.[49] Similarly, even though the Forgery and Counterfeiting Act (FCA) 1981 already punished the use of a false instrument,[50] the offences in the Identity Cards Act 2006 (IDCA 2006) were introduced specifically to address the possession of false identity documents.[51] The IA 1971 already included the offence of possession of a false passport[52] as a summary offence punishable with up to six months' imprisonment. However, this is barely used, as illustrated by the low rate of prosecutions.[53]

While the IDCA 2006 is not an immigration act, the offences contained in it are frequently used against non-citizens using forged or improperly obtained documents, or documents that belong to someone else (Macdonald 2010: Chapter 14.77).[54] The preference for the offences[55] under the IDCA 2006 over those in the IA 1971 and in the FCA 1981 in cases of document fraud is due to two reasons. First, the penalties of the offences under the IDCA 2006 are much higher (maximum of ten years' imprisonment) than those under the IA 1971. Second, the offences[56] in the IDCA 2006 are indictable only, whereas the offence in the FCA 1981 is triable either way.[57] Hence, defendants charged with the former are sent straight to the crown court, are less likely to get bail and more likely to attract harsher penalties (Wadham *et al.* 2006: 139).

Other immigration offences in this second group, such as assaulting a detainee custody officer,[58] and assaulting and obstructing an immigration officer,[59] reproduce those related to constables[60] and prison officers.[61] The creation of these offences is connected to the expansion of police-like powers to immigration officers and they were aimed to back up those powers. Even if they are rarely used, they provide immigration officers with leverage to enforce compliance. In fact, they were requested by operational officers who find it 'helpful' to have their authority backed up with a criminal sanction. As a UKBA official at the Policy and Strategy Group told me, they are also part of a 'presentational pack' which demonstrates that they are being 'looked after in the same ways as their police colleagues' (Respondent 14, 12/08/2010).

In this sense it is relevant to remember that, unlike other government agencies, the UKBA has retained its policy-making power and is therefore responsible for proposing, shaping and taking a bill through Parliament. Its role in the design of immigration policy is influenced by the agency's enforcement capacity. New legislation and new offences are frequently motivated and shaped by its enforcement work. Hence, the agency is an important actor in – and factor in – 'pragmatic criminalization' (Lacey 2009: 940; see also Stuntz 2001). New categories of offences are proposed to facilitate the exercise of the agency's work. A high-ranking official at the UKBA's Criminality and Detention Group told me that many of the recently created immigration offences are the product of loopholes and evidentiary difficulties that UKBA staff encounter in the exercise of immigration controls: '[W]e sometimes find through experience a gap in processes or a gap in law, and so we legislate and fix that. It's just through experience and through changes really . . .' (Respondent 5, 16/09/2010). He told me that this was the case with the offence of document fraud. The general offence of fraud under the FCA 1981 was difficult to use in the context of immigration, presumably because of its narrow scope and the requirement to prove the double intention by the defendant[62] (Wadham *et al.* 2006: 141). Because the IDCA 2006 was considered important for immigration enforcement, the agency was involved in its enactment.

Behind the cold and pragmatic language of the policy officials who emphasize the role of immigration offences in the effective and smooth regulation of immigration lies a more retributive and punitive rationale for the criminalization of these offences, particularly those involving fraud. An immigration barrister at Garden Court North Chambers articulated it in this way:

[The government has made] an absolutely fundamental statement that you . . . have to get people to tell the truth. And if they are not going to tell the truth, you are going to punish them. So I think they are trying very hard to engender an understanding that dishonesty does not pay in immigration terms. And I think that is partly because they have a problem here, as in many places, in just knowing who is here, you know, how many illegal entrants they have, where they are, you know, what is their true identity.

(Respondent 11, 29/04/2010)

More generally, making immigration breaches criminal offences has a broader symbolic function of drawing the moral boundaries of a political community. They function 'as a sort of "purifying filter" protecting the local and the national from threatening foreign elements' (Aas 2007: 288). This symbolic role is articulated in the image of the immigrant as abuser and cheat imprinted in recent policy documents. The targets are foreigners who, by appealing to fraud, 'abuse the hospitality' of the UK and 'cause harm' by 'living and working here illegally', 'abusing our public services or private businesses', or 'taking advantage of our free health services' (Home Office 2006b: 15; 2007b: 12; 2010d, 2010e: 32). The criminal law is elicited, at least at a rhetorical level, to enforce an implicit contract that immigrants sign with the 'people of the UK' (Home Office 2008b: 3). A trivial breach of immigration law is then conceived as a more serious wrong.

In this context, '[t]he enduring exclusionary bent of the criminal law is exacerbated by the demands for public protection and rebalancing in favour of the "law abiding majority" that are the hallmark of populist penal politics' (Zedner 2010: 390). Because of their weak status as residents, as opposed to citizens, those who are let in owe the receiving society the privilege of being hosted; they are in debt and on 'eternal probation' (Kanstroom 2000: 1907).[63] They are, in Matthew Gibney's (2009) term, 'precarious residents'. For that matter, breaches to their duties as good guests – epitomized by the violation of a civic contract – are sanctioned more harshly. The use of criminal law against immigration offenders for not living up to their obligations as guests – and their subsequent deportation – is a reminder of the line separating citizens from non-citizens and recreates the boundaries of membership (Anderson *et al.* 2011). Therefore, immigration offences are not merely regulatory. They are not only aimed at ensuring the good running of the immigration control system and preventing the undermining of the immigration control system. They convey a punitive rationale of moral wrongfulness and an element of blame against those who, by violating the boundaries of their status, engage in a breach of trust.

The motives reviewed above illustrate a less flamboyant, more pragmatic use of criminal law lying behind the expansion of formal criminalization in recent years. Such an expansion in the law on the books, though, is not reflected in the actual enforcement of these offences. In fact, the everyday practice of dealing with immigration offenders is bound by strategic decisions and a discretionary exercise of powers which casts doubts about a one-dimensional trend towards increased (substantive) criminalization.

On regulation and prevention: using criminal powers for immigration management

Criminal sanctions against immigration offenders are used primarily as threats, as the preferred choice to deal with them is through executive removal (Weber and Bowling 2004: 204). This is even more compelling at a time of tight budgets and squeezed public services. In terms of the 'benchmarks' of the agency's performance, removal numbers matter more than prosecution and conviction rates. A UKBA senior policy official explained to me that

> [A criminal proceeding] is expensive, is time consuming, and if there is an alternative such as administrative removal, that is still very clearly our first preference. We do not want to fill the UK's criminal justice system and prisons with foreign nationals whose offences are not very serious or very harmful.
>
> (Respondent 14, 12/08/2010)

Another high-ranking member of the force at the Criminality and Detention Group articulated the preference of the agency for removals over criminal prosecutions for minor offences because such a choice serves better 'the interest of justice':

> If we embark in a prosecution route we've got to wait for the prosecution to be over before we can remove the person and the motives of the person is only about staying in the country anyway . . . You know if the offence is not serious – these are victimless offences so there's no victim – and we have to have this person out of the country immediately, well normally we will take that course because it serves the interest of justice better, probably . . . [It] doesn't serve the interest of justice particularly to take it through the criminal justice system where they may or may not get a serious penalty. We are not talking about the most serious offences.
>
> (Respondent 5, 16/09/2010)

Expulsion is the primary form of intervention against immigration offenders because the ultimate goal of the UKBA in these cases is to remove those with no legal status, rather than sanctioning their wrongdoing. The punishment attached to an immigration breach works chiefly as a backup to the administrative sanction. In this context, criminal sanctions have a secondary role to that of civil or administrative sanctions. According to Carol Steiker (1997: 784), the recasting of the nature of civil and criminal sanctions as preventive reflects the dominance of consequentialist or utilitarian approaches in legal theory which 'portrays them as related parts of a unitary scheme of state control of private behaviour'. She argued that in this scheme, criminal punishment is relegated to perform a secondary or reinforcement role to that of civil sanctions:

> Just as economic analysis helped to shift conceptions of civil justice from compensation toward deterrence, so, too, it has begun to shift conceptions of criminal justice from retribution toward deterrence . . . [Law and economics advocates give] the criminal sanction a role secondary to that of the civil sanction; criminal law works as a 'backup' to civil law to induce deterrence in situations in which civil sanctions are likely to prove ineffective.
>
> (Steiker 1997: 785)

This observation holds true for regulatory offences in which criminal punishment reinforces the preventive role of the regimes underpinning these offences (Ashworth and Zedner 2011: 282). Likewise, the everyday practice of immigration offences reveals that criminal law is often used against foreigners who are in breach of immigration rules when immigration measures (the primary response) are ineffective or impracticable, in the same way that immigration measures such as removal or deportation are sometimes used against foreigners where the criminal law finds its limits.[64] The nature of the criminal sanction in the immigration arena does not only have a regulatory, preventive purpose. The rationale for the actual punishment of immigration wrongdoers is, as the magistrates and judges repeatedly emphasize in their decisions, deterrence.

While prevention of harm to others is a legitimate goal – and a duty – of the state and hence of the criminal law, prevention alone is a weak justification of criminal intervention on people's rights (Ashworth and Zedner 2011: 282; 2012). One of the purposes of any legal prohibition is to dissuade people from engaging in socially undesirable conducts and thus to orient their behaviour. While this is a pragmatic function of any social norm, by itself it is an unsatisfactory justification of criminal law (Ferrajoli 1989: 277; Duff 2011: 129). In the absence of strict limits – such as the requirement that the conduct being punished is a serious wrong, the proof of the agent's fault, and the proportionality of the sanction or retribution – the person subject to punishment risks being treated as a means to achieve particular social goals rather than as a rational and autonomous agent. The use of criminal law and punishment on purely preventive grounds is contested even by consequentialist theorists who proscribe punishments which are not necessary or represent a misuse of the criminal law (Kadish 1967: 169).

Criminal law regulation and punishment should not be based on effectiveness or bureaucratic convenience. Even when other non-criminal measures have proven unsuccessful, criminal law should be reserved for punishing the most serious wrongs (Ashworth 2008: 417; Ashworth and Zedner 2012). Because criminal wrongs are more serious than civil and administrative wrongs, the resort to criminal law should be subject to stricter limits (Stuntz 1996: 6). Criminal law is not a substitute or alternative to civil regulation, but it is a truly distinct form of regulation (Husak 2004: 211; Duff 2010a: 302). Concomitantly, in the case of serious wrongs, we should not wait until other non-criminal means fail to criminalize.

A correct interpretation of the principle of last resort should not license criminalization when non-criminal regulation fails, for instance, when criminalization provides an additional means to force compliance or as an alternative means of intervention when the primary sanction (removal) is frustrated for practical reasons. The conducts proscribed by immigration crimes are not serious wrongs, and hence criminalization of these conducts contravenes the principle of last resort. In fact, the conducts that are being criminalized – and punished – are not considered serious offences; they are made crimes in pursuit of other means. What is at stake is preventing the arrival of irremovable migrants. A similar rationale is behind the criminalization of aiders, facilitators, transportation companies and employers whose punishment is justified because of the impact that their conduct has on the system of controls over immigration. By displacing criminal law principles for immigration enforcement imperatives, '[t]he movement of states to make people themselves illegal shifts understandings of criminality' (Dauvergne 2008: 8).

Immigrants as criminal offenders: rhetoric, practices and symbolisms of criminalization

> *To prohibit a multitude of indifferent acts is not to prevent crimes that might arise from them, but is rather to create new ones.*[65]

While foreigners caught and removed by the state in breach of immigration laws are a small portion of the irregular resident population in the country, those who are actually prosecuted and convicted for breaches to immigration laws represent an even smaller percentage.[66] On the face of it, then, the criminalization of immigration is not a generalized phenomenon, as is sometimes claimed. Enforcement is inconsistent and random, and thus highly unpredictable for those who are potentially accused of immigration offences. Even when these offences are not enforced, criminalization carries a number of consequences.

At the rhetorical level, the reshaping of immigration law under the banner of crime has the consequence of demonizing migrants (Pratt and Valverde 2002). They are increasingly seen as criminals (Bosworth 2007: 208; Bosworth and Guild 2008; Dauvergne 2008). This is not only because of the borrowing of criminal justice jargon, methods and strategies for immigration enforcement. It is the potential use of criminal law – the prosecution, conviction and imprisonment – which has the most powerful effect in the representation of foreigners as cheats and abusers. Immigrants who violate immigration statutes are not only represented as criminal, dangerous and risky, but are also strictly speaking – in legal and institutional terms – criminal offenders. Making people criminal has the effect of expanding the category of 'criminals', forcing people to resort to illegal means and making them more vulnerable to exploitation (Dauvergne 2008; Weber and Grewcock 2012). At a practical level, the fact that the criminal route is not followed does not mean that the person goes scot-free – as may happen with minor, conventional offences. Because of the juxtaposed immigration controls, the label of 'immigration offender' justifies other measures – generally, detention and removal. The criminal label in this sense reinforces and legitimizes the need for administrative action and controls (Coutin 2005: 14).

When immigration-based offences are enforced, there is a further, symbolic implication of the criminalization of immigration status (Valverde 2010: 228). It enables the representation of the immigration drama on the public stage of a criminal hearing – even when it is a silent drama, since most of these cases are settled by guilty pleas. The very fact of being called, held to account and punished for entering the country by prohibited means uncovers the perils that those 'begging' for access are prepared to face to be in Britain. In doing so, these proceedings make possible the exposé of the receiving country as desirable, powerful and prosperous, and give the state the opportunity to display the last bastion of sovereign powers – the power to grant entry, and to punish and expel those who are not allowed in. As Bosworth (2011a: 592) argued in relation to the power to detain and deport, so too does the power to punish pose 'a virile, absolutist State, wielding great power over non-citizens' (see also Bosworth 2011c; Dauvergne 2004). Such representation is, however, quite misleading. A state whose main targets are destitute and helpless migrants barely imprints an image of a virile, powerful sovereign.

The criminalization of immigration status also makes apparent the importance of entitlement to enter and remain in certain nations. In the context of increased criminalization, the 'accident' of being born in the global South is reasserted as a moral, political and legal handicap which precludes those unfortunate ones from enjoying the rights reserved to the citizens of prosperous countries (Dauvergne 2008: 17), and licenses the use of state coercion against those who challenge the boundaries of their status.

While descriptions of criminalization practices generally take as their point of departure appeal court cases (e.g. Bye 1999; Webber 2008; Stoyanova 2012), the enquiry into everyday practices of prosecution and conviction of immigration defendants shows a much more mundane, bureaucratized, dull and far less glamorous exercise of state powers. Those who are detained, charged and brought to a criminal court for violating their immigration status are more often than not subject to an uncontested criminal process in which it seems that there is nothing to discuss, evidenced by the speed of the hearings and the concise volume of the court files. In this regard, the role of the judges – and criminal justice more generally – is literally to 'administrate' punishment. These cases often go unnoticed. While some of them do reach the courts of appeal and set case law, they are a minority.

The managerial or administrative approach underlying the immigration cases reviewed looks like the actuarial model theorized by Feeley and Simon (1992, 1994; see also Feeley 2004, 2006) or the 'new mode of bureaucratic management of crime' diagnosed by Harcourt (2003: 106). As a consequence of the 'administrativization' of the criminal procedure, immigration-based cases are predominantly handled through a downgraded criminal process in which some of the procedural guarantees germane to a criminal trial are diminished or slashed off (Greenspan 1991: 49; Duff *et al.* 2007; Ashworth and Zedner 2008). As Ashworth and Zedner (2008: 39) explain, '[t]his managerialist tendency is particularly dominant at the lower end of the tariff where the claim to normality is most plausible. Here, censure and hard treatment become less appropriate than the manipulation of costs or disincentives.' This 'assembly-line justice' model (Lydgate 2010) that has transformed the criminal courts, paraphrasing Husak (2008: 34), into 'sentences factories' is squarely fitted to 'process' the irrelevant, petty illegality of outsiders.

Conclusion

As Michel Foucault (1977) famously argued, criminal law has not always been the outcome of principles elaborated by Enlightenment thinkers. The dark side or authoritarian aspect of criminal law has been a constitutive part of it, rather than its perversion (Ericson 2007; Norrie 2009). An element of unaccountability and 'unlawlessness' has been inherent to the formation of modern criminal law conceived both as a control device and a source of protection for those affected by state coercion. This 'dark side' is exemplified by the extensive and unconstrained power that British law makers historically have had to criminalize an extensive range of conducts. In turn, this is reflected in the deployment of criminal punishment – or the threat of it – for purposes other than retribution or moral condemnation. While the goals of criminal law and punishment have never been absolutely 'pure' (Garland 1990; O'Malley 1999), a quick glance at the history of criminalization in Britain shows how utilitarian aims – particularly deterrence – were behind the broad use of criminal law for regulatory purposes.

These early developments are linked to more recent trends of excessive enactment of penal legislation, including immigration crimes. Underpinning the formal enactment of these offences and their enforcement in practice are both utilitarian and expressive conceptions of the (criminal) law (Hawkins 2002). Both are central to the justification of criminalization. However, as outlined above, alone they are an insufficient and improper base for criminal regulation and punishment as required by criminal law principles such as last resort, proportionality and harm. The disruption of these principles makes these offences questionable. I want to draw attention to two further fundamental problems in using criminal law to regulate immigration.

First, the great gap between formal criminalization (the expansion of criminal offences) and substantial criminalization (their actual enforcement) reveals the recurrent appeal to criminal legislation for symbolic and deterrence purposes. It can be argued that with the criminalization of immigration violations, there is an 'upgrade' of such breaches (formal condemnation). Their under-enforcement, however, suggests the opposite. For most immigration offenders, criminal punishment is more than anything a threat unlikely to be realized. Further, ever-increasing criminalization with limited resources (police, prosecutors, judges, defence counsels, etc.) means that those caught in breach are subject to substandard proceedings: access to poor legal defence, lack of knowledge about immigration and asylum law by police and practitioners, high incentives to plead guilty or to accept a caution, and subsequent removal. In December 2010, the government launched a pilot to divert cases of document fraud from the criminal justice system through 'simple caution'.[67] This proposal was not motivated by concerns about the pernicious effects of criminalization. Rather, its primary objective has been to reduce the burden on the criminal justice system and prison estate, and to facilitate removals. Both the 'administrativization' of the criminal process in immigration-related cases and the diversion of some of them from the criminal system seek to manage an increasing number of cases in a swift, effective way.

Second, in the cases in which these offences are used and the defendant is convicted, the purpose of punishment remains unclear. It is certainly not to reintegrate the convicted defendant, since the individual is usually due to be expelled. Neither is the aim to incapacitate or discipline him or her. The society that punishes a foreigner for violating the boundaries of status does not expect him or her to become a good member of it, but rather the opposite. The purpose is to expel this person from the community (Bosworth 2011a). Criminal punishment is then redundant and unfit to deal with immigration offenders. In the case of refugees, it is also against international and domestic law. The actual role of criminal punishment in relation to the individual offender is emptied of content. It can only play a more general function of (re)establishing the normative force of the violated norm (in positive terms) or as a deterrent (in negative terms). But are these enough justification for imposing criminal sanctions?

The problems outlined above suggest that immigration offences are not simply ancillary powers, nor are they inoffensive, harmless tools that only serve symbolic and political purposes. Even if they are not used, they 'create' crime and thus a pull of potential offenders liable to administrative or criminal sanctions. They license the use of coercive force with limited procedural safeguards, they are disproportionate to the 'wrong' done, and their normative justification remains weak. In fact, in the case of people subject to removal or deportation, imposing punishment does not serve retributive, incapacitating or rehabilitative aims.

Conclusion

In this book I have analysed the role of the criminal law in the immigration field and the different ways in which the two regimes converge. The banner of 'immigration crime' is certainly broad and therefore presents a number of challenges for researchers. It encompasses many offences with different features which are difficult to group together for analytic purposes. Further, foreigners using fraudulent documents are sometimes criminalized under offences that are part of non-immigration acts – such as the Identity Cards Act 2006 (IDCA 2006). Even though these crimes are not strictly speaking 'immigration offences', because they criminalize identity fraud they may be regarded as such. The purpose of this work has been to find common grounds for understanding the function (or functions) that the 'hybrid system' of administrative and criminal sanctions has served historically and in present conditions. In doing so, I have addressed immigration offences both as a general category and in relation to particular crimes.

As the literature on the criminalization of immigration shows, states from the economically developed West are increasingly deploying punitive measures against the 'hordes' coming from the global South. Low-skilled, poor, non-white immigrants are portrayed as security threats to the country's culture, identity and welfare. Yet this 'macro' or 'grand' analysis or theory needs to be grounded in the concrete and specific setting in which this phenomenon is taking place. The criminalization trend is rooted in legal, social and historical factors. In Britain, the shape of today's immigration system is the product of a long struggle to define its identity as a society *vis-à-vis* the outside. The post-war years are particularly crucial to understanding the mechanisms put in place to enforce such a boundary – including the appeal to criminal law.

At the same time, the criminalization of immigration is not a straightforward phenomenon. It is neither new nor generalized. While there is not much information about the actual use of criminal sanctions against immigration law-breakers in the pre-1900 period, evidence tends to suggest that these were very rarely used until the 1980s, with the exception of overstaying and the failure to observe the conditions of a leave (Home Office 1985: Table 21; see also Porter 1979: 4; Dummett and Nicol 1990: 161; Bloch and Schuster 2005: 494). Only since then, has the enforcement of both administrative and criminal provisions started to rise, particularly against people seeking asylum. However, it was not until New Labour came into office in 1997 that the powers to prosecute, detain, remove and deport immigration wrongdoers were more systematically used.

Immigration offences as the punitive regulation of the poor

Criminal law provisions have traditionally been inserted into immigration laws as backup sanctions. In this vein, immigration offences have historically served deterrent and regulatory purposes. Immigration crimes are part of what Ramsay has termed 'regulatory public welfare offences' for which punishment does not serve a retributive function. but acts as a deterrent against causing harm or creating a risk of harm to abstract or collective entities – as opposed to individual human beings (Ramsay 2006: 50). They resemble in many respects the 'police' or 'welfare' offences described by Dubber (2013) as an early manifestation of what he calls the 'police power'. Even though in recent years, the catalogue of immigration crimes has incorporated many offences that may not fit the regulatory model of criminal law – such as the assault on an immigration officer or trafficking-related offences – the role of criminal law in immigration enforcement remains primarily regulatory in nature.

The category of regulatory offences is controversial, as these offences have not been clearly defined (Ashworth 2000: note 12; Dubber 2005: 129). Still, a number of criminal law scholars have identified certain characteristics that may distinguish them from 'true', 'core' or 'paradigmatic' crimes. In his work on over-criminalization, Husak (2008: Chapter 1) divided the criminal law into a core and a periphery. The core is formed by crimes against the person and property, and the periphery is populated by an array of vaguely defined offences which he classified for analytical purpose into three groups: overlapping offences, crimes of risk prevention and ancillary offences. According to him, some of these 'peripheral' offences compromise various principles of liberal criminal law; because they criminalize trivial harms, they lack the *mens rea* requirement and they shift the burden of proof.

Many regulatory offences fall into the 'periphery' of the criminal law as outlined by Husak (Ashworth 2000: 228). Victor Tadros (2007: 16) excluded regulatory offences from his general theory of criminal responsibility because they 'do not carry with them any strong stigma, or often any great punishment' (see also Tadros 2010: 164). Similarly, Ashworth and Zedner (2011: 282) differentiate regulatory offences from other parts of the criminal law based on the function that each serves: '[in the former] it is not the seriousness of the wrongdoing that bolsters the case for criminalization but rather that of coordination and regulation of activities'. Other authors consider that the function of criminal law to regulate certain spheres – such as health and safety, environment, industry and finance – differs from the function of criminal law, for example, in punishing interpersonal violence (Ogus 2010). In the former domain, 'what is regulated could be described as performing a legitimate activity in an illegitimate way' in order to minimize danger and ensure fair practices (Ashworth 2008: 420); while in the latter, the conducts subject to condemnation are in themselves morally wrong and the purpose of punishment is censure.

The strict differentiation between so-called 'regulatory' offences and 'ordinary' offences, and the distinctive functions that each of them serve, is contested by others. Lindsey Farmer (2010a: 228), for instance, argued that regulatory offences are not '"merely technical" or morally neutral' but reflect a social consensus about the function of the criminal law and the role of the state in a particular historical and social setting (see also Farmer 2010b). Similarly, Stuart Green (1997: 1563) contended that 'regulatory offences' are morally neutral and argued that the moral wrongfulness of these offences derives from the mere disobedience to a legal command rather than from the underlying prohibited conduct. In turn, Andrew Sanders (2010: 44) asserted that the distinction between 'real' and 'regulatory' offences is untenable because of the difficulties in classifying certain conducts as either real or regulatory crimes. Further, as Celia Wells (2005: 7) observed, the distinction between conventional ('real') offences and regulatory ('quasi') offences has been unhelpful for holding corporations criminally accountable, and has perpetuated the perception that corporate crime is less serious than individual, conventional crime.

Even if this clear-cut distinction is useful for analytical purposes, its legal and empirical base is contentious as the exercise of differentiating one from the other has been unsuccessful so far (Dubber 2005: 129). In fact it is difficult to define the features of regulatory offences: are they strict liability? Does their sanction lack the stigma attached to that of ordinary offences? Are they non-serious offences? Are they harmless? (Green 1997; Ashworth 2000: note 12; Tadros 2007: 16). Some regulatory offences have been created to regulate activities which involve high risks for public safety[1] – for instance, food production and distribution, manufacturing of controlled medicines, etc. Others, including most immigration offences, do not entail harm or risk of harm to individuals or the general public and have been enacted for mere bureaucratic convenience to facilitate the work of regulators. The reproduction of these immigration offences has excessively expanded the breadth of the criminal law and disrupted its core function.

Although I have argued that the function of criminal law in the context of immigration is *predominantly* regulatory, immigration offences cannot be completely assimilated to regulatory offences. While their main function is to make possible the smooth and effective enforcement of border controls and immigration regulations, I have also argued that immigration offences play a distinct function in the reassertion of membership boundaries through punitive state coercion. Underlying the criminalization of immigration breaches is the idea of a breach of a contract. Criminal law is deployed to enforce that contract by punishing the foreigner for not abiding by the rules and failing in his or her obligations to the host society. This appeal to the criminal law represents 'a reversion to traditional visions of the social as unified, consensual and authoritative, and to traditional sovereign state strategies for reinforcing them' (O'Malley 2001: 94). The idea of the existence of a unified 'community of shared values' which should be guarded and protected against outsiders – be they the underclasses within or the aliens from outside – historically has been used to legitimize the exercise of state powers to punish and exclude (Aas 2007, 2011a;

Anderson *et al.* 2011: 554; Bosworth 2011a). This contractual conception has dominated recent government attempts to justify punitive measures such as deportation and punishment.

Hence, the role of punishment in immigration enforcement cannot be completely assimilated to its function in regulatory law. Criminal provisions in the latter are, broadly speaking, introduced to force private businesses or individuals to comply with (public) standards and regulations for safety or other public interest reasons. Instead, immigration regulations are entirely part of the public sphere. Criminalization in the immigration regulatory framework is not merely regulatory, but is embedded in the exercise of the sovereign state's power to punish and exclude. Thus, the crucial function of punishment is to '(ex)capacitate' non-members, as opposed to incapacitating or reintegrating. Locating these concepts in the regulatory state framework elaborated by Braithwaite (2003), immigration offences seem to be closer to the regulation of the poor, through mainly punishment (as legally defined) or punitive measures, than to the regulation of businesses. Within business regulatory enforcement, criminal prosecutions are barely pursued and the crimes of the powerful are usually dealt with through various 'soft' control devices, such as mediation, restitution, revocation of licences and other regulatory strategies. The hybrid system of immigration and criminal sanctions shares features of both regulatory regimes, but it is ultimately aimed at (punitively) excluding foreigners.

Situating the intertwining of penal and immigration policies in a broader geopolitical context, the appeal to criminal law for immigration enforcement by rich Western countries endeavours to maintain an increasingly stratified global order where the privilege of 'belonging' to the global North is jealously guarded against the hordes coming from the poor South. As Katja Franko Aas (2013) persuasively argued, punishment is one of the means to enforce the 'global hierarchies of citizenship'.

Contingency, discretion and the importance of membership in the interface between immigration and criminal laws

The appeal to criminal law by enforcement agencies is mainly justified by immigration imperatives, as criminal prosecutions are initiated only in certain specific cases. Actual immigration offenders – those who end up being prosecuted and eventually convicted – have done nothing different from those who are removed straightaway. The first group does not constitute particularly serious offenders: what they did and for what they are being sanctioned is essentially the same prohibited act as the one committed by those dealt with by the administrative route. They are doubly punished simply because they are harder to remove. Further, the first group is much smaller than the second one. Substantive criminalization is therefore a relatively infrequent and selective phenomenon, triggered by pragmatic and disparate considerations, rather than by a politically orchestrated decision to put more immigrants behind bars. In other words, the prosecution of immigration offenders – particularly those accused of document fraud – is an opportunistic use of the criminal law, and does not seek to castigate wrongdoing.

The decision-making process in cases involving immigration offences and its outcome are clear examples of the contingency of crime and criminalization: what is in fact a crime and who are the offenders largely depends on the process of definition and the actors involved in the labelling. More precisely, it depends on the *instrumentality* of the criminal law in *a particular case* to achieve a particular policy outcome (Sklansky 2012: 201). In this respect, Lacey (1995: 21) wrote: 'No unified set of principles constrains the range of discretionary powers which determine the course of a defendant's progress through this ideologically central path of criminal procedure.' In the case of immigration, the choice of criminalization is made even more 'artificial' by its unpredictability and highly discretionary nature.

While the analysis of the practices of punishment shows that they have as main targets foreigners without legal status, immigration laws are also used against legal residents and citizens – particularly naturalized British citizens aiding their relatives. As documented by the cases that reach the criminal courts, many of those nationals who are caught have been immigrants themselves. They are blamed for undermining immigration imperatives and so the ultimate goal of their prosecution and punishment is to bring down rates of illegal immigration. As in the case of undocumented immigrants, what is at stake is not the criminal wrong as such, but the impact that their conduct – facilitation – has on the overall system of immigration controls.

An important difference between the (foreigner) undocumented immigrant and the (citizen) facilitator is, however, that the former is subject to the dual system of criminal and administrative sanctions, whereas the latter is not. This parallel system of sanctions makes it impossible to predict which regime will be activated in a particular case. Such uncertainty is further accentuated by the wide margin of discretion held by enforcement officers and the instrumental use of the criminal law to pursue immigration enforcement objectives. In this sense, even though the institution of citizenship has been progressively eroded of its capacity to sort those who belong from those who do not (Soysal 1994; Dauvergne 2008: 101; Aas 2011a: 339), it remains important to differentiate the intensity and scope of sovereign state powers exercised over non-nationals versus nationals.

The problems of criminalization: are immigration offences different?

Formal criminalization of immigration breaches has a number of troubling consequences. Most importantly, it represents a departure from liberal criminal law principles, particularly last resort, harm, and proportionality of sanctions. Criminal law is used against non-serious, victimless conducts and the sanction of imprisonment on most immigration defendants is disproportionate to the wrong done. Many of these offences do not require proof of fault and so the principle of culpability is compromised as well. More generally, the great expansion of these offences in recent years has contributed to the phenomenon of over-criminalization described by some authors with all its worrisome consequences for the criminal law and those subject to it (Ashworth 2000, 2008; Husak 2008; Duff 2010a). The main function of criminal regulation in immigration is to dissuade people from 'wrongdoing' – that is, as a threat. When the threat materializes and people are charged with and convicted of immigration offences, the judiciary generally justifies their decision by the need to impose exemplary punishments against those who challenge immigration rules so that others do not follow the same track. The importance given to deterrence in the criminalization of immigration offences reveals an unbalanced emphasis on an utilitarian rationale which in turn risks leading to an unprincipled exercise of state power (Ashworth and Zedner 2011: 303).

Even if formally criminalized conducts are not punished, the expansion of the criminal law licenses punitive interventions against a whole population of so-defined 'immigration offenders'. As such, 'making people criminal' has not only a symbolic effect. Most importantly, it has legal and institutional consequences for those so labelled as they are candidates for expulsion. When immigration offences are used, people deserving of protection such as refugees and trafficking victims are at risk of being prosecuted and convicted for these offences. The cases analysed in this study reveal that these are not isolated 'mistakes', but the product of a system geared towards controlling the mobility of undesirable migrants (Dauvergne 2008) or the '*illegalized* global underclass' (Aas 2011a: 137, italics in original). While according to the government, the criminal law should be used against organized immigration criminality, and only those who cause the most harm – to society and to the foreigner him/herself – should be prosecuted, the cases that still crowd the criminal justice system's dockets are what the immigration agency classifies as 'low-level'. Indeed, those who end up being prosecuted and eventually punished, are largely immigrants and their relatives. Further, they are less likely to battle their cases successfully, and are equally more likely to be remanded in custody and get a custodial sentence as a sanction.

It could be argued that the problems of the criminalization of immigration breaches identified in this book are no different from those that affect the criminal law and its practice more generally. Over-criminalization and the use of criminal law for regulatory purposes; the expansion of strict liability offences and the emphasis on prevention; the high percentage of cases settled through the guilty plea and the erosion of criminal safeguards in the criminal process; and the disproportionate use of criminal law and imprisonment against the poor and the socially excluded are all features that have been denounced by criminal lawyers and criminologists for many years. Some legal scholars have explained them as a departure from or a perversion of liberal law principles (Duff *et al.* 2007; Duff 2010b; Steiker 2010; Ashworth and Zedner 2011); others have seen them as manifestations of the residue of an authoritarian, disciplinary power which constitutes the dark or illiberal side of the criminal law (Dubber 2005, 2013; Ericson 2007; Norrie 2009).

Seen as part of this perversion or authoritarian side of the criminal law, immigration offences are one tool among many to enforce exclusionary policies against unwelcome foreigners – the outcast or underclass coming from outside. Immigration offences are, though, a small part of the artillery of (immigration) controls and they are deployed when the other devices find their own limits. As such, they increase the flexibility and scope of immigration law (Stumpf 2011: 1729), a field which remains relatively unconstrained by legal norms and which authorizes broad discretionary power over those subject to it (Simon 1998; Kanstroom 2004: 641). Peter Schuck (1984: 1) defined in stark terms this feature of US immigration law: 'Probably no other area of American law has been so radically insulated and divergent from those fundamental norms of constitutional right, administrative procedure, and judicial role that animate the rest of our legal system.' Criminal (immigration) offences are part of immigration law, and as such, they contribute to exacerbating its pernicious features.

Because of the distinctive nature of immigration offences – they are part of both criminal and immigration law – they cannot be completely assimilated within other offences. The analysis of these offences thus should consider the regulatory scheme underpinning them and the specific function that criminal punishment is called to perform in the regulation of immigration.

Managerialism and the administrativization of immigration regulation

While the use of criminal law for immigration enforcement is not new, how criminal punishment – or the threat of it – is deployed and administered is novel. The 'administration of punishment' against immigration offenders is governed by a managerial approach which embraces risk and harm as measurements of the seriousness of certain conducts and as proxies for state action. As in the 'new penology' described by Feeley and Simon (1992, 1994), immigration offenders are divided into low-, medium- and high-risk categories in order to rationalize the use of the criminal law for immigration enforcement. The use of actuarial devices, such as the harm matrix, to identify the most harmful immigration offenders aims at achieving a certain political programme – the reduction of illegal immigration (O'Malley 2002). Even though the practice of immigration enforcement is messier and more ambiguous than its depiction in policy papers, the appeal to these clear-cut actuarial categories gives the idea of a perfectly designed system of controls and legitimizes enforcement actions.

Instead of being in stark opposition as posed by Feeley and Simon (1992: 451; see also Feeley 2004: 72), the language and methods of actuarialism and managerialism are linked to the rise of penal populism in crime and immigration policies and debates. The two trends are not contradictory, but intrinsically connected (O'Malley 1992: 258; 1999: 188; Zedner 2009: 43). At the centre of the government's immigration plans is a narrow policy objective (bringing down illegal immigration) and the proposal of practical enforcement strategies to achieve it. This effectively forecloses any discussion about the various other approaches to the same issue, such as tackling the social and economic causes of irregular migration. As Harcourt (2013: 270, italics in original) explains, this cost–benefit type analysis offers a 'common sense' approach to politically controversial issues, thus, '[a]n innocent and narrow objective has turned these political ideals into mere instrumental goods, it has displaced political contestation, wrangling, horse-trading, and debate, and it has imposed, under the veil of neutral, objective, positivistic science, a *political outcome*'. By representing immigration enforcement as a technical issue and emptying it of any political and moral considerations, the 'bureaucratic management' of immigration and crime (Harcourt 2007: 16; see also O'Malley 2004) hides the highly political and contested nature of immigration and its control. Thus it rules out alternative strategies that decouple immigration from control and enforcement.

The 'instrumentally rational, morally neutral, knowledge-based, pragmatic solutions' that characterize the managerial approach to control crime (Garland 2001: 182) are embedded in an anti-modern rhetoric: a populist discourse which represents immigrants as the source of a range of social ills – from unemployment to crime – that in turn justify a 'tough on immigration' approach. In this context, it is not difficult to link the cold, pragmatic language of the Home Office's position papers and the bureaucratic processing of immigration-crime cases by the criminal justice system with the heated debates on immigration in the Commons and the tabloid media (Huysmans and Buonfino 2008). While they seem distant from each other, they ultimately pursue similar goals.

Further, actuarial terminology and strategies provide a 'dispassionate management of population groups' (Bosworth and Guild 2008: 712) and an 'impersonal style of regulation' (Matthews 2005: 187) which effectively neutralize the concern about individual suffering and placate resistance (Simon 1988). Bosworth and Guild (2008: 709) argued that this managerial discourse in immigration 'effectively neutralizes the moral ambiguities of migration control. Rather than being treated as individuals with specific needs and experiences, foreigners are instead grouped together and managed collectively as a matter of administrative expediency.' This approach precludes the consideration of the 'individual wrong' in itself with all its complexities and nuances. By judging immigration-crime cases as part of an aggregate, judicial decisions assess them for their effects on broader policy purposes. Because these are considered as easy, unproblematic cases, they are dealt with through an impoverished criminal process which offers fewer constraints on punitive interventions (Pratt 2006: 134; Ashworth and Zedner 2008: 39).

———

In this book I sought to contribute to the body of literature on which I based my study: first, to the literature on the criminalization of immigration by looking at one specific manifestation of this phenomenon from a socio-legal perspective; and second, to the criminal law literature on criminalization by analysing the challenges that the criminalization of immigration poses to criminal law theory and by emphasizing the parallels and intertwining in the two fields. One of the problems that has contributed to an almost total indifference to the use of criminal laws against non-citizens – specifically through immigration offences – in academic circles is the seemingly disciplinary dominance of social scientists (sociologists, political scientists and anthropologists) in immigration studies and the retreat from this field of criminal law scholars.[2]

This epistemological division has been unhelpful for understanding the criminalization of immigration as part of a broader phenomenon of criminal law expansion and for developing limiting principles in the use of criminal powers against immigration wrongdoers. The criminal law remains circumscribed by state boundaries, and criminal law scholars have been focused on state criminal laws and its institutions (Valverde 2010; Farmer 2010b). Criminal law theory has been predominantly built on the idea of the 'citizen' as the main recipient of state protection through its criminal laws and the obbject of punishment (e.g. Duff 2010a, 2011; Ramsay 2010).[3] Social changes brought by globalization and the mechanisms put forth to police state boundaries should force a refocus on the criminal law as a discipline.

In this work, I attempted to breach these disciplinary boundaries by critically examining the function of criminal law in the enforcement of immigration laws from a socio-legal and normative perspective. I have argued that the criminal law has no role to play in the regulation of immigration. Most of the conducts criminalized are victimless and they do not even entail a risk of harm to the general public. Criminalization is a disproportionate measure to achieve an efficient system of immigration controls. The use of punishment against those who breach the boundaries of their immigration status is moot in practice because the ultimate sanction against them is expulsion. The goal of punishment is not to expiate a past guilt (through retribution); nor is it to prevent future wrongs (through incapacitation and rehabilitation). While deterrence appears to be an important consideration for policy makers and judges, I have shown that there is no evidence that criminal sanctions serve preventive purposes in the cases most usually prosecuted. Indeed, the threat of punishment is unlikely to act as a deterrent for undocumented migrants – either because many of them are unaware of these sanctions, or even if they are, they will often prefer to spend some time in a British prison to immediate return. Therefore, prevention remains a weak justification for punishment in these cases. Hence, the use of criminal law and punishment in immigration-related cases is unjustified in the light of the main theories of punishment. The chief purpose of punishment in immigration-related cases is ancillary and pragmatic: to facilitate the return of the accused.

The hybrid system of immigration and criminal sanctions should then be modified accordingly in order to reflect the purpose it chiefly serves. Criminal law should be used when harm or the risk of harm to others is involved – for example, against trafficking in human beings and certain cases of commercial smuggling. Punishment is not only ineffective and fruitless to address immigration wrongdoing, it is also highly damaging to those caught by this dual system of sanctions. Echoing the former EU Commissioner for Human Rights, Thomas Hammarberg, immigration breaches should remain administrative, and immigration management should largely be regulated through other, non-penal means.

Appendix
Brief account of the research process

Since I started this research project, I have been interested in looking at the mixed, hybrid or dual nature of immigration offences. Even though the shape and focus of the project has changed considerably since I started, the very existence of these offences sparked my attention from the outset. Being educated in law in Argentina, a country with a strong continental European legal tradition, where immigration regulations are a branch of administrative law and therefore are completely separate from penal law, I found the notion of 'immigration offences' a curious legal specimen worth investigating. My legal interest was complemented by my personal experience of being an immigrant myself and my interest in immigration and citizens' matters at a personal level. Even though, rightly or wrongly, I have barely felt any practical effects from these immigration provisions – perhaps due to my status as an EU citizen and my educational and socio-economic background – I always felt attracted and morally obliged to be engaged in debates touching on immigration issues. My condition as a foreigner and my legal background certainly influenced the approach to the research project, its design and outcomes.

Evolving design of the research project

From the beginning, the fieldwork stage was aimed at supplementing and enriching with empirical material the written text of policy documents and the understanding of the rationale behind the law. By looking at the concrete, practical reasons that guide and shape the decision making of the people that make and enforce the laws, I sought to scrutinize critically contemporary appeals to criminal law and the actual practices of punishment against immigrants. So besides looking at document-based data (legislation, policy papers, official statistics, parliamentary debates, case law, etc.), I analysed court cases (both hearings and court files) on immigration-related offences and conducted semi-structured interviews with government and non-government actors. Court data and interviews are important sources of information beyond the written texts of official documents. Research based on 'near data' contributes to understanding the way that the immigration enforcement system works in practice by contextualizing and bringing closer 'distant data' or 'mute evidence' 'manufactured' elsewhere – secondary data (Hodder 2003: 155; Daly 2011). Thus it serves the function of enriching the analysis of immigration legislation, policies and practices. Such qualitative data are also particularly important in this field where quantitative data are scarce and unreliable, as I explain below.

The design of the fieldwork phase was reviewed and modified according to the changing focus and emphasis of the research project. As such, it was not a 'one-off' decision, but an evolving process, like the project itself. While at the beginning, the collection of empirical evidence was limited to conducting interviews with key actors, soon after finishing this stage it was apparent that such data were insufficient and that they did not provide a comprehensible account of the decision-making process in cases involving immigration offences. Critically assessing the function of these offences and how they are being used against individuals became essential. This was the main reason for extending this stage by looking at the criminal justice system and the processing of cases involving immigration defendants. In this sense, the interviewing process not only provided data rich in detail on the experience and perceptions of my interviewees; it also made me rethink, redirect and focus the project and its design.

My enthusiasm for undertaking an enquiry on immigration offences often stumbled upon sceptical reactions. A member of the UK Border Agency finished an interview with his sincere doubts about where I would find evidence to draw any conclusions: '[This is a] difficult research [project] because it's not entirely tangible in ways. It's quite difficult too, because where are you going to get data from, really?' (Respondent 5, 16/09/2010). A barrister with expertise in immigration offences put it crudely: '[T]here's no such thing as an immigration crime. It's a crime. Immigration crime is a sort of handy tag, but it is not different than any other offence' (Respondent 15, 28/04/2010). Likewise, a senior member of the Crown Prosecution Service (CPS) told me that there is nothing different between the prosecution of immigration crimes and any other crimes: all are 'treated' in the same way and according to the same rules (Respondent 19, 14/06/2010). Many research participants and court staff did not appear to understand my interest in the subject, telling me there was little value in pursuing it. Such 'feedback' was discouraging at times. But their reactions also challenged me to research and disentangle the troubling functions of criminal punishment to regulate immigration, and to expose the perceived and seemingly unproblematic nature of immigration offences.

Interviewing the immigration elite

I started the interviewing process in April 2010. I endeavoured to interview both practitioners and legal advocates and high- to mid-ranked officials at the UKBA in order to have accounts from both sides of the immigration/criminal law practice. Participants were invited through a letter which explained the research project and the purpose of the interview. Before starting the interviews, a brief explanation of the research was given. The questionnaire was tailored to each particular group of interviewees. Participants were selected through purposeful sampling (Maxwell 2005: 88) and snowballing (Bachman and Schutt 2007: 126).

The first stage consisted of identifying through purposeful sampling people who were qualified to provide information about immigration reforms and enforcement. I selected the first sample of interviewees from secondary data (such as parliamentary debates, immigration websites, newspapers, scholarly articles). I singled out from these sources those actors who had been closely involved in the debates about immigration and, particularly, immigration enforcement in recent years. Some of the participants were also suggested by my doctoral supervisor. For example, I contacted a criminal law barrister specializing in immigration crimes who presented expert evidence to the Parliament's Standing Committee on the UK Borders Bill 2007. I also ranked MPs according to their interventions during parliamentary debates on immigration and asylum bills. The more they participated, the higher their rank. From this list, I selected a number of MPs from the mainstream parties (Conservative, Labour and Liberal Democrat). While I invited seven MPs and followed up my request by email and post, only one of them replied to my request and agreed to be interviewed.[1] The resulting sample was formed of criminal law and immigration practitioners and an MP. Most of the interviewees selected for the first round were practitioners (barristers and solicitors) and members of refugee and immigration organizations.

The second stage consisted of speaking to those people suggested by my initial interviewees from the first round of interviews. This technique of 'chain referral' or 'snowballing' not only facilitated the identification of key actors in a field where there are few people with knowledge or experience of immigration offences. It was also useful because it provided a degree of trust necessary to initiate contact, particularly important for accessing 'elite subjects' (Atkinson and Flint 2001; Harvey 2010). However, the value of these interviews was limited, as those referred were likely to share the views of the 'referee' and have similar professional and ideological backgrounds. Most of the people who were contacted in the second and third round of interviews were academics and practitioners generally critical of the government's approach to immigration. The homogeneity of the initial sample was a result of the method used to select participants – snowballing. People tend to suggest colleagues or people who are like-minded and with similar professional backgrounds. This is one of the weaknesses of snowballing: 'Because elements are not randomly drawn, but are dependent on the subjective choices of the respondents first accessed, most snowball samples are biased and do not therefore allow researchers to make claims to generality from a particular sample' (Atkinson and Flint 2001: 2).

Given this selection bias and in order to make the sample of informants more diverse, participants from the immigration agency (UKBA) were sought. I was particularly interested in speaking to people from the UKBA at different ranks and with different responsibilities (enforcement, policy design, etc.) in order to have a variety of experiences and views. I initiated the contact with UKBA staff through a number of methods. For example, my supervisor suggested a number of officials and put me in contact with them. I also got in touch with other officials directly, using the agency's 'organigram'. I then initiated a chain referral within the agency as well. The UKBA officials interviewed for this study ranged from junior staff (in the Criminality Policy Team and Immigration Policy) to senior members of the force with management positions in the Policy and Strategy Group, the Crime Directorate and the Criminality and Detention Group; there was also an official in an operational position (the head of a Local Immigration Team [LIT]). I also sought to interview caseworkers in charge of making decisions on immigration offenders. The head of the LIT passed on this request, but it was refused. He explained to me that caseworkers are generally not enthusiastic about talking to 'outsiders' because immigration is 'a very sensitive area', and there is concern that information will be made public and trigger a scandal (Respondent 18, 10/06/2010).

In fact, contacting people inside the immigration force was considerably more difficult than getting in touch with practitioners and academics. The access to officials in government bodies is in general more restrictive than to people with non-governmental affiliations. This is particularly so in the case of the police and similar law enforcement entities, such as the UKBA (Loftus 2009: 201). In gaining access to government officials, it was necessary to negotiate with gatekeepers (i.e. personal assistants, administrators, etc.). Even if they did not require any special procedure and an invitation with a brief description of the project sufficed, it was necessary to follow up the request closely. Reaching people inside the UKBA was also a long process because of the existence of many intermediaries who manage the contact with the official. For example, I sent my first request for an interview to the Director of Immigration Policy in April 2010. I followed this request up insistently and had various negative responses. Three months later I was finally put in contact with an official responsible for Policy and Strategy, who was not the person to whom I originally wrote. Fortunately, he was very cooperative, open and frank in his responses, and kindly helped me to contact other high-ranking personnel. Without his help, I would have been unlikely to reach the managerial levels. These difficulties in access that I encountered might explain the scant research done so far on the immigration force.

Once access is granted, researchers need to gain the trust of interviewees. Often people working in these enforcement agencies are suspicious and wary about research work, and how the outcomes will be used. They are also fearful of public exposure. The fact that I was a foreigner researching immigration policies might have been an additional reason for distrust. A member of the UKBA checked with me whether the data collected would be used only for my research and not 'for the media or anything like that' before allowing me to record the interview (Respondent 5, 16/09/2010). Another official requested my ID and took some information from my driving licence before starting the interview. He did not allow me to record it and also asked me if I was from the press: 'If you are, I'll have to arrest you.' (He did not laugh and neither did I) (Respondent 20, 28/04/2011). During the interview, he also implied that he knew I was from Argentina, which showed that he had done some background research on me before accepting my request.

In total, I interviewed 20 people: UKBA officials (six); practitioners (solicitors and barristers and members of asylum and immigration organizations) (ten); academics (two); an MP; and a legal adviser at the CPS. Additionally, I had some informal conversations with criminal lawyers when attending court hearings – i.e. prosecutors and solicitors. Except for two interviewees, everyone allowed me to record the interviews digitally. All interviews were conducted face-to-face, except for one that was done by telephone. Thereafter, I transcribed and coded them manually according to themes.

In order to gain access to and support from participants, they were promised confidentiality and anonymity. Because of the highly politicized and controversial nature of immigration in recent years, many of my interviewees asked me for confidentiality. Even though many of them are well-known advocates, academics or public officials whose names are in the public domain, without an assurance of confidentiality and that their names would remain anonymized, their participation would have been hindered. For example, the Head of Law of a charity working with asylum seekers asked me not to reveal his name to avoid any adverse impact on his work as an advocate before the UKBA. So interview notes and transcriptions were anonymized and research data were edited in order to remove all identifying information and thus ensure confidentiality. This is the reason why, when the data were incorporated into the book, some attributes of the interviewees – such as their professional background and institutional position – are mentioned, but not their names (Israel 2004: 719; Noaks and Wincup 2004: 48). Instead, when directly quoting them, I name them as Respondent 1, 2, 3 and so on, for internal identification, and provide the date of the interview.

The process of data collection was simultaneous to its analysis. In fact, conducting interviews with key actors allowed me not only to have a better knowledge about the subject, but also helped me to narrow down my research, find themes and structure my work (Noaks and Wincup 2004: 129). Interviews with senior criminal and immigration practitioners also allowed me to understand the origin and practice of immigration crimes in the past because they retain rich 'institutional memory' that cannot be captured through other methods (Tansey 2007).

Meeting 'real' immigration offenders

Until I attended hearings at criminal courts, I had only second-hand knowledge about how these offences are enforced and against whom. So I had very limited knowledge about whether and where I would find these cases. Thus, before starting the fieldwork, it was necessary to identify criminal courts dealing with immigration-related cases. I consulted the Oxford and Reading magistrates' courts; however, court staff did not seem to understand which cases I was after, and in one of them, the administrator told me that 'they don't have a lot of cases of document fraud'. Finally, I chose Uxbridge Magistrates' Court and Isleworth Crown Court because they have jurisdiction over Heathrow airport and thus were likely to deal with cases of immigration offences. The limited geographic scope of the review is a shortcoming of my research. The jurisdiction of the selected courts over a major port of entry certainly influenced the type of immigration-related cases that form part of the sample and makes claims of generalization questionable. However, because the number of cases involving immigration offences is so small nationally, a random selection of courts would have provided a much smaller sample of cases for analysis.

I attended Uxbridge Magistrates' Court during August and September 2010 for three to four days per week. I heard 15 cases on immigration-related offences in which 16 people were charged with these offences. The period of observation was relatively short because after two months I realized that few cases of interest were heard and the information disclosed in court was limited. So I subsequently decided to supplement the data obtained during the hearings with records in court files.

Ten of the cases which I heard at Uxbridge were sent to Isleworth Crown Court, either because the jurisdiction of the magistrates was insufficient or because the defendants chose to be judged by the crown court. I followed these cases through to the crown court as well. Six of the defendants were charged with possession of a false identity document with intent; five were charged with entering the country without a passport; two defendants with facilitation; two with assaulting an employee in a removal centre; and one with deception. Ten of the defendants pleaded guilty to these charges. While the IDCA 2006 is not an immigration act, I decided to consider cases of possession of false documents for my study, given their characteristics: the defendants were foreigners trying either to enter or leave Britain without proper documents. In fact, the offence of possession of a forged passport is frequently used in practice against undocumented migrants. Even though statistics for this offence do not show the nationality of the defendants, foreigners serving prison sentences are generally over-represented in the category of fraud and forgery offences (Hammond 2007: 821).[2]

In my fieldwork notes, I captured the details of each case I observed (such as the name of the defendant, criminal charges, and a brief description of the prosecution case and the response by the defence lawyer). I also wrote down my impressions and perceptions about the interactions between the parties, the interventions by the judges and magistrates, and the role of the defendant during the hearings. On some occasions, I had some difficulties in understanding oral interactions between the parties because they did not speak loud enough, they spoke very quickly or they used technical language with which I was not familiar. The focus of my observation was on the case overall and I did not have a set of specific questions to answer. Therefore, the aim of the observation was broad: to develop themes that might arise from it and to try to make sense of the criminal process in these cases.

As fieldwork sites, courts have the advantage of being open to the public and so it is easy to get access (Baldwin 2007: 237). I arrived in court without prior notice and did not have any difficulties in getting access to courtrooms. Attending hearings provided rich data about how these cases are dealt with by the courts, the way in which the different actors behave and interact, and the dynamics of the criminal process. Pieces of information – such as verbal and corporal expressions – that are not recorded in the court files may be captured during the hearings.

While hearings are public, in practice they usually proceed without members of the public. Family members of the defendant are sometimes present, but they leave when the hearing is over. So there is a huge variation in the people who sit in the public gallery each day. This is the reason why my presence throughout the day was noticed by court personnel, and by some practitioners, judges and magistrates. In the magistrates' court, I sat in only one room all the time as this was the court which decides cases that arrive daily to Uxbridge. While in the magistrates' court, different courtrooms deal with different types of case (juvenile cases, daily arrivals, trials, etc.). There is no such division of work at Isleworth Crown Court, where there are 13 courtrooms and cases are randomly distributed. The magistrates' court is a more informal environment than that of the crown court. It is smaller too. There is less variation of ushers, defence lawyers and prosecutors attending the court compared to the crown court where the parties and the staff fluctuate much more.

Because I sat every day in the same court at Uxbridge, the usher and lawyers were used to seeing me there and at some points asked me what I was doing. One of the magistrates asked the usher: 'Who is that lady at the back?', to which the usher replied: 'She's here to look at mainly passport cases, as the ones we saw this morning.' Another magistrate called me after a hearing. He asked me what I was doing in the court and talked to me about his experience as a non-stipendiary magistrate. Such questions were less common in the crown court. On one occasion, while I was sitting and taking notes in one of the courtrooms at Isleworth, the usher asked me who I was, what I was writing, and if I had any interest in the case. She also suggested that I announce myself to the usher before entering the courtroom as 'many judges want to know what people are writing about'. Even though my presence was noticed by court participants, the probability that it had an effect on how they behaved and conducted their roles during proceedings is fairly low because they follow standardized rituals which are relatively impermeable to 'external' factors.

Because of listing practices, there is no way to know in advance whether and when cases on immigration offences would be heard by the court on a particular day, as the public lists only provide limited information of the cases. They contain the name of the accused, the intervening authority, and a rough time at which the hearing will take place (morning or afternoon). The lists of cases in the crown court also contain the purpose of the hearing: trial, plea and case management, committal for sentence, etc. However, they do not provide information on the criminal charge. Also, these are daily public lists which are published by the court on the same day of the hearing. They are done the afternoon before the hearing. Some cases are taken off the list by the court without being publicly announced; other cases which are heard by the court are not on the list because the defendant was caught after the list was made.

This uncertainty was frustrating because in most of the days I attended the courts, none of these cases were heard. In fact, most of the cases I ended up watching were not related to my research. However, it forced me to sit in the court and look at the everyday work, the routines and the types of cases generally reaching the criminal justice system. Most of the matters before the criminal courts – particularly the magistrates' court – are motoring offences, breaches to bail conditions, theft, assault, possession of drugs and, in smaller numbers, immigration crimes. Hearings are brief, defence arguments are about 'mercy' rather than complex elucidations about factual or legal aspects of the cases, and generally, matters are solved the same day through plea bargains. These features were more evident in immigration-related cases as hearings were particularly short and dull.

Those immigration-offence cases I observed were largely dealt with in a few minutes without much examination of the circumstances and motives of the defendant. Occasionally, though, there were instances when the defence lawyer provided details of the circumstances in which the defendant left the country of origin and his or her journey to the UK which usually entailed persecution and abuses. On one occasion, the family member of a defendant in another non-immigration case, after hearing that the defendants received death threats by the Taliban, pronounced a loud 'Oh God!' Even so, it did not seem that the courts were in some sort of unease or a difficult position when dealing with these cases. By and large, court staff consider them as straightforward, easy cases. When I told one of the ushers I was interested in looking at this type of case, he explained that 'they are straightforward: cases of no-document are decided here and those involving false documents are sent to the crown court'.

One limitation of attending court hearings for data collection purposes is that some cases may be decided outside the courtroom without any public announcement – for example, a committal to the crown court – so I needed to rely on other sources, such as the court usher, clerk and administrators, to find out the outcome of a particular case. Moreover, only those issues discussed in open court can be accessed. A number of important aspects of a case are neither disclosed nor debated during the public hearing – such as the identity and background of the defendant or written statements by the parties and police and immigration files – and so are kept away from the researcher. This aspect of the court routines poses an important challenge to court-based research: '[r]esearchers are seriously handicapped when they are excluded from the significant action, and court procedures can be as baffling to them as to anyone else as a result' (Baldwin 2007: 245). A further weakness is that the attendance at court hearings provides only a snapshot of the cases that are actually dealt with by the designated courts and so observations can hardly be generalized (Payne and Williams 2005).

Looking inside the files: what do court cases reveal and obscure?

In order to tackle these difficulties, at a later stage, I requested access to review files on immigration-related cases at the designated courts. In order to gain access to case-files at Uxbridge Magistrates' Court and Isleworth Crown Court, it was necessary to submit an application to the Ministry of Justice through Data Collections and Research Requests to Her Majesty's Courts Service (HMCS) Data Access Panel and Performance Board. These requests were granted in November 2010 and May 2011, respectively. The search on court files provided quantitative and qualitative data about the number and types of cases heard in those courts during a longer time-period, and the decisions made in such cases. I conducted this search over files initiated during the period from 1 January 2008 to 31 December 2009 at both courts. In England and Wales, criminal court files have been computerized since January 2001 in an electronic database held by the Office for Criminal Justice Reform, and so it was relatively easy to identify cases of interest. I requested access to files in which the defendants were charged with offences under immigration acts and were subject to immigration control (that is, persons who do not have right of abode in the UK).[3] I requested full files, but was particularly interested in certain parts of them, such as statements of the case, written records of public examinations, reports by the official receiver and judgments. Due to the small number of cases that the search threw up, I decided to consider them all rather than to draw a sample out of them. Files were reviewed manually and data were stored in Excel files. The data recorded comprised: the offence; the ethnic background and gender of the defendant; whether she or he had residence in the UK and needed an interpreter; a brief description of the facts; whether the defence raised defences; the defendant's plea, the bail decision and the final judgment.

At the magistrates' court, I reviewed 229 cases in which 232 defendants were charged with immigration offences. When a single person was accused of more than one offence, I considered the principal offence. People were charged with the following offences:

- entering without a passport (159 defendants);
- assisting unlawful immigration (40);
- failing to comply with [a] requirement of the Secretary of State (20);
- deception (8);
- helping an asylum seeker to enter the country (3); and
- entering the UK without a leave (2).

Sixty-one defendants in these cases were committed to Isleworth Crown Court, while 171 defendants were dealt with in the magistrates' court. Of the latter, 163 of them (95 per cent) pleaded guilty to those charges. In the rest of the cases, the defendant pleaded not guilty in three; in three others, the prosecution was withdrawn or discontinued; and in two other cases, there was no information. The rate of guilty pleas was particularly high among those who were charged with entering without a passport: 149 defendants out of 154 pleaded guilty at the magistrates' court (97 per cent).

At Isleworth Crown Court, I reviewed 99 court files with 106 people charged with various immigration offences. Sixteen of them were committed for sentence from Uxbridge Magistrates' Court, while 90 defendants were sent for trial. Defendants were accused of the following offences:

- assisting unlawful immigration (58 defendants);
- entering without a passport (17);
- failing to comply with [a] requirement of the Secretary of State (14);
- deception (13); and
- helping an asylum seeker to enter the country (4).

Forty-eight defendants (53.3 per cent) of the 90 whose cases were sent to trial pleaded guilty to the charges. Of those who pleaded not guilty, 56 per cent of them were found not guilty, while 44 per cent were found guilty.

According to recent policy papers (Home Office 2007b, 2008b, 2010d), criminal law should be used against serious immigration crimes – such as smuggling, trafficking or illegal employment. However, none of the cases reviewed involved organized immigration crimes. In my sample, none of the defendants were charged with offences like trafficking in human beings or illegal employment. In a large proportion of immigration-offences cases, undocumented immigrants were prosecuted and punished, particularly those arriving to the country without a passport. In the vast majority of cases of assisting unlawful immigration, only one person was accused, and in some of them, the defendant was charged with assisting a family member.

The permission to access court files was subject to a number of conditions. One of them was the prohibition to reveal any personal information about the parties involved. The reference numbers of the files are considered personal data and as such are covered by data protection rules. Because of this limitation, I did not include this information when quoting the files reviewed. Instead, when I refer to them throughout the book, I provide the following information: the name of the court, whether the reference relates to a court file or a public hearing,[4] and a number. This number is for internal identification purposes, but does not correspond to the real reference number given by the court.[5]

The search of the court files was not as ethnographically rich as the hearing stage because it was very solitary work without much contact with the court environment. In both courts, I was given a room where I spent the whole day examining files. However, from my brief contacts with court staff – particularly administrative personnel working in the 'backyard' of the courts – I perceived the perplexity that my research topic caused. One of the administrative staff at Isleworth Crown Court directly asked me why I was doing this research and what was interesting about immigration offences.

The quantification of criminalization: undeserving numbers and undeserving words

One of the most important obstacles I encountered throughout this project concerned the difficulty of accurately quantifying the criminalization phenomenon. While successive governments have been enthusiastic in including criminal law provisions in immigration legislation, apparently they were less interested in learning whether and how such provisions were enforced, evidenced by the scarce statistical data on these offences. Because of this, it has been difficult to trace the 'enforcement side' of the history of immigration crimes. These are numbers that evidently were undeserving of collection, crimes unworthy to be counted.[6] In fact, while immigration controls statistics have been systematically compiled since the early 1960s, until 1984, Home Office data on people proceeded against for these offences were not included in the annual volume on the 'Control of Immigration

Statistics'. So I relied on the personal experiences of practitioners doing immigration law prior to the 1980s to learn what the enforcement of these offences looked like at that time.

While immigration statistics now include a table on people proceeded against and convicted for offences in immigration acts both at magistrates' and crown courts, because of counting practices, there have been some inconsistencies and under-recording. For example, in the sample of court files reviewed, I counted 20 cases of non-cooperation with removal proceedings in the magistrates' court and 14 such cases in the crown court. In total, 34 defendants were proceeded against for this offence between 2008 and 2009 in only two courts of justice. National statistics for 2008 and 2009 throw up an even smaller rate of prosecutions: in 2008, there were 46 defendants proceeded against for this offence; and in 2009, only 15. These numbers make one suspicious about the reliability of statistics on immigration crimes. Unfortunately, though, they are the only source of quantitative data on the enforcement of these offences. In a recent review of immigration statistics, the government proposed the cessation of a number of data sets including those related to people proceeded against and convicted for offences under immigration acts due to 'resource constraints'. Following the response to that consultation, it was decided to retain information on court proceedings as part of the immigration statistics published by the Home Office (Home Office 2010a: 3).

Another problem is that while many immigrants are proceeded against for document fraud under non-immigration legislation (particularly the IDCA 2006), statistics about prosecutions and convictions are not disaggregated by the nationality of the defendant. Consequently it is not possible to quantify the criminalization of immigration through non-immigration, 'mainstream' criminal laws. There are also no statistics about the number of foreign national prisoners (FNPs) who have been convicted for immigration-related offences, nor for those who have been victims of trafficking or are asylum seekers.

The lack of quantitative data and the weakness of the available data represent an important obstacle to understanding the dimension and extent of the criminalization phenomenon. In the absence of these data, I have been forced to rely on testimonies of practitioners and qualitative data about particular cases. The mere absence of these data, though, is a 'rich' piece of information. Interpreted together with other evidence, it reinforces the view put forward in this book that immigration offences historically have been considered as a non-issue, not deserving of scrutiny or debate. The problems raised in this work, however, cast doubts over such indifference and apathy on the subject.

Notes

1 Introduction

1 In a speech on immigration in April 2011, British Prime Minister David Cameron referred to the need to limit the immigration flows to Britain while opening up 'a new route for people of exceptional talent – like scientists, academics and artists' and introducing a 'new entrepreneur visa, to roll out the red carpet for anyone who has a great business idea and serious investment'. Transcription of the speech is available at: http://www.guardian.co.uk/politics/2011/apr/14/david-cameron-immigration-speech-full-text (accessed 13 May 2011).

2 The perils of forced migration involve people being left to criminal gangs, subject to exploitation and humiliation, forced to trade with their own bodies and being abused, raped and tortured. In many cases, this journey leads to family break-downs and children being left behind and abandoned (see e.g. Khosravi 2010; also De Genova 2002; Calavita 2005).

3 For a critique of the 'criminologies of catastrophe' and the 'dystopias' of grand criminological theories, see O'Malley (2000); Zedner (2002).

4 Criminalization literature is mainly produced in criminology and sociology. Scholars in disciplines such as political science, international relations and security studies have identified a similar process of 'securitization' of immigration (see e.g. Huysmans 1995, 2000, 2006; Ibrahim 2005; Muller 2004; D'Appollonia and Reich 2008; also Boswell 2007). Jef Huysmans (2006: 80) explains that immigration has been identified in public discourse as a 'societal security threat'; that is, a threat to the cultural identity of European societies.

5 Perhaps the clearest attempt to link national security to immigration and border controls was the provision in the Anti-Terrorism, Crime and Security Act 2001 which, as enacted, authorized the detention of a person deemed to be a suspected international terrorist over whom an order of removal or deportation might be taken but could not be executed either temporarily or indefinitely. The British Parliament subsequently had to modify this provision on indeterminate detention – which was replaced by control orders – following a judgment by the European Court of Human Rights (ECHR, *A and others v the United Kingdom*, judgment of 19 February 2009, Application 3455/05).

6 See e.g. Guild and Minderhoud (2006); Ruhs and Anderson (2010); Anderson (2010a, 2012).

2 Tracing the history of immigration controls in Britain (from the late 1700s to the mid-1990s)

1 Intervention by Major Evans Gordon, Hansard, HC Deb 2/05/1905, col. 717.
2 Public Act 33, George III, c. 4 1793 (AA 1793).

3 The concept of 'alien' was introduced in eighteenth-century legislation and it is still very much in use today. It has an enormous symbolic power. It is used in the law and in public discourse as a synonym of foreigner, but has a pejorative meaning often coupled with 'undesirable', 'criminal', or 'terrorist'. In a sense, not all foreigners are aliens. This 'chilling extraterrestrial category' (Cohen 1994: 34) has historically served the purpose of demarcating the frontiers of 'us' and 'them', insiders and outsiders. Further, as a manifestation of the state's sovereign authority, it constitutes a linguistic device to justify the exercise of discretionary executive powers on a certain group and their exclusion from a series of rights guaranteed to nationals.

4 See S. XII, AA 1793. 'Transportation for life' – a form of banishment – was widely used as a criminal sanction against foreigners and citizens alike, particularly during the eighteenth century (Markowitz 2008: 320).

5 S. XI, AA 1793.

6 S. XXXVIII, AA 1793.

7 Such as the Aliens Act 1814 (Public Act 55, George III, c. 54 1814–1815); the Aliens Act 1826 (Public Act 7, George IV, c. 54 1826); and the Aliens Act 1848 (Public Act 11 & 12, Victoria I, c. 20 1848).

8 S. VII, AA 1814.

9 S. II, AA 1826.

10 S. II, AA 1826.

11 Ss VI, VII, VIII and IX, AA 1826; S. XIX, AA 1814.

12 S. XIII, AA 1826, and Ss XVII and XXIX, AA 1814, respectively.

13 Ss II, III and V, AA 1814.

14 S. XVII, AA 1814.

15 S. XX, AA 1848.

16 Statistical data on foreigners convicted for offences under immigration acts is not available for this period (personal correspondence with Mark Pearsall, The National Archives).

17 See Hansard, HC Deb 2/05/1905, col. 708.

18 S. 1(3), AA 1905. There were further two grounds for expulsion, following a recommendation of a court: first, conviction for a crime punished with imprisonment; and second, for vagrancy (S. 4(1)).

19 Respectively, Ss 1(5), 3(2) and 7(4), AA 1905.

20 S. 7(1), AA 1905.

21 Respectively, Ss 1(5), 4(3), 5(2) and 7(4), AA 1905.

22 Ss 4(2) and 7(1), AA 1905.

23 See Hansard, HC Deb 5/08/1914.

24 Between 1914 and 1919, 28,744 foreigners were repatriated, of whom 23,571 were Germans (Holmes 1988: 96).

25 S. 1(1), ARA 1914.

26 Intervention by Reginald Paget in Hansard, HC Deb 26/11/1953, col. 531.

27 Ss 1(3) (g) and 18(1) (b), Aliens Order 1920. See the decision on *Larsonneur* (1934) 24 Cr. App. R. 74 in which the Court of Appeal held that the circumstances in which the defendant arrived in the UK (she was escorted from Ireland to the UK by the Irish police and handed over to the British police) 'are perfectly immaterial, so far as this appeal is concerned' and dismissed the appeal against conviction for the offence of being found unlawfully in the UK [at 78]. This decision has been widely criticized for upholding situational liability, that is liability for a state of affairs – rather than an act or omission – over which the defendant has no control. See for example, Sim (1962).

28 See *The King v Inspector of Leman Street Police Station, Ex parte Venicoff. The King v Secretary of State for Home Affairs, Ex parte Same* [1920] 3 KB 72 (on the validity of a deportation order on the grounds of being 'conducive to the public good'; the court upheld the discretionary power of the Secretary of State to issue a deportation order);

also *The King v Secretary of State for Home Affairs. Ex parte Duke of Chateau Thierry* [1917] 1 KB 922 (quoted in Griffith 1960: 163).

29 During debates on the 1914 Bill, the then Home Secretary Reginald McKenna promised that '[t]his measure applies only to a state of war . . . The Order will cease to have effect as soon as the war ceased or a state of national danger or grave emergency no longer exists' (Hansard, HC Deb 5/08/1914, col. 1990).

30 While Irish people were not subject to immigration controls in the early twentieth century, the Irish population in Britain has been historically perceived as 'others'. They have been considered an ethnic minority and stereotyped as dirty, drunk, lazy and violent. The 'Irish foreignness' was built upon their religion, and their distinct culture and ethnic background (Ghaill 2000: 138). While until 1962, they were not liable to deportation, since the 1920s when Ireland gained independence from Britain, many Irish were 'repatriated' to Ireland (Hickman 1998: 292).

31 Intervention by Peter Mahon MP in Hansard, HC Deb 27/02/1968, col. 1314.

32 The concept of 'subject' is related to the relationship between the monarch and his or her subjects: the King or Queen grants rights and privileges to his or her subjects. All subjects are equal in the bond that links them to the monarch (Dummett and Nicol 1990: 22).

33 Quoted by Andrew Turner MP in Hansard, HC Deb 19/03/2003, col. 270WH.

34 While non-white immigrants arrived before then, they did so in smaller numbers. For example, by the late eighteenth century, there were only 20,000 black people in London (Dummett and Nicol 1990: 79; see also Walvin 1973; Shyllon 1977).

35 However, John Solomos argues that the government engaged in a 'concerted campaign' to stop non-white immigration, rather than merely responding to public or economic pressure (Solomos 1989).

36 Quoted by Andrew Turner MP in Hansard, HC Deb 19/03/2003, col. 270WH.

37 While Labour's Clement Attlee governed from 1945 to 1951, Conservative administrations dominated the post-war period: Winston Churchill (1951–1955); Anthony Eden (1955–1957); Harold Macmillan (1957–1963); and Alec Douglas-Home (1963–1964).

38 He said:

> [O]ne of the problems of such groups who form a new community in a town is that, if they are easily identifiable, they come constantly to the notice of the community . . . People from European or near-European stock are not so easily identifiable . . . Wherever they live, the local inhabitants can identify them. This tends to become impressed on people's minds, who then say that there are a number of strangers in their midst . . . They fear that they will be overwhelmed by them. Wrongly or rightly, these views are held and we must be aware of them.
>
> (Hansard, HC Deb 27/02/1968, col. 1318)

39 The system of vouchers for Commonwealth citizens was different from the work permit system which applied to aliens. Aliens were required to obtain a work permit which was subject to a strict pre-admission labour market test, while Commonwealth citizens could access the labour market by obtaining a voucher in any of the following three categories: a pre-arranged job, special skills, or where there were specific domestic needs for unskilled workers. These vouchers were not subject to labour market conditions (Salt and Kitching 1990). However, they were severely reduced after 1964 and eliminated in 1973, when the two systems merged, so both aliens and Commonwealth citizens were equally required to obtain a work permit.

40 S. 4, CIA 1962.

41 Hansard, HC Deb 16/11/1961, col. 698.

42 Hansard, HC Deb 7/02/1962, col. 435.

43 See Hansard, HC Deb 7/02/1962, col. 436.

44 See Hansard, HL Deb 20/03/1962, col. 476.
45 In fact, the first and second Race Relations Acts which sanctioned anti-discriminatory measures were passed under Wilson's administration in 1965 and 1968, respectively, at the time when the debate on whether to maintain and tighten immigration controls was taking place.
46 One of the main critiques of the CIA 1962 was its ineffectiveness. Even if it helped to reduce 'primary immigration', it did not deal with the dependents of those Commonwealth citizens already residing in Britain as it did not set limits on their entry.
47 In a case against the UK, the European Commission on Human Rights found that the CIA 1968 had racial motives because it singled out a group for differential treatment on racial grounds and thus violated article 3 of the European Convention on Human Rights (see European Comm HR, *East African Asians v The United Kingdom* (3 EHRR 76) 15 December 1973, known as 'the *East African Asians* case'). For a comment on this case, see Lester (2002).
48 Between 1965 and 1967, the number of people exercising the right to settle in Britain jumped from 6,150 to 13,600. In the first two months of 1968, the number of entries was calculated at 12,800 (Lester 2002: 54). In 1972, President Idi Amin expelled 40,000 Ugandan Asians, and Britain accepted 28,000 of them, as an attempt to loosen up the already damaged relations with the Commonwealth and in response to domestic pressures (Gupta 1974).
49 Home Secretary Callaghan paraphrasing former Home Secretary Butler (Hansard, HC Deb 27/02/1968, col. 1249).
50 Interventions by Charles Mapp and John Farr, Hansard, HC Deb 28/02/1968, cols 1655–1656. See S. 4, CIA 1968.
51 Hansard, HC Deb 27/02/1968, col. 1245.
52 The only action available against immigration decisions was by way of *certiorari*, *mandamus* or a *declaration* to question the 'unreasonable' exercise of discretion by an immigration officer (Macdonald 1969: 237).
53 A term already used by Republican candidate Richard Nixon in his presidential campaign (Dallek 2008).
54 S. 2(1) (a) to (d), IA 1971.
55 It established the principle of *ius sanguinis* (citizenship is transmitted through blood – parenthood) as the basis to grant citizenship. The act also created two residual categories: British Dependent Territories Citizenship and British Overseas Citizenship. People with such citizenships did not have the right anymore to enter and settle in the UK.
56 S. 3(5), IA 1971.
57 S. 15(3), IA 1971.
58 S. 24(1), IA 1971. Moreover, 'illegal entry' was interpreted extensively by the courts later on, encompassing lying to obtain leave to enter and entering by deception of a third party. The courts also allowed the retrospective application of the IA 1971, thus permitting the criminalization of those who entered the country illegally before the act was in force (Couper 1984; Gordon 1985).
59 S. 25(1) and 25(2), IA 1971.
60 S. 26(1), IA 1971. This provision was interpreted by the courts as requiring from the accused granted entry clearance 'a positive duty of candour on all material facts which denote a change of circumstances since the issue of the entry clearance'. Non-disclosure of changes – such as getting married – was considered a breach of that positive duty and thus a criminal offence (*Zamir v Secretary of State for the Home Department* [1980] AC 930).
61 S. 27(a), (b) and (c), IA 1971.
62 See intervention by Lord Windlesham in Hansard, HL Deb 02/08/1971, col. 975.
63 Two central intelligence units were established within the Home Office: the Drugs Intelligence Unit and the Illegal Immigration Intelligence Unit (IIIU). Drugs and people

trafficking were considered to be related because of their transnational nature and the need for greater enforcement coordination to deal with them. The IIIU was first created by a Home Office press release in October 1972 (see below in chapter).

64 Hansard, HC Deb 31/01/1973, col. 1532.
65 Respondents 6, 8 and 11, interviews held on 20/04, 17/5 and 29/04/2010, respectively.
66 See Hansard, HC Deb 4/08/1976, col. 786W.
67 See Hansard, HC Deb 08/03/1971.
68 Likewise, housing authorities were reluctant to police immigrants when granting accommodation to them before legislation enacted in the 1990s made these controls compulsory (Morris 1998: 966).
69 Intervention by Michael Morris MP, Hansard, HC Deb 16/03/1987, col. 746.
70 The Conservative Party's 1979 election manifesto contained a number of measures to restrict immigration.
71 For example, in 1986, the Minister of State at the Home Office, David Waddington, issued four sets of guidelines in order to cut down the number of representations by MPs on behalf of members of their constituencies on immigration matters (Cohen 1994: 64).
72 S. 24(1A), IA 1971. This provision was enacted in response to the interpretation made by the courts of the offences of overstaying and illegal entry. They were considered as non-continuing ones and so the three-year prosecution bar started to count on the day the person illegally entered or overstayed his/her visa (*Grant v Borg* [1982] 2 All ER 257).
73 S. 5, IA 1988.
74 See Home Office (1984: Table 21); Home Office (1985: Table 21).
75 It could be argued though that many immigrants arriving before then from former colonies were *de facto* refugees – particularly Asians from East Africa – even though their 'shady' status as British citizens would have impeded them from being recognized as such. See Porter (1979).
76 Visa requirements are now in place for citizens of over 100 nations worldwide.
77 E.g. Ss 1(5), 4(3) and 5(2), AA 1905.
78 See e.g. *R v Richter* (1906) *The Times*, 27 January 1906; and *Attorney-General v Sutcliffe* (1907) *The Times*, 20 July 1907 (quoted in Dummett and Nicol 1990: 161, fns 4 and 5).
79 S. 25(1), IA 1971.
80 Official Journal L 239 of 22/09/2000 ('Schengen Convention') (article 26). The provisions in the Schengen Convention were later supplemented by Council Directive 2001/51/EC of 28 June 2001 supplementing the provisions of Article 26 of the Convention implementing the Schengen Agreement of 14 June 1985, Official Journal L 187 of 10/7/2001 ('Carrier Liability Directive').
81 The problems arising from establishing such sanctions against airlines with the UK's obligations under Article 31 of the Refugee Convention are clearly exposed in *R v Uxbridge Magistrates' Court, Ex parte Adimi; R v Crown Prosecution Service, Ex parte Sorani; R v Secretary of State for the Home Department, Ex parte Kaziu* [1999] INLR 490 ('Adimi'), and *R v Asfaw (United Nations High Commissioner for Refugees intervening)* [2008] UKHL 31 ('Asfaw'). See Chapter 3.
82 Intervention by Home Secretary Douglas Hurd in Hansard, HC Deb 16/03/1987, col. 734.
83 In 1989, Britain received around 11,640 applications; whereas for 1990 and 1991, the figures jumped to 26,205 and 44,840, respectively. With the adoption of the AIAA 1993, these rates decreased as refusal rates increased from 14 per cent in 1992 to 74 per cent in 1994 (Bloch 2000: 30, 35).
84 A third piece of legislation was introduced in 1997: The Special Immigration Appeals Commission Act 1997 (SIACA 1997). This act created the Special Immigration Appeals Commission (SIAC) and regulates its operation. The SIAC examines appeals

against decisions to deport someone on national security grounds and for other public interest reasons, and against decisions to stop someone becoming a British citizen. The SIACA 1997 was modified by the Anti-Terrorism, Crime and Security Act 2001.

85 Schedule 1, paragraph 5, AIAA 1993.

86 S. 24(1a)(a), IA 1971.

87 In 1997, only one prosecution – though unsuccessful – was brought under this provision in magistrates' and crown courts. In subsequent years, prosecution and conviction rates increased, but at a slow pace: in 1998, seven prosecutions and one conviction; in 1999, 19 prosecutions and 11 convictions; and in 2000, four prosecutions and no conviction (Home Office 2001: Table 7.5).

88 S. 25(1) (b) and (c), IA 1971.

89 See *R v Naillie; R v Kanesarajah* [1993] AC 674, HL [at 680].

90 This drop is in part due to legislative changes and the use of other offences to deal with 'humanitarian' or 'commercial' smugglers, analysed in more detail in Chapter 3.

91 See Hansard, HC Deb 08/07/1996, vol. 281 cc 31–2W, quoted in Dunstan (1998: 208).

92 For instance, legislative changes introduced in 1996 contributed to the reduction in the number of asylum applications to 14,320 applicants that year (Hansard, HC Deb 11/05/1999).

93 See S. 8(1), AIA 1996.

94 See S. 24(1) (b), IA 1971.

95 See Chapter 3.

96 See Cabinet Papers, 'Conclusions of a Meeting of the Cabinet held at 10 Downing Street, S.W.1, on Thursday, 13 May, 1971, at 10.30 a.m.' (HM Government 1971: 5–6). In this meeting, the Secretary of State for Employment affirmed that, because of the various 'incentives' to employ foreigners, businesses were less likely to hire nationals. He proposed to introduce a quota to fill unskilled seasonal vacancies in the hotel and catering industries to tackle the increasing domestic unemployment.

97 What some commentators have called 'Fortress Europe' (e.g. Albrecht 2002).

98 See Chapter 6.

99 Similar depictions can be found in recent media reports (e.g. Harper and Leapman 2007; Malkin 2007; Whitehead 2008).

100 In 1979, the JCWI proposed the decriminalization of immigration offences and the use of administrative powers to deal with immigration offenders. It was held that decriminalization would send a message that 'breaches to immigration law do not in any sense represent the serious threat to society which crime in the ordinary sense of the word does' (quoted in Couper 1984: 450).

3 The Labour years: contemporary contours of immigration policy and enforcement from 1997 to 2010

1 The BNP is a right-wing party formed as a splinter group from the National Front in 1982. Like the National Front, it advocates for a halt on further immigration and for the return of immigrants to their country of origin.

2 Particularly working classes and trade unions. The latter has been one of the most combative groups against immigration, concerned with the economic effect that immigration has on internal wages and its alleged distortion of fair competition. The racist exclusion from trade unions experienced by ethnic minorities during the post-war years, together with the reluctance of the unions to engage in more radical action to address the exploitation of non-white workers later on have contributed to a hostile relationship between unions and ethnic minority workers (Wrench 2000). However, others argue that this is not any longer true (see e.g. Avci and McDonald 2000).

3 Applications for asylum, excluding dependants, rose by 25,000 in 1999. There was an increase of 55 per cent and nearly 119 per cent in claims, compared to 1998 and 1997, respectively (Woodbridge *et al.* 2000: 2).

4   In 2002, immigration and asylum appeared as the second most important issue for the British public – after health care (Ipsos Mori 2002).
5   See Home Office 1998: Chapter 11.
6   The first centre to hold immigrants, opened in 1969 next to Heathrow airport, was Harmondsworth Immigration Removal Centre with a capacity to hold between 40 and 50 detainees at a time (Hansard, HC Deb 22/01/1969, col. 559). More than two decades later, the government reopened former juvenile prisons as detention centres: Haslar in 1989 and Campsfield in 1993, and it opened Tinsley House in 1996. After that, four more establishments were opened: Oakington in 2000, Yarl's Wood in 2001, Colnbrook in 2004 and Brook House in 2009. Additionally, three other centres were redesignated to accommodate immigrants (Lindholme, Dungavel and Dover). More recently, the UKBA opened Morton Hall, which was previously a women's prison. Nowadays there are 11 removal centres throughout the country under the authority of the UKBA. See http://www.ukba.homeoffice.gov.uk/managingborders/immigrationremovalcentres/ (accessed: 18 October 2011).
7   In fact, a famous motto of the Labour Party was 'tough on crime, tough on the causes of crime', a reference to the idea that combating social exclusion as a cause of crime is not contradictory to punishing offenders and defending society from them (Aliverti 2008).
8   See, for instance, intervention by Parliamentary Under-Secretary of State for the Home Department, Mike O'Brien, during the debates on the 1999 Bill in Hansard, HC Deb 22/02/1999, col. 122.
9   See examples in Home Office (1998); Home Office (2002); Home Office (2005c); Home Office (2006b); Home Office (2007a); Home Office (2008b); and Home Office (2010d).
10 For example, the government rejected proposals to introduce exemptions to carrier liability regimes in cases where the undocumented or clandestine entrant was a refugee (see Hansard, HC Deb 20/04/1999, col. 712; HL Deb 18/10/1999, col. 862).
11 In fact, one of the objectives of the Ministry of Justice's Public Service Agreement was to 'Reduce unfounded asylum claims as part of a wider strategy to tackle abuse of the immigration laws and promote controlled legal migration' (Ministry of Justice 2007: 2).
12 The department was criticized for its malfunctioning and inefficiency, apparent in the finding that 16,000 pieces of mail were unopened, the failure to computerize files due to problems with the contractor (Siemens), and delays in enforcement actions in as many as 67,000 cases. See e.g. Hansard, HC Deb 22/2/1999, col. 105; and HL Deb 2/11/1999, col. 773.
13 See Hansard, HC Deb 22/02/1999, col. 37.
14 Until 1999, the legislation that introduced the highest number of immigration crimes – 21 offences – was the IA 1971, followed by the CIA 1962 which added 14 offences to the statute book.
15 S. 24A(1), IA 1971.
16 S. 24(1) (aa), IA 1971.
17 Ss 105–108, IAA 1999.
18 Schedule 11, paragraphs 4 and 5; and Schedule 12, paragraphs 3, 4, 5 and 6, IAA 1999.
19 See Hansard, HC Deb 16/3/1999.
20 Ss 32 and 40, respectively, IAA 1999.
21 S. 25(1), IA 1971.
22 This provision was subsequently amended by the Asylum and Immigration (Treatment of Claimants, etc.) Act 2004 (AI(TC)A 2004) which made hiring an illegal worker a triable either way offence (S. 8(4), AIA 1996). The Accession (Immigration and Worker Authorisation) Regulation 2006 (11) introduced similar offences for workers from Romania and Bulgaria (Ss 12, 13 and 14).
23 For 2000, there were ten prosecutions and four convictions; for 2001, five and two; for 2002, two and one; for 2003, two and one; for 2004, 11 and eight; for 2005, 23 and 13;

and for 2006, ten and six (see Home Office 2005a: Table 6.5; Home Office 2008a: Table 6.7).

24 A similar pattern is observed in the United States where the numbers of prosecutions and convictions for knowingly hiring 'unauthorized aliens', under the Immigration Reform and Control Act 1986, has been historically low. Medina (1997) explains low enforcement rates as a function of the moral tension arising from the employment prohibition, given that private labour relations are at the core of the US economic system and constitutionally protected from state intervention (Medina 1997; see also Welch 2003: 329).

25 While in 2008, the UKBA imposed 1,164 civil penalties against employers, worth £11.2 million, in 2009, the number almost doubled: 2,210 fines were levied amounting to a total of £22.1 million (according to a Freedom of Information [FOI] request by Giant Precision). However, the Independent Chief Inspector of the UKBA, John Vine, recently launched a report in which he uncovered that in 2010 only just over £5 million in fines have been effectively recovered and at least 23 per cent of penalties have been reduced or cancelled following an objection (Vine 2010: 12).

26 Since the provisions in S. 21 (criminal offence) and S. 15 (civil penalty) of the IANA 2006 came into force on 29 February 2008, in 2008 only two successful prosecutions were recorded. From 2009 to 2011, five convictions per year were recorded (Home Office 2010b: Tables 3.11a and b; Home Office 2012: Table pr.01).

27 Some businesses, though, are more frequently penalized under this regime: for example, Asian or Chinese take-away restaurants or off-licence stores. Because they usually hire foreign workers and in many cases do not keep proper paperwork, they are regularly targeted (Webber 2009). See, for example, the names of businesses fined by UKBA in London and the South East on the agency's website at: http://www.ukba.homeoffice. gov.uk/sitecontent/documents/employersandsponsors/listemployerspenalties/civil-penalties-region/london-and-southeast.pdf?view=Binary (accessed: 15 January 2011).

28 These cases are criminalized under various provisions of the IA 1971 and the AI(TC)A 2004. Where there is document fraud involved, immigrants may also be prosecuted under other acts – such as the IDCA 2006.

29 See Hansard, HC Deb 1/03/2007, col. 82.

30 Hansard, HC Deb 20/04/1999.

31 Simon Brown LJ in *R v Uxbridge Magistrates' Court, Ex parte Adimi*; *R v Crown Prosecution Service, Ex parte Sorani*; *R v Secretary of State for the Home Department, Ex parte Kaziu* [1999] INLR 490 (henceforth 'Adimi') [at 523].

32 The 'Refugee Convention' was adopted on 28 July 1951 and entered into force on 22 April 1954. The UK ratified this convention on 11 March 1954.

33 That refugees come 'directly from a territory where their life or freedom was threatened', 'present themselves without delay to the authorities' and 'show good cause for their illegal entry or presence'.

34 See, respectively, the amendment proposed by Lord Bishop of Southwark, in Hansard, HL Deb 18/10/1999, col. 845, and the position of the applicants as summarized in 'Adimi' [at 530].

35 See the position of the government in 'Adimi' [at 534] and in the debate in the House of Lords (Hansard, HL Deb 18/10/1999, col. 856).

36 S. 31(1) (c), IAA 1999.

37 S. 31(2), IAA 1999.

38 For England, Wales and Northern Ireland, offences under (a) Part I, FCA 1981 (forgery and connected offences); (b) S. 24A, IA 1971 (deception); or (c) S. 26(1) (d), IA 1971 (falsification of documents) (S. 31(3), IAA 1999); and for Scotland, offences (a) of fraud, (b) of uttering a forged document, (c) under S. 24A, IA 1971 (deception), or (d) under S. 26(1) (d), IA 1971 (falsification of documents), and any attempt to commit any of those offences (S. 31(4), IAA 1999). The explanatory notes state that the Secretary of State may amend this list.

39 The House of Lords in the 'Asfaw' case, however, found such list to be only enumerative and extended the catalogue of offences in S. 31 to those 'attributable to the attempt of a refugee to leave the country in the continuing course of a flight from persecution even after a short stopover in transit' (*R v Asfaw (United Nations High Commissioner for Refugees intervening)* [2008] UKHL 31 [at 1087]).

40 This defence is equal to the common law defence of necessity, providing immunity for criminal offences that are considered reasonable responses to an imminent harm.

41 See APIs on section 31 of the Immigration and Asylum Act 1999 and Article 31 of the 1951 Refugee Convention: p. 5. The APIs were launched in 2006 (and modified in 2009) to assist caseworkers on asylum decisions. These instructions adopt a restrictive approach towards the content of article 31, stating that:

> The correct approach is that the protection afforded to refugees is found solely in section 31 of the Act and that there is no scope, in any case, for superimposing on the statutory protection the protection contained in Article 31 of the Convention.

For example, against the terms of the Refugee Convention and the 'Adimi' case, they establish that a stopover en route to the UK in a safe country precludes the application of section 31.

42 In many criminal cases examined for this study, the accused had claimed or was intending to claim asylum (see Chapter 5).

43 See APIs: p. 7 (bold in original). Similarly, the legal guidance for Crown Prosecutors in this regard states: 'the fact that a defendant's application for asylum remains undetermined should not of itself prevent or delay prosecution or conviction'. However, it advises prosecutors that:

> [W]here a suspect's refugee status remains to be determined by the Home Office or is the subject of an appeal to the Immigration Appellate Authority, yet the suspect has complied with all the conditions set out in sub-sections 31(1) and (2) it would normally be appropriate to await the outcome of the asylum proceedings before commencing a prosecution.

Available at: http://www.cps.gov.uk/legal/h_to_k/immigration/index.html:tatu (accessed: 8 April 2011).

44 See Hansard, HL Deb 2/11/1999, col. 784.

45 See e.g. *R (on the application of Hussain) v Secretary of State for the Home Department and others* [2001] EWHC Admin 555; *R (on the application of Gjovalin Pepushi) v Crown Prosecution Service* [2004] EWHC 798 (Admin); *R v Navabi; R v Embaye* [2005] EWCA Crim 2865. In these cases, British courts established the prevalence of statutory provisions – i.e. S. 31, IAA 1999 and S. 2, AI(TC)A 2004 – over international obligations arising from the Refugee Convention. See, however, *R v Asfaw* (cited in note 39).

46 See, e.g. *R (on the application of Hoverspeed) v Secretary of State for the Home Department* [1999] INLR 591 (on carrier liability); and *R (on the application of European Roma Rights Centre) and others v Immigration Officer at Prague Airport and another* [2004] UKHL 55 (on the decision to refuse leave to enter to asylum seekers in the country of origin by liaison officers).

47 The number of work permits for high-skilled migrants increased significantly after 1995 and new channels were opened for low-skilled workers – mainly, the Seasonal Agricultural Workers Scheme and the Sectors Based Scheme workers (Somerville 2007: 30).

48 See decision by the Court of Appeal dismissing the appeal and confirming the conviction for manslaughter: *R v Wacker (Perry)* [2002] EWCA Crim 1944.

49 S. 25(1), IA 1971. This offence covers a broad range of conduct: assisting illegal entry

or assisting someone to remain by deception and other forms of assistance which facilitate a breach of immigration laws. It includes harbouring (S. 25(2), IA 1971) which was thereon abolished. The maximum penalty for the new 'generic' offence of assisting was increased from 10 to 14 years of imprisonment, the same maximum penalty for helping an asylum seeker and trafficking for exploitation. By an amendment introduced in the UK Borders Act 2007, this offence may be committed overseas and regardless of nationality.

50 S. 25A(1), IA 1971.

51 S. 25B(1) and (3), IA 1971.

52 S. 145(1), (2) and (3), NIAA 2002. Other trafficking offences are included in the Sexual Offences Act 2003 (SOA 2003) (for sexual exploitation) and in the AI(TC)A 2004 (for exploitation).

53 Respectively, Council Directive 2002/90/EC of 28 November 2002 defining the facilitation of unauthorized entry, transit and residence, Official Journal L 328 of 5/12/2002 ('Directive on unauthorised entry, transit and residence') and Council Framework Decision 2002/946/JHA of 28 November 2002 on the strengthening of the legal framework to prevent the facilitation of unauthorized entry, transit and residence, Official Journal L 328 of 5/12/2002 ('Framework Decision on unauthorised entry, transit and residence').

54 Neither do other international instruments. For example, the Directive on unauthorized entry, transit and residence (see note 53) does not preclude Member states from penalizing 'humanitarian assistance' (article 1, 2). The Protocol against the Smuggling of Migrants by Land, Sea and Air, Supplementing the United Nations Convention against Transnational Organized Crime ('UN Protocol against smuggling') prescribes the criminalization of smuggling without subjecting that imperative to any exceptions (article 6). In contrast, Switzerland, for instance, exempts both refugees and those assisting them from penalty (article 23(3), Swiss Asylum Law).

55 S. 25A(1) and (3), IA 1971.

56 According to information in the file, this family is originally from Iraq. Some years ago, the mother and eldest son left Iraq and were granted refugee status in Britain. They are naturalized British citizens.

57 As evidenced by the number of people helping family members charged with facilitation: see Chapter 4. In *R v Van Binh Le; R v Stark* [1999] 1 Cr. App. R. (S.) 422 [at 3], the fact that facilitation is committed for gain and the person assisted is not a family member are considered aggravating factors for this offence.

58 For the difference between 'asylum claimant' and 'illegal entrant' in the jurisprudence, see *R v Naillie; R v Kanesarajah* [1993] AC 674, HL [at 680C].

59 *R v Alps* [2001] All ER (D) 29 (Feb) [at 23 and 24]. See also *Sternaj and Sternaj v Crown Prosecution Service* [2011] EWHC 1094 (Admin) confirming that a defence grounded on the Refugee Convention is not available for a person charged with S. 25 [at 33] but leaving open the possibility for the Crown to question whether it was in the public interest to prosecute [at 39]. In *R v Kapoor and others* [2012] EWCA Crim 435 the Court of Appeal stated that S.2 (AI(TC)A 2004) is not an 'immigration law' for the purpose of S. 25..

60 Ss 137 and 138, NIAA 2002, respectively.

61 S. 26A(3), IA 1971.

62 S. 26B(1) and (2), IA 1971.

63 Schedule 3, paragraph 13, NIAA 2002.

64 Ss 152–154, NIAA 2002.

65 Particularly, it increased the fine imposed on carriers that transport passengers without proper documents from £1,000 to £2,000 (Schedule 8, paragraph 13, NIAA 2002).

66 Some of the behaviours criminalized by the AI(TC)A 2004 are already contained in the IA 1971 under the title of 'General offences in connection with administration of

Act' (S. 26(1)). Further offences related to the possession of false identity documents, providing false information and tampering with the Register were later criminalized by the IDCA 2006 (Ss 25, 28 and 29, respectively).

67 *R v Naillie; R v Kanesarajah* [1993] AC 674, HL. This offence is in S. 2(1), AI(TC)A 2004. A similar offence in S. 2(2) of the act relates to dependent children arriving without passports.

68 Magistrates' courts report the following numbers of prosecutions for this offence: 492 (2006), 272 (2007), 177 (2008), 131 (2009), 104 (2010) and 94 (2011) (Home Office 2010b: Table 3.11a; Home Office 2012: Table pr.01).

69 The government envisaged from the outset that between 10,000 and 12,000 asylum applicants would be subject to such provision (see Hansard, HC Deb 13/01/04, cols 99–100).

70 See intervention by the Minister for Immigration, Beverly Hughes in Hansard, HC Deb 8/01/2004, cols 44–75.

71 S. 8(3) (a) and (c), AI(TC)A 2004.

72 S. 2(4) (c), (d) and (e), AI(TC)A 2004.

73 See respectively, Hansard, HC Deb 13/01/2004, col. 119; HC Deb 1/03/2004, cols 620–621; and HL Deb 5/04/2004, cols 1629–1630. See also *R v Navabi and Embaye* [2005] EWCA Crim 2865.

74 See, e.g. *R (on the application of K) v Croydon Crown Court* [2005] EWHC 478 (Admin) [at 11].

75 S. 2(7) (b)(iii), AI(TC)A 2004.

76 The influence of the agent has been considered as a mitigating factor in *R v Ai* [2005] EWCA Crim 936 [at 14]. While an outstanding asylum claim has not been considered as a ground for impunity, it has been taken into account as a mitigating factor together with the age of the applicant in *R v Wang* [2005] EWCA Crim 293 [at 11].

77 *Soe Thet v Director of Public Prosecutions* [2006] EWHC 2701 (Admin).

78 See also House of Commons (2004: 4–8).

79 *R v Farida Said Mohammed; R v Abdullah Mohamed Osman* [2007] EWCA Crim 2332 [at 36].

80 In 2011, 81 per cent of defendants charged with this crime in magistrates' courts were found guilty; 100 per cent of them were found guilty in crown courts. Similar percentages are recorded for previous years: 85 and 100 per cent (2010); and 78 and 100 per cent (2009); 92 and 64 per cent (2008); 93 and 100 per cent (2007); and 97 and 92 per cent (2006) (see Home Office 2010b: Tables 3.11a and b; Home Office 2012: Table pr.01).

81 S. 35(3), AI(TC)A 2004. See *R v Tabnak* [2007] All ER (D) 223 (Feb), interpreting the scope of such defence as limited to inability to comply, not unwillingness to do so. The Appeal Court states that 'fear of persecution' under the Refugee Convention is not considered 'reasonable excuse' [at 2].

82 It involves complying with the following:

(a) provide information or documents to the Secretary of State or to any other person; (b) obtain information or documents; (c) provide fingerprints, submit to the taking of a photograph or provide information, or submit to a process for the recording of information, about external physical characteristics (including, in particular, features of the iris or any other part of the eye); (d) make, or consent to or cooperate with the making of, an application to a person acting for the government of a State other than the United Kingdom; (e) cooperate with a process designed to enable determination of an application; (f) complete a form accurately and completely; (g) attend an interview and answer questions accurately and completely; (h) make an appointment.

See S. 35(2), AI(TC)A 2004.

83   See Hansard, HL Deb 27/04/2004, col. 274.
84   Since the entry into force of this offence, the number of prosecutions in magistrates' courts has been very low: 9 (2005); 14 (2006); 12 (2007); 35 (2008); 11 (2009); 8 (2010); and 1 (2011) (Home Office 2010c: Table 3.11a; Home Office 2010b: Table pr.01).
85   This is a problem facing other countries. Identity stripping has been identified as a main reason for long periods of immigration detention in Holland and Germany (Broeders 2010). While non-cooperation is not a criminal offence in those countries, the Dutch and German governments use administrative detention to force foreigners to cooperate.
86   *R (on the application of Feridon Rostami) v Secretary of State for the Home Department* [2009] EWHC 2094 (QB) (henceforth 'Rostami').
87   Quoted in 'Rostami' [at 54].
88   'Rostami' [at 73].
89   The IANA 2006 introduced six offences: illegal employment (S. 21(1)), failure to comply with requirement to provide information (S. 34(1)), absconding from detention (S. 41(6) (a)), absconding while carrying arrangements to put the person in detention (S. 41(6) (b)), and obstructing (S. 41(6) (c)) and assaulting an authorized person performing immigration powers (S. 41(6) (d)). The UK Borders Act 2007 introduced the following offences: absconding from immigration detention (S. 3(1) (a)), assaulting an immigration officer in the exercise of power of arrest (S. 3(1) (b)), obstructing an immigration officer in the course of an arrest (S. 3(1) (c)) and assaulting an immigration officer (S. 22(1)). It also modifies a number of offences already in the statute book (helping an asylum seeker to enter the UK (S. 29), assisting unlawful immigration (S. 30) and people trafficking (S. 31)). The Borders, Citizenship and Immigration Act 2009 (BCIA 2009) included only one offence: the wrongful disclosure of information (S. 18(1)).
90   See e.g. *Daily Mail* (2006).
91   See e.g. interventions by the Minister of State, Baroness Scotland in Hansard, HL Deb 13/06/2007, col. 1697; and by the Minister for Immigration, Citizenship and Nationality, Liam Byrne in Hansard, HC Deb 20/03/2007, col. 440.
92   In 2007, there were only two 'hub' prisons (Bulwood Hall in Essex and Canterbury Prison in Kent) holding exclusively FNPs. In 2009, six other prisons were designated as 'hubs' in which the FNP population is concentrated: HMP Risley (North West); Hewell (West Midlands); Morton Hall (East Midlands); The Mount (Eastern region); The Verne (South West); and Wormwood Scrubs (London region). There are also 36 'spoke' prisons holding a number of foreigners.
93   S. 32, UK Borders Act 2007.
94   See *R (on the application of Abdi and others) v Secretary of State for the Home Department* [2008] EWHC 3166 (Admin) which uncovered an unpublished policy of the Home Office which mandated continued detention for FNPs awaiting deportation on public security grounds. According to this policy, FNPs should be detained as a matter of principle to protect the public and due to a high risk of absconding. This 'secret policy' that operated between April 2006 and November 2008 was a direct consequence of the FNP scandal. The High Court declared it unlawful because it was contrary to legal provisions in relation to FNPs and because it was not made public.
95   Currently there are no data available on the percentage of FNPs who have been convicted for immigration offences. In 2009, there were 7,502 foreigners serving immediate custodial sentences in prison establishments, and 928 were serving a custodial sentence for 'fraud and forgery' offences – that is, 12.4 per cent of the FNP population (Ministry of Justice 2010a: Table 7.23). However, the category of 'fraud and forgery' offences does not completely cover the range of immigration offences. According to Home Office data obtained by the author, in March 2012, 1,053 people were in prison for a number of offences under immigration acts and other related offences – such as deception and document fraud. It is not clear, however, if these

data relate to foreigners only. Estimates on foreigners in removal centres suggest that around 50 per cent of the population has criminal convictions (NAO 2009a: 8). However, there are no disaggregated data according to criminal offences.

96 Intervention by Mick Chatwin (JCWI) during the debates on the Immigration and Asylum Bill 1999: Hansard, HC Deb 16/03/1999.

97 With that aim, the government launched the 'Simplification Project' in 2007. It was supposed to revise both primary and secondary legislation. It included a review of criminal offences under immigration legislation in order to group them in one place, eliminate overlapping and duplication, and close loopholes (Home Office 2009b). The product was a Draft Immigration Bill – that reduced the number of immigration offences – which was presented to Parliament in November 2009. However, the project – including the Draft Bill – was discontinued by the present Coalition government.

98 An institutional parallel is the reorganization of the US Immigration and Naturalization Service (INS) as part of the US Department of Homeland Security in 2003 which incorporated security and crime-related considerations into immigration enforcement (Tumlin 2004: 1179; Coutin 2005: 15).

99 They cover the powers to arrest with or without warrant, to detain a suspect for a limited time, and to enter and search premises, and seize evidence. These powers granted by the IA 1971 have been progressively extended by the IAA 1999, NIAA 2002, AI(TC)A 2004 and UK Borders Act 2007. The BCIA 2009 furnished UKBA officers with new powers similar to those exercised by HM Revenue and Customs staff.

100 With the creation of UKBA and its restructuring as a police-like enforcement agency at the border, the cooperation between the two agencies – the police and UKBA – has been strengthened (see e.g. ACPO and UKBA 2008).

101 The identification of illegal immigration as a main security threat appeared early on at the European level, particularly at the Schengen Convention. The strengthening of the external borders against organized crime, terrorism and illegal immigration were measures to 'compensate' for the lifting of Europe's internal borders (Anderson *et al.* 1995; also Bigo 1994).

102 Defined as 'all the potential negative consequences of illegal migration' (Home Office 2007b: 10).

103 In the agency's policy statement, it is made clear that 'enforcement priority would be to take action against the most harmful people first and deny the privileges of the UK to those here illegally' (Home Office 2007b: 10).

104 In a response to an FOI request, David Goggin from the UKBA's Criminality and Detention Group explained that:

> [Ex-foreign national prisoners] are subject to a *risk assessment process* and will only be transferred if it is assessed that they present no specific risks. Those considered presenting a *high security risk* due to the nature of their offence or behaviour will remain in prison on completion of their sentences. The type of offences range from drug related offences and robbery to individuals using false documentation.

> (Letter dated 18 August 2010, italics added, Ref. 15678)

105 An actuarial instrument has also been introduced to assess the suitability of an enforcement visit ('scoring matrix'). See UKBA Enforcement Instructions and Guidance (EI&G), Chapter 31.4 (Joint Intelligence Units).

106 This trend is not so clear in crown courts, where there was a drop in 2005 and a new upward trend starting in 2006.

107 Response to an FOI request, letter dated 2 March 2012 (Ref. 21732). Conditional

cautions are now available for 'relevant foreign offenders' under the Legal Aid, Sentencing and Punishment of Offenders Act 2012 (S.134).

108 A recent poll reported Britain as 'by far' the country least happy with immigrants among six European countries plus America and Canada (*The Economist* 2009a).

109 Even after numerous reforms to speed up the resolution of asylum claims, huge backlogs make it impossible to achieve the UKBA targets (*The Economist* 2009b; BBC News 2009; Travis 2010). Moreover, the measures introduced to expedite asylum claims, such as the fast-track procedure, have been applied improperly to cases that deserved more in-depth examination, leaving a lot of people, particularly women, unprotected (Human Rights Watch 2010).

4 The use of criminal law powers against immigration offenders: the decision to prosecute

1 See S. 28(4), IA 1971; see also UKBA EI&G, Chapter 33.4.

2 See respectively, S. 3(5) (a) and 3(6), IA 1971; and S. 32, UK Borders Act 2007. Family members of a deportee are also liable to deportation (S. 3(5) (b), IA 1971).

3 Other non-nationals who can be removed are: family members of those liable to removal; persons who attempted but failed to obtain leave to remain by deception; and UK-born children of all those liable to removal. See Schedule 2, IA 1971 and S. 10, IAA 1999.

4 The general grounds for refusal in HC 395, paragraph 320, were amended during 2008 by HC 321. HC 321 amended paragraph 320 by the insertion of paragraph 320(7B) to provide for the mandatory refusal of applications in which deception has been used (quoted in Macdonald 2010: Ch. 3.57).

5 In order to be able to exercise these powers, immigration officers are required to attend a three-week training course and annual two-day training courses. For a recent inspection of an arrest team by the Independent Chief Inspector of the UKBA, see Vine (2011).

6 A senior member of the UKBA's Crime Directorate told me that in April 2011, this department had 183 seconded police officers and 147 UKBA officers. By 2015, the Crime Directorate plans to increase the participation of the latter to 237 and decrease that of the former to only 80 (Respondent 20, 28/04/2011). See also Home Office 2010c.

7 These powers are sanctioned by different acts, such as S. 23(2), Misuse of Drugs Act 1971; S. 1, Police and Criminal Evidence Act 1984; and S. 60, Criminal Justice and Public Order Act 1994.

8 See UKBA EI&G, Chapter 31.19.1.

9 This case is not part of the ones analysed for this study as the defendant, Mr Singh, was not charged with immigration offences. The hearing was held on 3 September 2010 before Uxbridge Magistrates' Court.

10 CPS, 'Legal Guidance: Immigration'. Available at: http://www.cps.gov.uk/legal/h_to_k/immigration/ (accessed: 23 October 2011).

11 Chapter 33.6 (italics in original). The EI&G is a policy document which gives guidance to caseworkers on the exercise of discretionary powers established in statutes. There is also a comprehensive code of guidance on the application of immigration rules, such as the IDIs, considered below, or the Asylum Policy Instruction (APIs), mentioned in Chapter 3.

12 S. 1, Chapter 20, IDIs (paragraph 3.1).

13 S. 1, Chapter 20, IDIs (paragraph 2.5).

14 See 'Amended Instructions for Documenting Removals and the Implementation of section 35 of the Asylum and Immigration (Treatment of Claimants, etc.) Act 2004 in Non-Compliant Cases'. Available at: http://www.ukba.homeoffice.gov.uk/sitecontent/

documents/policyandlaw/enforcement/oemsectionc/section-35?view=Binary (accessed: 8 March 2011).
15 UKBA EI&G, Chapter 17.11.5. This document states that:

> This department has assured Parliament that the Secretary of State will only request an individual to take such steps as are required to document him/her if the department intends/is able to remove or deport the individual. If policy, instructions or a significant legal judgement prevent removal then such cases will not qualify for Section 35 action.

16 Standard Acceptable Criteria (SAC), Version 1.0, 28 April 2009 (unpublished document).
17 Standard Acceptable Criteria (SAC), Version 1.0, p. 5.
18 Although in recent years there has been a drift towards more 'punitive' regulation: see Baldwin (2004); Macrory (2006).
19 Standard Acceptable Criteria (SAC), Version 1.0, p. 3.
20 See Chapter 3.
21 See *R v Governor of Durham Prison Ex parte Singh* [1984] 1 All ER 983 [at 706]. This leading case states three fundamental temporal limits to administrative detention of foreigners: the detention should be imposed only when the making of a deportation order or a removal is pending; detention should be limited to a 'reasonably necessary' period to undertake that action; and when it is apparent that the removal of the person will not take place within a reasonable period, detention will cease to be lawful. See also the decision by the European Court in ECHR, *Chahal v the United Kingdom*, judgement of 15 November 1996, Application 22414/93, paragraph 113.
22 See also UKBA EI&G, S. 3(10): 'Where leave to remain has been obtained by deception, administrative removal . . . will be the correct course of action.'
23 See Home Office (2010b: Tables 3.11a and b); Home Office (2012: Table pr.01).
24 S. 5, IA 1988 and S. 10, IAA 1999.
25 See Chapter 2.
26 S. 24(1) (a), IA 1971.
27 While the number of people refused entry at port and subsequently removed in 2010 was 18,276, the total number of prosecutions for the offence of entering the UK without a leave was 38 for the same year at both magistrates' (25) and crown courts (13) (Home Office 2010b: Tables 3.1, 3.11a and 3.11b; Home Office 2011b: Table pr.01).
28 The nationality of people subject to enforcement action also has an effect on the length of post-conviction detention. Nationals of certain countries – such as Zimbabwe, Algeria, Iraq, Somalia and Iran – with a criminal conviction are less likely to obtain bail and more likely to remain in administrative detention for longer periods because of the impossibility of deporting them (London Detainee Support Group 2009: 12).
29 Data on the nationality of the defendant are not systematically compiled by the courts. However, from certain documents in court files (e.g. photocopies of passport, defendants' statement, references by immigration or police officers, etc.) it was possible to establish the nationality of the defendants. These documents suggest that nationals from certain countries were over-represented in the sample. At the magistrates' court, most of those accused of immigration offences claimed to come from China, Somalia, Iran and Sri Lanka. At the crown court, most immigration-related defendants claimed to be Somalis, Iranian, Sri Lankan, and Kuwaiti. Some of the defendants, though, are naturalized British citizens, particularly in the cases before the crown court.
30 See Chapter 3.
31 Respectively, a barrister at Doughty Street Chambers (Respondent 15, interview held

on 28/04/2010) and the director of an organization supporting immigration detainees (Respondent 9, interview held on 16/07/2010).

32 'Forged passport attempt foiled at Bristol Airport' (19 May 2010). Available at: http://www.ukba.homeoffice.gov.uk/sitecontent/newsarticles/2010/may/06-forged-passport-bristol (accessed: 10 March 2011).

33 See UKBA, respectively, 'Christchurch takeaway facing possible fine' (2 July 2010) and 'Illegally working in Loughborough' (5 July 2010). [Online source no longer accessible.]

34 Home Office/UKBA Crime Directorate: p. 7 (unpublished document from 2011).

35 Within immigration law, it is possible to think of the dual system of civil penalties and prosecution for illegal employment which applies to citizens and non-citizens alike. However, under this regime, criminal charges can only be pressed against those who 'knowingly' employ a person without entitlement to work. The rest of the cases of illegal employment are dealt with through civil penalties. As such there is no overlap between the two regimes.

36 An early example of the broad executive powers over non-citizens in Britain is the extension of emergency legislation from 1919 until 1971 on the entry and residence of 'aliens'. The then Under-Secretary of State for the Home Department argued against the introduction of permanent legislation on the premise that the emergency regime provided more flexibility and that new legislation would entail that 'the powers of the Home Secretary should be more precisely defined than they are today' (Hansard, HC Deb 26/11/1953, col. 560). See Chapter 2.

37 Keith Best, then Chief Executive of the Immigration Advisory Service (IAS) in Hansard, HC Deb 27/02/2007, col. 65.

38 See Chapter 3.

39 See, for example, the campaigns by 'No One is Illegal' and 'London NoBorders' (respectively at: http://www.noii.org.uk/ and http://www.london.noborders.org.uk) (accessed: 22 October 2011).

40 In an interview with BBC Radio 4, a senior official in the Immigration Services Union puts it this way:

> I think there is certainly a feeling amongst senior civil servants in the Home Office that immigration is not an area you want to work in. You don't want to go to a dinner party and when people say, 'Oh what are you working on?', you don't want to say, 'Oh I work in immigration.'
> (BBC4, 'Current Affairs', 8/02/2010, transcripts available at http://news.bbc.co.uk/nol/shared/spl/hi/programmes/analysis/ transcripts/08_02_10.txt [accessed: 6 March 2011])

He explains that this is so because immigration is 'not liberal. It's not seen as a nice thing to do. You're not helping people. You are actually enforcing the law and not allowing people into the country.'

41 Such as the TV programme 'UK Border Force', and the coverage of its operation on the agency's website and in the press. References like 'customer satisfaction', 'customer approach' and 'customer service' are also very much present in recent policy papers (Home Office 2006b: 4; Home Office 2009c; Home Office 2010e; Home Office 2011a).

42 Even within the EU, the former Commissioner for Human Rights has repeatedly verbalized his opposition to the criminalization of immigration breaches (e.g. Council of Europe 2010).

43 Katja Franko Aas finds a similar contradiction between the rationale behind the construction of the mass surveillance architecture within the EU (allegedly created to disrupt organized criminality relating to immigration) and the targets of such systems in practice (the undocumented migrant) (Aas 2011a: 137).

44 See trafficking in prostitution (S. 145, NIAA 2002); trafficking into the UK, within the UK, and out of the UK for sexual exploitation (respectively, Ss 57, 58 and 59, SOA 2003); and trafficking people for exploitation (S. 4(1), (2) and (3), AI(TC)A 2004). In addition, the Coroners and Justice Act 2009 criminalized slavery, servitude and forced or compulsory labour (S. 71(1)).

45 In addition, 41 cases from arrests in 2009 and 2010 were pending a decision (see Hansard, HC Deb 13/09/2010, c882W, data up until 31/07/2010). In 2007, there were 25 prosecutions for trafficking for sexual exploitation (Barnardos 2009: 6). The government claims that between 2010 and 2011 there have been 116 prosecutions for offences involving sexual and labour exploitation and other kinds of exploitation, but it is not clear from these data if all of them are under trafficking charges (Home Office 2011c: 6).

46 It is difficult to ascertain with confidence the number of people charged with document offences who are actually trafficking victims because of the difficulties involved in their identification (Nelken 2010).

47 These are two protocols that are part of the Code for Crown Prosecutors: on Prosecution of Defendants charged with offences who might be Trafficked Victims; and on Prosecution of Young Defendants charged with offences who might be Trafficked Victims. According to them, prosecutors are under a duty to be proactive in establishing if a person subject to a criminal prosecution is a potential victim of trafficking. The principle of non-prosecution of victims of trafficking for immigration crimes or other offences is also contained in the UN HCHR Principles and Guidelines on Human Rights and Trafficking, guideline 5; and in the Directive 2011/36/EU of the European Parliament and of the Council of 5 April 2011 on preventing and combating trafficking in human beings and protecting its victims, and replacing Council Framework Decision 2002/629/JHA, article 8.

48 The settlement reached by the parties in the case on 11 April 2011 and approved by Mrs Justice Cox remains confidential. This case is registered in the High Court as *ELS v The Home Office*, claim HQ09X01333. See press coverage of the case: *Daily Mail* (2011); BBC News (2011); Travis (2011).

49 As Marie Segrave observes, the discussions over the regulation of trafficking at the international level have been dominated from the outset by a concern with transnational organized crime, border surveillance and, to a lesser extent, the sexual exploitation of 'innocent' women. While human rights approaches were put forward, they have been less successful (Segrave 2009: 74).

50 Review carried out on 7 June 2010 based on the UKBA's website: 'Latest News: Enforcing the Law'. Available at: http://www.ukba.homeoffice.gov.uk/news-and-updates/?area=Enforcingthelaw (accessed: 8 March 2011).

51 S. 25, IA 1971.

52 See Home Office (2010b: Table 3.11a and b); Home Office (2012: Table pr.01). The most frequent offences at magistrates' courts are entering the UK without a passport and deception. This coincides with the findings of the review of court cases for this study.

53 At Uxbridge, only three out of 40 defendants had no address in the UK; at Isleworth, seven out of 58 had no address in the country.

54 In many cases, people accused of document offences are interviewed by officers at the Human Smuggling Unit at Heathrow police station. Most questions are related to the 'agent', his/her identity, the itinerary, who paid for the trip and how much, etc.

55 See Chapter 5.

56 S. 25(1) and (5), IDCA 2006, respectively. However, I did not examine court files on these offences as they are not technically considered immigration offences.

57 According to the leading case *R v Van Binh Le; R v Stark* [1999] 1 Cr. App. R. (S.) 422 [at 3], aggravating features include: repeat offending; committed for financial gain; involving strangers rather than family members; a high degree of planning/

sophistication; the number of immigrants involved; and the level of involvement of the offender. See also CPS Guidance, 'Human Trafficking and Smuggling'. Available at: http://www.cps.gov.uk/legal/h_to_k/human_trafficking_and_smuggling/#a05 (accessed: 10 December 2010).

58 Standard Acceptable Criteria (SAC), Version 1.0, p. 3.
59 This is also the logic behind the recent crusade against illegal employment. See Chapter 3.

5 Practices of punishment: immigration defendants before the criminal courts

1 Under article 31 of the Refugee Convention, and S. 31, IAA 1999. See Chapter 3.
2 However, some asylum applications are decided through the 'fast-track' procedure. So if the claimant is 'fast tracked', the applicant will be administratively detained until a decision is made. This process usually takes two weeks. Often the decision to 'fast track' a claim is based on the country of origin of the applicant. Applications by nationals of certain listed countries are in principle considered as unfounded. See http://www.bia.homeoffice.gov.uk/sitecontent/documents/policyandlaw/asylumprocessguidance/detention/guidance/dftanddnsaintakeselection?view=Binary (accessed: 25 November 2011).
3 See Chapter 6.
4 This first interview is designed to determine eligibility for benefits. It involves questions on personal details of the applicant, health, employment, journey, education, and immigration history. No questions are asked about the substantive claim for asylum. Those questions are asked in the Statement of Evidence Form which is handed to the applicant in the first interview and should be filled in within ten working days of the claim. A second interview happens shortly afterwards (Bohmer and Shuman 2008: 47).
5 In this regard, the Dublin Convention determines the Member state responsible for assessing an asylum claim, thus restricting the choice by asylum seekers on the country of application (Council Regulation (EC) No. 343/2003 of 18 February 2003 establishing the criteria and mechanisms for determining the Member State responsible for examining an asylum application lodged in one of the Member States by a third-country national, Official Journal L 050 of 25/02/2003). This is an example of how European harmonization on immigration and asylum policies has limited local access to international protection. Other bilateral agreements authorize the rejection of asylum applicants if they have passed through a 'safe country'. The Home Office deems certain countries as 'safe' and asylum applicants who have travelled through them may be returned there. See Hailbronner (2004); Achermann and Gattiker (1995).
6 The accused was later discharged. He claimed he was tortured in Iran and was diagnosed with post-traumatic stress disorder (PTSD).
7 See Chapter 3.
8 See IND Guidance issued to immigration officers on S. 2 of the Asylum and Immigration (Treatment of Claimants, etc.) Act 2004, quoted in the Immigration Law Practitioners' Association (ILPA) 'Information on new immigration offences for criminal practitioners'. Available at: http://www.ilpa.org.uk/s2infocrimpractsamend. htm (accessed: 3 May 2011).
9 See S. 2(7) (b) (iii), AI(TC)A 2004.
10 Criminal law and immigration solicitor (Respondent 4, 16/07/2010).
11 In many other cases, such an intention might not have been recorded in the file.
12 154 defendants pleaded guilty; one pleaded not guilty and was found guilty by the court.
13 See *R v Makuwa (Liliane)* [2006] EWCA Crim 175 [at 3] in which Moore-Bick LJ stated that 'Provided the defendant adduced sufficient evidence in support of her claim to refugee status to raise the issue, the prosecution bore the burden of proving to the usual standard that she was not in fact a refugee'. For a comment, see Fitzpatrick

(2006). See, however, Stoyanova (2012: 13), where she argues that the evidentiary threshold required is actually quite high.

14 *Soe Thet v Director of Public Prosecutions* [2006] EWHC 2701 (Admin).

15 This legal intertwining also raises difficulties for those serving a prison sentence. In fact, the lack of knowledge and training on immigration matters has been identified as one of the main problems in dealing with foreign national prisoners (FNPs) by prison staff and by the prisoners themselves (HMIP 2006: 23, 28; see also Bosworth 2011c). A research report on foreigners in prison commissioned by the HM Inspectorate of Prisons states that '[p]risoners were generally given little information during criminal proceedings about the potential immigration consequences' (HMIP 2006: 34).

16 For instance, until recently, the main textbooks for criminal law practitioners made no reference to the protocols on trafficking victims prosecuted for immigration crimes, incorporated into the Code for Crown Prosecutors.

17 See *R v Uxbridge Magistrates' Court, Ex parte Adimi; R v Crown Prosecution Service, Ex parte Sorani; R v Secretary of State for the Home Department, Ex parte Kaziu* [1999] INLR 490 [at 526]. See also Chapter 3.

18 See *R v El Hudarey* [2008] EWCA Crim 1761 [at 9].

19 *Mohamed & Ors v R* [2010] EWCA Crim 2400. These were four separate appeals which were considered jointly because of the similarity of the facts at stake.

20 Cases of MV, Rahma Abukar Mohamed and Mohsen Nofallah.

21 Cases of Abdalla Mohamed and MV.

22 Case of Abdalla Mohamed.

23 See e.g. *R v Kishientine* [2004] EWCA Crim 3352 [at 10], where Pill LJ noted that the assessment of the asylum claim is

> a question for the Home Office and the appellate system provided in relation to decisions of the Secretary of State. In our judgment, it is not appropriate that the Court should routinely assess the genuineness and strength of asylum claims.

24 This is the case of Mr Elmi from Somalia who, when he filed an asylum application, was caught in possession of a Norwegian passport that related to someone else and was charged for this offence. He pleaded guilty and was convicted to 12 months' imprisonment and automatic deportation.

25 See *R v Wang* [2005] EWCA Crim 293 [at 12] in which the Appeal Court reduced the sentence imposed by the lower court from ten months to two months due to mitigating circumstances, including an extant asylum claim.

26 In 2009, it was 67.6 per cent and in 2010, 67.8 per cent (see Crown Prosecution Service 2012: Annex B, Chart 3).

27 In 2009, it was 73.5 per cent and in 2010, 72.5 per cent (Crown Prosecution Service 2012: Annex B, Table 7).

28 On the English system of sentencing guidelines, see Ashworth (2006).

29 In one case, the plea was vacated and the case was sent back to the Uxbridge Magistrates' Court (Isleworth Crown Court, court file, Case 7).

30 This case is not part of my sample as I did not hear the whole trial and only sat in on the hearing when the sentence was read by chance – because I was waiting for one of the cases I was following up. This hearing was held at Isleworth Crown Court against Mr Ahmed on 13 September 2010. Similarly, in *R v Kalonga* [2004] EWCA Crim 1250, the Court of Appeal referred to the decision by the lower court in which the judge said he gave the defendant full credit for 'being honest enough to plead guilty' [at 4].

31 In the sample, only 1 out of 232 defendants before the magistrates' court was white; only 3 out of 106 defendants before the crown court were white.

32 Free legal advice is provided from duty solicitors for people in police stations, regardless of their financial situation.

33 See Legal Services Commission website: http://www.legalservices.gov.uk/about_ legal_aid.asp; and the Citizens Advice Bureau website: http://www.adviceguide.org.uk/ index/your_rights/legal_system/help_with_legal_costs.htm (accessed: 29 October 2011).

34 More generally, the view that legal aid fees are low compared to other legal work is the main reason for the withdrawal of solicitor firms from criminal legal aid contracts (NAO 2009b).

35 The letter refers to article 33(1) of the Refugee Convention which prescribes the prohibition of expulsion or return (*non-refoulement*) of a refugee to a place where 'his life and freedom would be threatened'. Paragraph (2) of the Refugee Convention excludes from this protection a refugee

> whom there are reasonable grounds for regarding as a danger to the security of the country in which he is, or who, having been convicted by a final judgement of a particularly serious crime, constitutes a danger to the community of that country.

36 *Padilla v Kentucky,* 000 US 08-651 (2010). The US Supreme Court understood that, although it is not a criminal sanction, 'deportation is an integral part – indeed, sometimes the most integral part – of the penalty that may be imposed on noncitizens defendants who plead guilty to specified crimes', not just a collateral consequence [p. 6]. Deportation is, according to the court, 'intimately related to the criminal process' [p. 8] and therefore, it concluded that counsel advice on the immigration consequences of a criminal conviction is part of the right to effective assistance of counsel [p. 17]. For a comment, see Chin (2011).

37 For analysis on the impact of 'foreignness' on the rates of imprisonment among non-citizens in Europe, see Albrecht (1997: 73); Albrecht (2000); Melossi (2003); Guillén and Vallès (2003); Wacquant (2006); Silveira Gorski (2009); De Giorgi (2010).

38 He was probably referring to S. 142(1), Criminal Justice Act 2003, which lists the purposes of sentencing (italics added):

> (a) the punishment of offenders; (b) the reduction of crime (*including its reduction by deterrence*); (c) the reform and rehabilitation of offenders; (d) the protection of the public; (e) the making of reparation by offenders to persons affected by their offence.

39 For example, in Uxbridge Magistrates' Court, court file, Cases 124, 128, 129, 135 and 146.

40 For example, in Uxbridge Magistrates' Court, court file, Cases 118, 125, 133, 134 and 150.

41 For example, in Uxbridge Magistrates' Court, court file, Cases 151, 155 and 198.

42 The motives given by crown court judges in their decisions were not available in files. There was only information about the sanction imposed in the case of conviction.

43 *R v Kolawole* [2004] EWCA Crim 3047 [at 6]. According to this judgment, the appropriate range for this offence should be between 12 and 18 months' imprisonment. This ruling superseded *R v Daljit Singh* [1999] 1 Cr. App. R. (S.) which fixed the penalty tariff at six to nine months' imprisonment [at 490]. See also *R v Kishientine* [2004] EWCA Crim 3352, where Pill LJ states that in the case of document fraud, deterrent sentences are needed: 'There is clearly a public interest in the maintenance of immigration control' [at paragraph 10].

44 *R v Van Binh Le; R v Stark* [1999] 1 Cr. App. R. (S.) 422 [at 3]. See also Sentencing Guidelines Council (2005: 101).

45 *R v Wang* [2005] EWCA Crim 293 [at 10].

46 For example, Uxbridge Magistrates' Court, court file, Cases 170 and 178. In relation to

the offence of failure to cooperate, magistrates referred to the fact that this offence 'challenges the deportation system and repatriation of failed asylum seekers' (Uxbridge Magistrates' Court , court file, Case 146).

47 This is connected to the introduction of the logic of prevention or pre-emption in the criminal justice system, much discussed in recent criminology and criminal law literature. See, among others, Steiker (1998); Zedner (2005, 2007); Harcourt (2007); Ashworth (2009); McCulloch and Pickering (2009); O'Malley (2013: Chapter 16).

48 For example, Uxbridge Magistrates' Court, court file, Cases 52, 136 and 182.

49 For example, Uxbridge Magistrates' Court, court-file, Cases 2 and 126.

50 For example, Uxbridge Magistrates' Court, court-file, Case 229.

51 The 'custodial threshold' is reached when the offence is 'so serious that neither a fine alone nor a community sentence can be justified for the offence' (S. 152(2), CJA 2003). The notion of 'serious offence' and the offences falling into this category, though, are not unequivocal. There are no fixed criteria to rank 'seriousness' in the legislation and sentencing data (Francis *et al.* 2001).

52 While magistrates should decide whether to recommend deportation for convicted non-citizens, many are uncertain about these powers and usually they do not make such recommendation (Ashford 1993: 22). In one of the cases heard at Uxbridge Magistrates' Court, the magistrates asked their legal adviser about this aspect and the chair noted: 'I've never heard that before' (Uxbridge Magistrates' Court, hearing, Case 5). The fact that they do not make this recommendation in many cases involving foreigners was one of the reasons for introducing the automatic deportation against certain convicted non-nationals in 2007.

53 Rehabilitation or reintegration has never been among the purposes of punishment for foreigners. For instance, the Carlisle Committee – appointed to analyse the British parole system and to suggest changes – recommended the exclusion of foreign nationals liable to deportation from this system because their punishment has no rehabilitative purposes (Carlisle 1988: paragraph 470). More recently, in a parliamentary debate about foreign prisoners in the UK, Conservative MP Philip Hollobone made the point that the number of foreigners in British prisons contributes to their overcrowding and thus undermines the rehabilitative aims of punishment for 'British prisoners, who are likely to stay in this country for a long time'. The government representative, MP Crispin Blunt, added that rehabilitation of foreigners is 'not a duty owed by the United Kingdom taxpayer to foreigners in the same way as it is owed to our own citizens' (Hansard, HC Deb 22/06/2010, cols 55WH and 56WH).

54 In several US jurisdictions, being undocumented is a ground for ineligibility for non-prison sentences: see Chin (2011: 1430). In Italy, the judiciary is reluctant to apply procedural possibilities for leniency in favour of undocumented migrants – particularly the suspension of a prison sentence or alternatives to prison (Nelken 2009: 308).

55 The Court of Appeal held that sentencing decisions should not consider the effect that the sentence can have on deportation. In *R v Kiril Mintchev* [2011] EWCA Crim 499, the court stated: 'if once the decision is reached that the sentence of the judge was otherwise appropriate, then it cannot be right to reduce it simply to avoid the application of the automatic deportation provisions' [at 23]. See also *R v Lyla Turner* [2010] EWCA Crim 2897 [at 28].

6 Explaining the role of criminal law in the control of immigration

1 See, however, Zedner (2010).

2 Hildebrandt argues that in mediaeval Europe – and Germany, in particular – a clear line was drawn between 'police' and 'justice', each subject to different regimes and limitations. Criminal law belonged to the domain of 'justice' where a number of legal rules applied. The domain of 'police', instead, was 'based on the authority of the

sovereign to command his subjects and seemed to be situated outside the realm of law' (Hildebrandt 2009: 53). Regulatory offences were part of the police ambit or the administration: they were not aimed at protecting public goods, but the integrity of the administrative order.

3 While this expression seems novel, it has been used earlier by criminal law scholars critical of the pace of the expansion of substantive criminal law: see Kadish (1967).

4 This consultation paper was primarily aimed at reviewing the system of sanctions – and particularly the role of criminal justice – in regulatory contexts. It follows the report prepared by Richard Macrory (2006) in which he called for a limitation of the role of criminal justice in dealing with regulatory non-compliance and the creation of a more diversified penalty system.

5 Excluding motoring offences.

6 One of them being a partial amendment to S. 25(1), IA 1971.

7 E.g. interventions by Neil Gerard in Hansard, HC Deb 24/04/2002, cols 387–388 and HC Deb 17/12/2003, col. 1636; and Damian Green in Hansard, HC Deb 05/02/2007, col. 601.

8 Public opinion surveys show that UK-born, white Britons with lower levels of education and income are more likely strongly to prefer restrictive immigration policies (e.g. McLaren and Johnson 2007; Blinder 2011).

9 8 USC Sec. 1325(a), US Code.

10 8 USC Sec. 1326, US Code.

11 8 USC Sec. 1253, US Code.

12 18 USC Sec. 758, US Code.

13 8 USC Sec. 1253, US Code.

14 *Arizona et al. v United States* 000 U.S. 11-182 (2012). On the constitutionality of state regulation of immigration, see Chin and Miller (2011); Eagly (2011).

15 Division 12, Migration Act 1958.

16 Part 3, Immigration and Refugee Protection Act 2001. See Pratt (2005).

17 There are signs of convergence in other aspects of immigration policies. Welch and Schuster noticed a 'conservative shift' in the treatment of asylum seekers and an increase in detention rates in the United States, the UK, France, Germany and Italy (Welch and Schuster 2005b).

18 Article 83, Law 3386/2005 (Immigration Act).

19 Article 10 bis, Law No. 94/2009 (modifying Law Decree No. 286/1998).

20 Article 5(1), Law No. 94/2009 (modifying Law Decree No. 286/1998) (non-official translation).

21 Article 14(5b), Law Decree No. 286/1998. The original version of this provision, which ordered the compulsory arrest of foreigners in breach of deportation orders, was modified to the current version following a decision by the Italian Constitutional Court ruling that such provision was discriminatory (Italian Constitutional Court, Decision No. 222, 8–15 July 2004, quoted in Ventrella McCreight 2006: 162).

22 Article 1(f), Law Decree No. 92/2008.

23 Article 197, Dutch Penal Code. After much debate, in October 2012, the Dutch coalition government announced its plans to make illegal residence a criminal offence punishable by imprisonment of up to four years or a fine of up to €3,800.

24 Article 318 bis, Criminal Code. While the scope of criminal law against migrants is limited in Spain, Spanish courts have interpreted this provision broadly, imposing sanctions on those who help family members and in other cases of 'humanitarian smuggling' (Martínez Escamilla 2009: 9).

25 Article 6(1), UN Protocol against Smuggling which prescribes the criminalization of smuggling without subjecting that imperative to any exception.

26 Article 5, Protocol to Prevent, Suppress and Punish Trafficking in Persons, Especially Women and Children, supplementing the United Nations Convention against Transnational Organized Crime ('UN Protocol against Trafficking').

27 See articles 3(2), 26(2) and 27(1), respectively, Schengen Convention.
28 Article 4(1), Carrier Liability Directive.
29 See, respectively, article 1(1), Directive on unauthorized entry, transit and residence; and article 1(1), Framework Decision on unauthorized entry, transit and residence.
30 Such as when the infringement is continued or is persistently repeated; involves a significant number of workers; involves exploitative conditions; relates to a victim of trafficking or involves a minor. See article 9(1), Directive 2009/52/EC of the European Parliament and of the Council of 18 June 2009 providing for minimum standards on sanctions and measures against employers of illegally staying third-country nationals, Official Journal L 168/24 of 30/6/2009.
31 See articles 18–21, European Convention on Action against Trafficking in Human Beings.
32 Article 1(1), Council Framework Decision 2002/629/JHA of 19 July 2002 on combating trafficking in human beings, Official Journal L 203 of 1/8/2002.
33 See article 4(a) and article 3(a), respectively, UN Protocol against Trafficking.
34 IACHR, *Vélez Loor v Panama*. Preliminary Objections, Merits, Reparations, and Costs. Judgment of 23 November 2010. Series C No. 218, paragraph 172.
35 Directive 2008/115/EC of the European Parliament and of the Council of 16 December 2008 on common standards and procedures in Member States for returning illegally staying third-country nationals, Official Journal L 348 of 24/12/2008.
36 ECJ, Judgment of 28 April 2011. *Hassen El Dridi*. Case C-61/11, paragraph 62.
37 ECJ, Judgment of 28 April 2011. *Hassen El Dridi*. Case C-61/11, paragraph 52.
38 See ECHR, *SD v Greece*, judgment of 11 June 2009, Application 53541/07.
39 Some authors have criticized the punitive inclination of international human rights bodies which prescribe penal sanctions on virtually any human rights violation without considering principles of substantive criminal law and criminal responsibility (see e.g. Pastor 2005; Aliverti 2007; also Sebba 2009).
40 See, however, a recent landmark decision in which the Court recognized the right of third-country parents without legal residence to reside and work in the country of citizenship of their dependent children (ECHR, *Ruiz Zambrano v Belgium*, judgment of 8 March 2011, Case C-34/09, paragraphs 42–44).
41 ECHR, *Amuur v France*, judgment of 25 June of 1996, Application 19776/92, paragraph 41; *Saadi v the United Kingdom*, judgment of 29 January 2008, Application 13229/03, paragraph 64.
42 See e.g. ECHR, *Engel et al v the Netherlands*, judgment of 23 November 1976, Applications 5100/71, 5101/71, 5102/71, 5354/72, 5370/72, paragraph 81; and *Öztürk v Germany*, judgment of 21 February 1984, Application 8544/79, paragraph 53. For a comment on *Öztürk v Germany*, see Duff (2007).
43 In a leading case involving non-nationals suspected of terrorism who were indefinitely detained under the UK's Anti-Terrorism, Crime and Security Act 2001, the ECHR supported 'less intrusive' measures to address the terrorist threat that led to the detention of the petitioners, including the recourse to the criminal justice system through the creation of specific offences. See ECHR, *A and others v the United Kingdom*, judgment of 19 February 2009, Application 3455/05, paragraph 145.
44 Schedule 4, paragraph 8, IAA 1999.
45 Schedule 12, paragraph 3, IAA 1999.
46 S. 137(1), NIAA 2002.
47 S. 34(1), IANA 2006.
48 Ss 15(1), 15A, 16(1) and 20(2), Theft Act 1968; Ss 1(1) and 2(1), Theft Act 1978; and Ss 2(1), 3 and 4(1), Fraud Act 2006.
49 S. 24A, IA 1971 (S. 28, IAA 1999). The reproduction of fraud-based offences in regulatory contexts has been identified as one of the causes of the expansion of criminal law in recent years (Law Commission 2010: 11).
50 S. 3, FCA 1981.

51 S. 25(1) and (5), IDCA 2006. The IDCA 2006 was repealed by the Identity Documents Act 2010 which introduced three separate offences of document fraud, similar to those repealed and with the same penalties (Ss 4 and 6).

52 S. 26(1) (d), IA 1971.

53 See Home Office (2001: Table 7.5); Home Office (2006a: Table 6.7); Home Office (2010b: Tables 3.11a and 3.11b); Home Office (2012: Table pr.01).

54 Before then, S. 3, FCA 1981 was preferred (see Chapter 3).

55 Particularly the offences of possession with intent under S. 25(1) and (5), IDCA 2006.

56 Excluding the offence of simple possession of a false, an improperly obtained or another's identity document without reasonable excuse, which is triable either way. See S. 25(5) and (7), IDCA 2006.

57 In English criminal law, offences are classified into three categories: summary only (triable only before magistrates' courts), indictable only (triable only on indictment before crown courts) or hybrid (triable either way).

58 Schedule 11, paragraph 4, IAA 1999.

59 S. 3(1) (b) and (c) and S. 22(1), respectively, UK Borders Act 2007.

60 S. 89(1), Police Act 1996.

61 S. 8, Prison Act 1952.

62 Evidentiary difficulties were mentioned as one of the motives for introducing a civil penalty regime on carriers responsible for clandestine entrants and people without proper documentation. See Chapter 3.

63 In a similar line, Daniel Kanstroom (2000: 1907) argued that deportation is based on a contractual model in US legislation and case law. It is a social control device on non-citizens who are conceived as 'eternal guests', with limited rights and subject to expulsion. The consequence (deportation) bears no link or proportion to the cause (breach to the entry conditions). Its main goal is to return the individual to the *status quo ante*.

64 This is evident in cases involving national security issues where the person subject to investigation cannot be criminally prosecuted and is removed from the country for alleged breaches to immigration rules instead. For example, in April 2009, 12 Pakistani men were arrested following an anti-terrorist operation in Manchester. They were not charged with criminal offences, but deported to Pakistan (see media coverage in O'Neill *et al.* 2009). Other similar examples of how removal has been used against terrorist suspects in the United States are described in Chacón (2008: 1861). Equally, one of my interviewees working on FNP policy at UKBA told me that they usually 'get an immigration solution to a criminal problem'. This happens when

> the police [are] looking for us to prioritize a particular case or [someone] who doesn't have any leave because that individual is known to be an offender or a low level offender in the community . . . The police might ask us to shift that up in our priorities.
>
> (Respondent 2, 18/05/2010)

On the use of immigration enforcement for crime control, see also Quassoli (2004).

65 Beccaria ([1764]1963: Chapter XLI: 94).

66 A recent estimation of the UK irregular resident population for 2007 was 618,000, of whom 442,000 were calculated to be based in London (Gordon *et al.* 2009: 8). In 2009, 67,215 people were subject to removal and voluntary departure, while only 549 people were proceeded against and 433 were convicted of immigration offences (Home Office 2010b: Tables 3.1, 3.11a and 3.11b).

67 In order to be eligible, the individual has to admit the charge and accept voluntary removal. The offence forms part of the person's criminal records. Cautions have been extensively used in recent years as a means to unclog the criminal justice system (Duff *et al.* 2007; Ashworth and Zedner 2008).

Conclusion

1 The fact that a certain type of activity involves a potential danger to public safety has been one of the reasons for displacing the general presumption under English law that *mens rea* is required for every offence (*Gammon Ltd v A-G of Hong Kong* [1985] 1 AC 1 [at 14]). In *Sweet v Parsley* [1970] AC 132 [at 163], Lord Diplock justified the displacement of this presumption and favoured absolute liability for offences in which the defendant is voluntarily involved in activities entailing a potential danger to the public and which thus require a 'higher duty of care'. Thus, the substance matter of a particular activity justifies not only the decision to criminalize, but also the imposition of strict liability (thus the reference to a higher duty of care as opposed to the ordinary duty of care required for negligence). See Simester *et al.* (2010: 192).

2 See, however, the special issue of the *New Criminal Law Review* on 'Citizenship and Criminalization' (2010: vol. 13, issue 2) as a promising starting point.

3 See, however, Dubber (2010b).

Appendix: brief account of the research process

1 A low level of response is a common feature of research relying on interviews with MPs: see Williams (1984).

2 Criminal justice data are disaggregated by groups of crimes, one of them being 'fraud and forgery'. While FNPs are not significantly represented in other offence categories, compared to British prisoners, they are over-represented in drug, and fraud and forgery offences. In 2005, FNPs comprised 51 per cent of all prisoners for fraud and forgery. Moreover, the largest increase in convicted FNPs between 2000 and 2005 was for drug offences (from 1,736 to 2,538) followed by fraud and forgery (from 139 to 611) (Hammond 2007: 821). Similarly, in 2009, half of those serving an immediate custodial sentence for 'fraud and forgery' offences were foreigners (Ministry of Justice 2010a: 78).

3 However, this 'filter' had apparently not been considered for the search, as I found that some of those charged with these offences – particularly 'facilitation' offences – were British nationals.

4 When referring to court hearings, I mention the name of the defendant as this is information that has been revealed during the hearings and thus made public.

5 Cases before Uxbridge Magistrates' Court are referred to as: Uxbridge Magistrates' Court, court file/hearing, Case X. Cases before Isleworth Crown Court are referred to as: Isleworth Crown Court, court file/hearing, Case X.

6 I borrow this expression from Katja Franko Aas which so nicely captures the lack of interest in these offences. I also thank her for making me aware of this aspect of my research.

References

Aas, K. F. (2007). Analysing a World in Motion: Global Flows Meet 'Criminology of the Other'. *Theoretical Criminology*, 11, 283–303.

Aas, K. F. (2011a). 'Crimmigrant' Bodies and Bona Fide Travelers: Surveillance, Citizenship and Global Governance. *Theoretical Criminology*, 15, 331–346.

Aas, K. F. (2011b). Victimhood of the National? Denationalizing Sovereignty in Crime Control. In A. Crawford (ed.) *International and Comparative Criminal Justice and Urban Governance: Convergence and Divergence in Global, National and Local Settings*. Cambridge: Cambridge University Press, pp. 389–412.

Aas, K. F. (2012). (In)security-at-a-Distance: Rescaling Justice, Risk and Warfare in a Transnational Age. *Global Crime*, 13, 235–253.

Aas, K. F. (2013). The Ordered and the Bordered Society: Migration Control, Citizenship and the Northern Penal State. In K. F. Aas and M. Bosworth (eds) *The Borders of Punishment: Criminal Justice, Citizenship and Social Exclusion*. Oxford: Oxford University Press.

Achermann, A. and Gattiker, M. (1995). Safe Third Countries: European Developments. *International Journal of Refugee Law*, 7, 19–38.

ACPO and UKBA (2008). Police and United Kingdom Border Agency Engagement to Strengthen the UK Border. A Memorandum of Understanding between the Association of Chief Police Officers of England, Wales and Northern Ireland (ACPO) and the United Kingdom Border Agency (UK Border Agency). London: ACPO/UKBA. Available at: http://www.ukba.homeoffice.gov.uk/sitecontent/documents/aboutus/ workingwithus/Policeandukbaengagement/ (accessed: 7 February 2013).

Aharonson, E. and Ramsay, P. (2010). Citizenship and Criminalization in Contemporary Perspective: Introduction. *New Criminal Law Review*, 13, 181–189.

Albrecht, H. (1997). Ethnic Minorities, Crime and Criminal Justice in Germany. *Crime and Justice*, 21, 31–100.

Albrecht, H. (2000). Foreigners, Migration, Immigration and the Development of Criminal Justice in Europe. In P. Green and A. Rutherford (eds) *Criminal Policy in Transition*. Oxford and Portland, OR: Hart, pp. 131–150.

Albrecht, H. (2002). Fortress Europe? Controlling Illegal Immigration. *European Journal of Crime, Criminal Law and Criminal Justice*, 10, 1–22.

Aliverti, A. (2007). Responsabilidades Limitadas: La Responsabilidad Estatal e Individual a Través de la Lente de la Corte Interamericana de DD HH. In J. Otero and P. Eiroa (eds) *Memoria y Derecho Penal*. Buenos Aires: Del Puerto, pp. 239–267.

Aliverti, A. (2008). What Type of Prevention? Early Intervention Programs in the United Kingdom and the Eclectic Character of Crime Prevention in Late Modernity. Unpublished MSc in Criminology and Criminal Justice Thesis, University of Oxford.

Alschuler, A. (1975). The Defense Attorney's Role in Plea Bargaining. *The Yale Law Journal*, 84, 1175–1314.

Amnesty International (2010). *Greece: Irregular Migrants and Asylum-Seekers Routinely Detained in Substandard Conditions*. London: Amnesty International Publications.

Amoore, L. (2006). Biometric Borders: Governing Mobilities in the War on Terror. *Political Geography*, 25, 336–351.

Anderson, B. (2007). A Very Private Business. *European Journal of Women's Studies*, 14, 247–264.

Anderson, B. (2010a). Mobilizing Migrants, Making Citizens: Migrant Domestic Workers as Political Agents. *Ethnic and Racial Studies*, 33, 60–74.

Anderson, B. (2010b). Migration, Immigration Controls and the Fashioning of Precarious Workers. *Work, Employment & Society*, 24, 300–317.

Anderson, B. (2012). Where's the Harm in That? Immigration Enforcement, Trafficking, and the Protection of Migrants' Rights. *American Behavioral Scientist*, 56, 1241–1257.

Anderson, B. and O'Connell Davidson, J. (2003). *Is Trafficking in Human Beings Demand Driven? A Multi-Country Pilot Study*. IOM Migration Research Series No. 15. Geneva: International Organization for Migration.

Anderson, B., Gibney, M. and Paoletti, E. (2011). Citizenship, Deportation and the Boundaries of Belonging. *Citizenship Studies*, 15, 547–563.

Anderson, M. (2000). The Transformation of Border Controls: A European Precedent? In P. Andreas and T. Snyder (eds) *The Wall around the West. State Borders and Immigration Controls in North America and Europe*. Oxford: Rowman & Littlefield Publishers Inc., pp. 15–29.

Anderson, M., den Boer, M., Gilmore, W. and Walker, N. (1995). *Policing the European Union*. Oxford: Oxford University Press.

Ashford, M. (1993). *Detained without Trial: A Survey of Immigration Act Detention*. London: Joint Council for the Welfare of Immigrants.

Ashworth, A. (1987). The 'Public Interest' Element in Prosecutions. *Criminal Law Review*, September, 595–607.

Ashworth, A. (1988). Criminal Justice and the Criminal Process. *British Journal of Criminology*, 28, 111–123.

Ashworth, A. (1989). Criminal Justice and Deserved Sentences. *Criminal Law Review*, May, 340–355.

Ashworth, A. (2000). Is the Criminal Law a Lost Cause? *Law Quarterly Review*, 226, 225–256.

Ashworth, A. (2006). The Sentencing Guideline System in England and Wales. *South African Journal of Criminal Law*, 19, 1–22.

Ashworth, A. (2007). Sentencing. In M. Maguire, M. Morgan and R. Reiner (eds) *The Oxford Handbook of Criminology*, 4th edn. Oxford: Oxford University Press, pp. 990–1023.

Ashworth, A. (2008). Conceptions on Overcriminalization. *Ohio State Journal of Criminal Law*, 5, 407–425.

Ashworth, A. (2009). Criminal Law, Human Rights and Preventive Justice. In B. McSherry, A. Norrie and S. Bronnit (eds) *Regulating Deviance. The Redirection of Criminalisation and the Futures of Criminal Law*. Oxford: Hart, pp. 87–108.

Ashworth, A. and Player, E. (2005). Criminal Justice Act 2003: The Sentencing Provisions. *Modern Law Review*, 68, 822–838.

Ashworth, A. and Redmayne, M. (2010) *The Criminal Process*, 4th edn. Oxford: Oxford University Press.

Ashworth, A. and Zedner, L. (2008). Defending the Criminal Law: Reflections on the Changing Character of Crime, Procedure, and Sanctions. *Criminal Law and Philosophy*, 2, 21–51.

Ashworth, A. and Zedner, L. (2011). Just Prevention: Preventive Rationales and the Limits of the Criminal Law. In R. Duff and S. Green (eds) *Philosophical Foundations of the Criminal Law*. Oxford: Oxford University Press, pp. 279–303.

Ashworth, A. and Zedner, L. (2012). Prevention and Criminalization: Justifications and Limits. *New Criminal Law Review*, 15, 542–571.

Atkinson, R. and Flint, J. (2001). Accessing Hidden and Hard-to-Reach Populations: Snowball Research Strategies. *Social Research Update*, 33. Available at: http://sru.soc.surrey.ac.uk/SRU33.html (accessed: 9 February 2013).

Avci, G. and McDonald, C. (2000). Chipping Away at the Fortress: Unions, Immigration and the Transnational Labour Market. *International Migration*, 38, 191–213.

Bachman, R. and Schutt, R. (2007). *The Practice of Research in Criminology and Criminal Justice*, 3rd edn. Thousand Oaks, CA: Sage.

Bacon, C. (2005). The Evolution of Immigration Detention in the UK: The Involvement of Private Prison Companies. RSC Working Paper No. 27. Available at: http://www.rsc.ox.ac.uk/publications/working-papers-folder_contents/RSCworkingpaper27.pdf (accessed: 9 February 2013).

Baldwin, J. (2007). Research on the Criminal Courts. In R. King and E. Wincup (eds) *Doing Research on Crime and Justice*. Oxford: Oxford University Press, pp. 237–255.

Baldwin, R. (2004). The New Punitive Regulation. *Modern Law Review*, 67, 351–383.

Baratta, A. (2002). *Criminología Crítica y Crítica del Derecho Penal. Introducción a la Sociología Jurídico-Penal*. Buenos Aires: Siglo Veintiuno.

Barnardos (2009). *Whose Child Now? Fifteen Years of Working to Prevent the Sexual Exploitation of Children in the UK*. Barkingside, Essex: Barnardos.

BBC News (2009). Border Agency Bonuses Criticised by MPs. 8 December 2009.

BBC News (2011). Sex Trafficking Victim Gets Damages from Home Office. BBC News. 11 April 2011.

Beccaria, C. ([1764] 1963). *On Crimes and Punishments*. Indianapolis, IN: Bobbs-Merrill.

Benhabib, S. (1999). Citizens, Residents, and Aliens in a Changing World: Political Membership in the Global Era. *Social Research*, 66, 709–744.

Benhabib, S. (2002). In Search of Europe's Borders. *Dissent*, Fall 2002, 33–39.

Bigo, D. (1994). The European Internal Security Field: Stakes and Rivalries in a Newly Developing Area of Police Intervention. In M. Anderson and M. Den Boer (eds) *Policing Across National Boundaries*. London: Pinter Publishers, pp. 161–173.

Bigo, D. (2005). Frontier Controls in the European Union: Who is in Control? In D. Bigo and E. Guild (eds) *Controlling Frontiers: Free Movement into and within Europe*. Aldershot: Ashgate, pp. 49–99.

Bigo, D. and Guild, E. (2005). Policing at a Distance: Schengen Visa Policies. In D. Bigo and E. Guild (eds) *Controlling Frontiers. Free Movement into and within Europe*. Aldershot: Ashgate, pp. 233–263.

Black, J. (2002). Critical Reflections on Regulation. *Australian Journal of Legal Philosophy*, 27, 1–35.

Black, R. (2003). Breaking the Convention: Researching the 'Illegal' Migration of Refugees to Europe. *Antipode*, 35, 34–54.

Blinder, S. (2011). UK Public Opinion toward Migration: Determinants of Attitudes. The Migration Observatory. Available at: http://www.migrationobservatory.ox.ac.uk/sites/files/migobs/Public%20Opinion-Determinants%20of%20Attitudes%20Briefing.pdf (accessed: 28 June 2011).

Bloch, A. (2000). A New Era or More of the Same? Asylum Policy in the UK. *Journal of Refugee Studies*, 13, 29–42.

Bloch, A. and Schuster, L. (2005). At the Extremes of Exclusion: Deportation, Detention and Dispersal. *Ethnic and Racial Studies*, 28, 491–512.

Bohmer, C. and Shuman, A. (2008). *Rejecting Refugees. Political Asylum in the 21st Century*. London and New York: Routledge.

Boswell, C. (2003). *European Migration Policies in Flux: Changing Patterns of Inclusion and Exclusion*. Oxford: Blackwell.

Boswell, C. (2005). Migration in Europe. Paper prepared for the Global Commission on International Migration. Geneva: Global Commission on International Migration. Available at: http://www.iom.int/jahia/webdav/site/myjahiasite/shared/shared/mainsite/policy_and_research/gcim/rs/RS4.pdf (accessed: 16 November 2011).

Boswell, C. (2007). Migration Control in Europe after 9/11: Explaining the Absence of Securitization. *Journal of Common Market Studies*, 45, 589–610.

Boswell, C. (2008). Migration, Security, and Legitimacy. In G. Freeman, T. Givens and D. Leal (eds) *Immigration Policy and Security: US, European and Commonwealth Perspectives*. New York: Routledge, pp. 93–106.

Bosworth, M. (2007). Immigration Detention in Britain. In M. Lee (ed.) *Human Trafficking*. Cullompton: Willan, pp. 159–177.

Bosworth, M. (2008). Border Control and the Limits of the Sovereign State. *Social & Legal Studies*, 17, 199–215.

Bosworth, M. (2011a). Deportation, Detention and Foreign-National Prisoners in England and Wales. *Citizenship Studies*, 15, 583–595.

Bosworth, M. (2011b). Ambivalence and Detention. Seminar paper presented at 'A Chrysalis for Every Kind of Criminal? Mobility, Crime and Citizenship', Centre on Migration, Policy and Society (COMPAS), University of Oxford, 20 October 2011.

Bosworth, M. (2011c). Human Rights and Immigration Detention in the UK. In M. Dembour and T. Kelly (eds) *Are Human Rights for Migrants? Critical Reflections on the Status of Irregular Migrants in Europe and the United States*. London: Routledge, pp. 165–183.

Bosworth, M. and Guild, M. (2008). Governing through Migration Control: Security and Citizenship in Britain. *British Journal of Criminology*, 48, 703–719.

Bottoms, A. (1995). The Philosophy and Politics of Punishment and Sentencing. In C. Clarkson and M. Morgan (eds) *The Politics of Sentencing Reform*. Oxford: Oxford University Press, pp. 17–49.

Bottoms, A. and McClean, J. (1976). *Defendants in the Criminal Process*. London: Routledge & Kegan Paul.

Braithwaite, J. (2003). What's Wrong with the Sociology of Punishment? *Theoretical Criminology*, 7, 5–28.

Braithwaite, J. (2010). Foreword. In H. Quirk, T. Seddon and G. Smith (eds) *Regulation and Criminal Justice: Innovations in Policy and Research*. Cambridge: Cambridge University Press, pp. xiii–xviii.

Braithwaite, J. and Ayres, I. (1992). *Responsive Regulation: Transcending the Deregulation Debate*. Oxford: Oxford University Press.

Brandariz García, J. and Fernández Bessa, C. (2009). L'immigrato come Categoria di

Rischio nel Sistema Penale Spagnolo. In S. Palidda (ed.) *Razzismo Democratico. La Persecuzione degli Stranieri in Europa*. Genoa: AgenziaX, pp. 142–154.

Brennan, R. (2006). *Immigration Advice at the Police Station*. London: The Law Society.

Broeders, D. (2010). Return to Sender? Administrative Detention of Irregular Migrants in Germany and the Netherlands. *Punishment & Society*, 12, 169–186.

Broeders, D. and Engbersen, G. (2007). The Fight Against Illegal Migration. *American Behavioral Scientist*, 50, 1592–1609.

Brown, D. (2007). Democracy and Decriminalization. *Texas Law Review*, 86, 223–275.

Buckland, B. (2008). More than Just Victims: The Truth about Human Trafficking. *Public Policy Research*, 15, 42–47.

Burgess, E. ([1925] 1967). The Growth of the City: An Introduction to a Research Project. In R. Park and E. Burgess (eds) *The City: Suggestions for Investigation of Human Behavior in the Urban Environment*. London: University of Chicago Press, pp. 47–62.

Bye, E. (1999). Putting Right an Asylum Wrong. *Law Society Gazette*, 36, p. 36.

Cabinet Office (2007). *Security in a Global Hub. Establishing the UK's New Border Arrangements*. London: Cabinet Office.

Calavita, K. (2003). A 'Reserve Army of Delinquents': The Criminalization and Economic Punishment of Immigrants in Spain. *Punishment & Society*, 5, 399–413.

Calavita, K. (2005). *Immigrants at the Margins: Law, Race, and Exclusion in Southern Europe*. New York: Cambridge University Press.

Carens, J. (2003). Who Should Get In? The Ethics of Immigration Admissions. *Ethics & International Affairs*, 17, 95–110.

Carling, J. (2002). Migration in the Age of Involuntary Immobility: Theoretical Reflections and Cape Verdean Experiences. *Journal of Ethnic and Migration Studies*, 28, 5–42.

Carlisle, M. (1988). *The Parole System in England and Wales* [The Carlisle Report]. London: HMSO.

Carson, W. (1970). White-Collar Crime and the Enforcement of Factory Legislation. *British Journal of Criminology*, 10, 383–398.

Carter, B., Harris, C. and Joshi, S. (1987). The 1951–55 Conservative Government and the Racialisation of Black Immigration. Policy Papers in Ethnic Relations No. 11, Centre for Research in Ethnic Relations, University of Warwick.

Carter, B., Green, M. and Halpern, R. (1996). Immigration Policy and the Racialization of Migrant Labour: The Construction of National Identities in the USA and Britain. *Ethnic and Racial Studies*, 19, 135–157.

Cecchi, D. (2011). The Criminalization of Immigration in Italy: Extent of the Phenomenon and Possible Interpretations. *Italian Sociological Review*, 1, 34–42.

Cesarani, D. (1993). An Alien Concept? The Continuity of Anti-Alienism in British Society before 1940. In D. Cesarani and T. Kushner (eds) *The Internment of Aliens in Twentieth Century Britain*. London: Frank Cass, pp. 25–52.

Chacón, J. (2007). Unsecured Borders: Immigration Restrictions, Crime Control and National Security. *Connecticut Law Review*, 39, 1827–1891.

Chacón, J. (2008). The Security Myth. Punishing Immigrants in the Name of National Security. In A. D'Appollonia and S. Reich (eds) *Immigration, Integration, and Security: America and Europe in Contemporary Perspectives*. Pittsburgh, PA: University of Pittsburgh Press, pp. 145–163.

Chan, W. (2005). Crime, Deportation and the Regulation of Immigrants in Canada. *Crime, Law and Social Change*, 44, 153–180.

Chin, G. (2011). Illegal Entry as Crime, Deportation as Punishment: Immigration Status and the Criminal Process. *UCLA Law Review*, 58, 1417–1460.

Chin, G. and Miller, M. (2011). The Unconstitutionality of State Regulation of Immigration through Criminal Law. *Duke Law Journal*, 61, 251–314.

Clayton, G. (2012). *Textbook on Immigration and Asylum Law*. Oxford: Oxford University Press.

Cohen, R. (1994). *Frontiers of Identity. The British and the Others*. Harlow, Essex: Longman.

Cohen, R. (2006). *Migration and Its Enemies: Global Capital, Migrant Labour and the Nation-State*. Aldershot: Ashgate.

Cole, R. and Maslow-Armand, L. (1997). The Role of Counsel and the Courts in Addressing Foreign Language and Cultural Barriers at Different Stages of a Criminal Proceeding. *Western New England Law Review*, 19, 193–228.

Coleman, D. and Salt, J. (1992). *The British Population. Patterns, Trends and Processes*. New York: Oxford University Press.

Council of Europe (2010). *Criminalisation of Migration in Europe: Human Rights Implications*. Strasbourg: Office of the Commissioner for Human Rights, Council of Europe.

Couper, K. (1984). An Elusive Concept: The Changing Definition of Illegal Immigrants in the Practice of Immigration Control in the United Kingdom. *International Migration Review*, 18, 437–452.

Coutin, S. B. (2005). Contesting Criminality: Illegal Immigration and the Spatialization of Legality. *Theoretical Criminology*, 9, 5–33.

Craies, W. (1890). The Right of Aliens to Enter British Territory. *Law Quarterly Review*, XXI, 27–41.

Crown Prosecution Service (2012). Crown Prosecution Service Annual Report 2011–2012. London: CPS.

D'Appollonia, A. (2008). Immigration, Security, and Integration in the European Union. In A. D'Appollonia and S. Reich (eds) *Immigration, Integration, and Security: America and Europe in Comparative Perspectives*. Pittsburgh, PA: University of Pittsburgh Press, pp. 203–228.

D'Appollonia, A. and Reich, S. (2008). The Securitization of Immigration. Multiple Countries, Multiple Dimensions. In A. D'Appollonia and S. Reich (eds) *Immigration, Integration, and Security: America and Europe in Comparative Perspectives*. Pittsburgh, PA: University of Pittsburgh Press, pp. 1–22.

Daily Mail (2006). Home Office Blunders Left Foreign Rapists in UK. 26 April 2006. Available at: http://www.dailymail.co.uk/news/article-384183/Home-Office-blunders-left-foreign-rapists-UK.html (accessed: 9 February 2013).

Daily Mail (2011). Sex Trafficking Victim Wins Damages from Home Office after Being Deported Back to Sex Gang in Moldova. 11 April 2011. Available at: http://www.dailymail.co.uk/news/article-1375850/Sex-trafficking-victim-wins-damages-Home-Office-deported-sex-gang-Moldova.html (accessed: 9 February 2013).

Dallek, R. (2008). *Nixon and Kissinger. Partners in Power*. London: Penguin Books.

Daly, K. (2011). Shake It Up, Baby: Practising Rock 'N' Roll Criminology. In M. Bosworth and C. Hoyle (eds) *What Is Criminology?* Oxford: Oxford University Press, pp. 111–124.

Darlington, A. (2006). Passport to Prison. *Criminal Law & Justice Weekly*, 33, August.

Dauvergne, C. (2004). Sovereignty, Migration and the Rule of Law in Global Times. *Modern Law Review*, 67, 588–615.

Dauvergne, C. (2008). *Making People Illegal. What Globalization Means for Migration and Law*. New York: Cambridge University Press.

Davidson, L. (2010). Big Rise in Early Guilty Pleas after Legal Aid Reforms. *The Sunday Times*. 2 March 2010.

Daw, R. and Solomon, A. (2010). Assisted Suicide and Identifying the Public Interest in the Decision to Prosecute. *Criminal Law Review*, October, 737–751.

De Genova, N. (2002). Migrant 'Illegality' and Deportability in Everyday Life. *Annual Review of Anthropology*, 31, 419–447.

De Giorgi, A. (2006). *Re-Thinking the Political Economy of Punishment: Perspectives on Post-Fordism and Penal Politics*. Aldershot: Ashgate.

De Giorgi, A. (2010). Immigration Control, Post-Fordism, and Less Eligibility: A Materialist Critique of the Criminalization of Immigration across Europe. *Punishment & Society*, 12, 147–167.

De Giorgi, A. (2011). Post-Fordism and Penal Change: The New Penology as a Post-Disciplinary Social Control Strategy. In D. Melossi, M. Sozzo and C. Sparks (eds) *Travels of the Criminal Question. Cultural Embeddedness and Diffusion*. Oxford: Hart, pp. 113–143.

Demleitner, N. (2004). Misguided Prevention: The War on Terrorism as a War on Immigrant Offenders and Immigration Violators. *Criminal Law Bulletin*, 40, 550–575.

Demleitner, N. and Sands, J. (2002). Non-Citizen Offenders and Immigration Crimes: New Challenges in the Federal System. *Federal Sentencing Report*, 14, 247–254.

Dery, L. (1996). Disinterring the 'Good' and 'Bad Immigrant': A Deconstruction of the State Court Interpreter Laws for Non-English-Speaking Criminal Defendants. *University of Kansas Law Review*, 45, 837–896.

De Smith, S. (1972). Case and Comment. *Cambridge Law Journal*, 30, 1–4.

Dinwiddy, J. (1968). The Use of the Crown's Power of Deportation under the Aliens Act, 1793–1826. *Historical Research*, 41, 193–211.

Dubber, M. (2005). *The Police Power. Patriarchy and the Foundations of American Government*. New York: Columbia University Press.

Dubber, M. (2010a). Criminal Law between Public and Private Law. In R. A. Duff, L. Farmer, S. E. Marshall, M. Renzo and V. Tadros (eds) *The Boundaries of the Criminal Law*. Oxford: Oxford University Press, pp. 191–213.

Dubber, M. (2010b). Citizenship and Penal Law. *New Criminal Law Review*, 13, 190–215.

Dubber, M. (2011). Regulatory and Legal Aspects of Penality. In A. Sarat, L. Douglas and M. Merrill Umphrey (eds) *Law as Punishment/Law as Regulation*. Stanford, CA: Stanford University Press, pp. 19–49.

Dubber, M. (2013). Preventive Justice: The Quest for Principles. In A. Ashworth, L. Zedner and P. Tomlin (eds) *Prevention and the Limits of the Criminal Law*. Oxford: Oxford University Press, pp. 47–68.

Duff, R. (2007). Crimes, Regulatory Offences and Criminal Trials. In H. Müller-Dietz, E. Müller and K.-L. Kunz (eds) *Festschrift für Heike Jung*. Nomos: Verlagsgesellschaft, pp. 87–98.

Duff, R. (2010a). A Criminal Law for Citizens. *Theoretical Criminology*, 14, 293–309.

Duff, R. (2010b). Perversions and Subversions of Criminal Law. In R. A. Duff, L. Farmer, S. E. Marshall, M. Renzo and V. Tadros (eds) *The Boundaries of the Criminal Law*. Oxford: Oxford University Press, pp. 88–112.

Duff, R. (2011). Responsibility, Citizenship, and Criminal Law. In R. Duff and S. Green (eds) *Philosophical Foundations of Criminal Law*. Oxford: Oxford University Press, pp. 125–148.

Duff, R., Farmer, L., Marshall, S. and Tadros, V. (2007). *The Trial on Trial: Towards a Normative Theory of the Criminal Trial*. Oxford: Hart.

Duff, R., Farmer, L., Marshall, S., Renzo, M. and Tadros, V. (2010). Introduction: The Boundaries of the Criminal Law. In R. A. Duff, L. Farmer, S. E. Marshall, M. Renzo and V. Tadros (eds) *The Boundaries of the Criminal Law*. Oxford: Oxford University Press, pp. 1–26.

Dummett, A. and Nicol, A. (1990). *Subjects, Citizens, Aliens and Others: Nationality and Immigration Law*. London: Weidenfeld and Nicolson.

Dunstan, R. (1998). United Kingdom: Breaches of Article 31 of the 1951 Refugee Convention. *International Journal of Refugee Law*, 10, 205–213.

Düvell, F. (2007). United Kingdom. In A. Triandafyllidou and R. Gropas (eds) *European Immigration. A Sourcebook*. Aldershot: Ashgate, pp. 347–359.

Eagly, I. (2010). Prosecuting Immigration. *Northwestern University Law Review*, 104, 1281–1360.

Eagly, I. (2011). Local Immigration Prosecution: A Study of Arizona Before SB 1070. *UCLA Law Review*, 58, 1749–1818.

Ellermann, A. (2010). Undocumented Migrants and Resistance in the Liberal State. *Politics & Society*, 38, 408–429.

Ericson, R. (2007). *Crime in an Insecure World*. Cambridge: Polity Press.

Evans, J. (1983). *Immigration Law*. London: Sweet & Maxwell.

Farmer, L. (1996). The Obsession with Definition: The Nature of Crime and Critical Legal Theory. *Social & Legal Studies*, 5, 57–73.

Farmer, L. (2010a). Criminal Wrongs in Historical Perspective. In R. A. Duff, L. Farmer, S. E. Marshall, M. Renzo and V. Tadros (eds) *The Boundaries of the Criminal Law*. Oxford: Oxford University Press, pp. 214–237.

Farmer, L. (2010b). Time and Space in Criminal Law. *New Criminal Law Review*, 13, 333–356.

Feeley, M. (1979). *The Process is the Punishment: Handling Cases in a Lower Criminal Court*. New York: Russell Sage Foundation.

Feeley, M. (2004). Actuarial Justice and the Modern State. In G. Bruinsma, H. Elffers and J. de Keijser (eds) *Punishment, Places, and Perpetrators: Developments in Criminology and Criminal Justice Research*. Cullompton, Devon: Willan, pp. 62–77.

Feeley, M. (2006). Origins of Actuarial Justice. In S. Armstrong and L. McAra (eds) *Perspectives on Punishment*. Oxford: Oxford University Press, pp. 217–232.

Feeley, M. and Simon, J. (1992). The New Penology: Notes on the Emerging Strategy of Corrections and Its Implications. *Criminology*, 30, 449–474.

Feeley, M. and Simon, J. (1994). Actuarial Justice: The Emerging New Criminal Law. In D. Nelken (ed.) *The Futures of Criminology*. London: Sage, pp. 173–201.

Fekete, L. and Webber, F. (2009). Foreign Nationals, Enemy Penology and the Criminal Justice System. *European Race Bulletin*, 69, Autumn. Available at: http://www.irr. org.uk/pdf2/ERB_69_FNP_all.pdf (accessed: 2 February 2010).

Feldman, D. (2003). Was the Nineteenth Century a Golden Age for Immigrants? In A. Fahrmeir, O. Faron and P. Weil (eds) *Migration Control in the North Atlantic World: The Evolution of State Practices in Europe and the United States from the French Revolution to the Inter-War Period*. New York: Berghahn Books, pp. 167–177.

Ferrajoli, L. (1989). *Diritto e Ragione. Teoria del Garantismo Penale*. Rome: Giuseppe Laterza & Figli.

Fionda, J. and Ashworth, A. (1994). The New Code for Crown Prosecutors: Part 1: Prosecution, Accountability and the Public Interest. *Criminal Law Review*, December, 894–903.

Fitzpatrick, B. (2006). Burden of Proof: Immigration – Using False Instrument – Statutory Defence. *Criminal Law Review*, October, 911–917.

Flynn, D. (2005). New Borders, New Management: The Dilemmas of Modern Immigration Policies. *Ethnic and Racial Studies*, 28, 463–490.

Foucault, M. (1977). *Discipline and Punish: The Birth of the Prison*. London: Allen Lane.

Foucault, M. (1991). Governmentality. In G. Burchell, C. Gordon and P. Miller (eds) *The Foucault Effect: Studies in Governmentality.* Hemel Hempstead: Harvester Wheatsheaf, pp. 87–104.

FRA Europa (2011). *Fundamental Rights of Migrants in an Irregular Situation in the European Union*. Comparative Report. Luxembourg: FRA – European Union Agency for Fundamental Rights. Available at: http://fra.europa.eu/sites/default/files/fra_uploads/1827-FRA_2011_Migrants_in_an_irregular_situation_EN.pdf (accessed: 16 October 2012).

Francis, B., Soothill, K. and Dittrich, R. (2001). A New Approach for Ranking 'Serious' Offences. The Use of Paired-Comparisons Methodology. *British Journal of Criminology*, 41, 726–737.

Fraser, D. (2000). The Postwar Consensus: A Debate Not Long Enough? *Parliamentary Affairs*, 53, 347–362.

Freeman, G. (1994). Commentary. In W. Cornelius, P. Martin and J. Hollifield (eds) *Controlling Immigration: A Global Perspective*. Stanford, CA: Stanford University Press, pp. 297–302.

Gallagher, A. and Karlebach, N. (2011). Prosecution of Trafficking in Persons Cases: Integrating a Human Rights-Based Approach in the Administration of Criminal Justice. Background Paper. Geneva: OHCHR.

Gardner, C. (2006). Can the Government Manage Migration? A Study of UK Legislation and Policy from 1996–2006. Working Paper No. 34. Oxford: Centre on Migration, Policy and Society (COMPAS), University of Oxford.

Garland, D. (1990). *Punishment and Modern Society: A Study in Social Theory*. Oxford: Oxford University Press.

Garland, D. (1996). The Limits of the Sovereign State: Strategies of Crime Control in Contemporary Society. *British Journal of Criminology*, 36, 445–471.

Garland, D. (2001). *Culture of Control: Crime and Social Order in Contemporary Society*. Oxford: Oxford University Press.

Garoupa, N., Ogus, A. and Sanders, A. (2011). The Investigation and Prosecution of Regulatory Offences: Is there an Economic Case for Integration? *Cambridge Law Journal*, 70, 229–259.

Ghaill, M. (2000). The Irish in Britain: The Invisibility of Ethnicity and Anti-Irish Racism. *Journal of Ethnic and Migration Studies*, 26, 137–147.

Gibney, M. (1988). *Open Borders? Closed Societies? The Ethical and Political Issues*. New York: Greenwood Press.

Gibney, M. (2008). Asylum and the Expansion of Deportation in the United Kingdom. *Government and Opposition*, 43, 146–167.

Gibney, M. (2009). *Precarious Residents: Migration Control, Membership and the Rights of Non-Citizens*. Human Development Research Paper No. 10. New York: UNDP.

Gibney, M. and Hansen, R. (2003). *Deportation and the Liberal State: The Forcible Return of Asylum Seekers and Unlawful Migrants in Canada, Germany and the United Kingdom*. New Issues in Refugee Research Working Paper No. 77. Geneva: UN High Commissioner for Refugees.

Gilroy, P. (1982). Police and Thieves. In J. Solomos, B. Findlay, S. Jones and P. Gilroy (eds) *The Empire Strikes Back: Race and Racism in 70s Britain*. London: Hutchinson in association with the Centre for Contemporary Cultural Studies, University of Birmingham, pp. 143–182.

Gonzalez, W. (2002). Trafficking: Criminalization of Victims in the Sex Industry. *Buffalo Women's Law Journal*, 11, 19–26.

Goodey, J. (2003). Migration, Crime and Victimhood. *Punishment & Society*, 5, 415–431.

Goodwin-Gill, G. (2001). *Article 31 of the 1951 Convention Relating to the Status of Refugees: Non-Penalization, Detention and Protection*. Geneva: UNHCR.

Gordon, I., Scanlon, K., Travers, T. and Whitehead, C. (2009). *Economic Impact on the London and UK Economy of an Earned Regularisation of Irregular Migrants to the UK*. London: Greater London Authority.

Gordon, P. (1985). *Policing Immigration: Britain's Internal Controls*. London: Pluto Press.

Green, P. and Grewcock, M. (2002). The War against Illegal Immigration: State Crime and the Construction of European Identity. *Current Issues in Criminal Justice*, 14, 87–101.

Green, S. (1997). Why it's a Crime to Tear the Tag off a Mattress?: Overcriminalization and the Moral Content of Regulatory Offenses. *Emory Law Journal*, 46, 1533–1615.

Greenspan, R. (1991). The Transformation of Criminal Due Process in the Administrative State: The Targeted Urban Crime Narcotics Task Force. Unpublished PhD thesis, University of California at Berkeley.

Grewcock, M. (2009). *Border Crimes. Australia's War on Illicit Immigrants*. Sydney: University of Sydney Law School.

Griffith, J. (1960). Legal Aspects of Immigration. In J. Griffith, J. Henderson, M. Usborne and D. Wood (eds) *Coloured Immigrants in Britain*. London: Oxford University Press, pp. 159–177.

Guild, E. (2003). International Terrorism and EU Immigration, Asylum and Borders Policy: The Unexpected Victims of 11 September 2001. *European Foreign Affairs Review*, 8, 311–346.

Guild, E. and Geyer, F. (2008). Introduction: The Search for EU Criminal Law – Where Is it Headed? In E. Guild and F. Geyer (eds) *Security versus Justice? Police and Judicial Cooperation in the European Union*. Aldershot, Hampshire: Ashgate, pp. 1–15.

Guild, E. and Minderhoud, P. (2006). *Immigration and Criminal Law in the European Union: The Legal Measures and Social Consequences of Criminal Law in Member States on Trafficking and Smuggling in Human Beings*. Leiden: Martinus Nijhoff.

Guillén, F. and Vallès, L. (2003). Seguretat, Delinqüència i Immigració: Aprendre a Llegir les Dades. In E. Aja and M. Nadal (eds) *La Immigració a Catalunya Avui. Anuari 2002*. Barcelona: Mediterrània, pp. 327–362.

Gupta, A. (1974). Ugandan Asians, Britain, India and the Commonwealth. *African Affairs*, 73, 312–324.

Hagan, J. and Palloni, A. (1998). Immigration and Crime in the United States. In J. Smith and B. Edmonston (eds) *The Immigration Debate: Studies on the Economic, Demographic, and Fiscal Effects of Immigration*. Washington, DC: National Academy Press, pp. 367–387.

Hailbronner, K. (2004). Asylum Law in the Context of a European Migration Policy. In N. Walker (ed.) *Europe's Area of Freedom, Security and Justice*. Oxford: Oxford University Press, pp. 41–88.

Hales, L. (1996). *Refugees and Criminal Justice?* Cropwood Occasional Paper No. 21. Institute of Criminology, University of Cambridge.

Hales, L. and Gelsthorpe, L. (2011). Research on Criminalisation of Migrant Women. *Prison Service Journal*, November, 33–37.

Hall, S., Critcher, C., Jefferson, T., Clarke, J. and Roberts, B. (1978). *Policing the Crisis. Mugging, the State, and Law and Order.* London: Macmillan.

Hammarberg, T. (2008). It Is Wrong to Criminalize Migration. *Viewpoints*, 29 September 2008. Available at: http://www.coe.int/t/commissioner/Viewpoints/080929_en.asp (accessed: 2 February 2013).

Hammond, N. (2007). United Kingdom. In A. van Kalmthout, F. Hofstee-van der Meulen and F. Dünkel (eds) *Foreigners in European Prisons.* Nijmegen: Wolf Legal Publishers, Chapter 26.

Hampshire, J. (2005). *Citizenship and Belonging. Immigration and the Politics of Demographic Governance in Postwar Britain.* Basingstoke: Palgrave Macmillan.

Hansen, R. (2000). *Citizenship and Immigration in Post-War Britain: The Institutional Origins of a Multicultural Nation.* Oxford: Oxford University Press.

Harcourt, B. (1999). The Collapse of the Harm Principle. *The Journal of Criminal Law and Criminology*, 90, 109–194.

Harcourt, B. (2003). The Shaping of Chance: Actuarial Models and Criminal Profiling at the Turn of the Twenty-First Century. *The University of Chicago Law Review*, 70, 105–128.

Harcourt, B. (2007). *Against Prediction: Punishing and Policing in an Actuarial Age.* Chicago, IL: University of Chicago Press.

Harcourt, B. (2013). Punitive Preventive Justice: A Critique. In A. Ashworth, L. Zedner and P. Tomlin (eds) *Prevention and the Limits of the Criminal Law.* Oxford: Oxford University Press, pp. 252–272.

Harper, T. and Leapman, B. (2007). Foreigners 'Commit Fifth of Crime in London'. *The Telegraph.* 23 September 2007. Available at: http://www.telegraph.co.uk/news/uknews/1563890/Foreigners-commit-fifth-of-crime-in-London.html (accessed: 9 February 2013).

Harrison, B. (2010). *Finding a Role? The United Kingdom 1970–1990.* Oxford: Oxford University Press.

Harvey, C. (2000). *Seeking Asylum in the UK. Problems and Prospects.* London: Butterworths.

Harvey, W. (2010). Methodological Approaches for Interviewing Elites. *Geography Compass*, 4, 193–205.

Hathaway, J. (2005). *The Rights of Refugees under International Law.* Cambridge: Cambridge University Press.

Hawkins, K. (1984). *Environment and Enforcement: Regulation and the Social Definition of Pollution.* Oxford: Oxford University Press.

Hawkins, K. (2002). *Law as Last Resort: Prosecution Decision-Making in a Regulatory Agency.* Oxford: Oxford University Press.

Hayter, T. (2003). No Borders: The Case against Immigration Controls. *Feminist Review*, 73, 6–18.

Hepple, B. (1969). Immigration Appeals Act 1969. *Modern Law Review*, 32, 668–672.

Hickman, M. (1998). Reconstructing Deconstructing 'Race': British Political Discourses about the Irish in Britain. *Ethnic and Racial Studies*, 21, 288–307.

Hildebrandt, M. (2009). Justice and Police: Regulatory Offenses and the Criminal Law. *New Criminal Law Review*, 12, 43–68.

HM Government (1971). Conclusions of a Meeting of the Cabinet Held at 10 Downing Street, S.W.1, on Thursday, 13 May, 1971, at 10.30 a.m. Available at: http://filestore.

nationalarchives.gov.uk/pdfs/small/cab-128-49-cm-71-25-25.pdf (accessed: 5 February 2013).

HM Government (2009). PSA Delivery Agreement 3: Ensure Controlled, Fair Migration that Protects the Public and Contributes to Economic Growth. London: HMSO.

HMIP (2006). *Foreign National Prisoners: A Thematic Review*. London: HM Inspectorate of Prisons.

Hodder, I. (2003). The Interpretation of Documents and Material Culture. In N. Denzin and Y. Lincoln (eds) *Collecting and Interpreting Qualitative Materials*, 2nd edn. London: Sage, pp. 155–175.

Hollifield, J. (1992). *Immigrants, Markets, and States: Political Economy of Postwar Europe*. Cambridge, MA: Harvard University Press.

Holmes, C. (1988). *John Bull's Island: Immigration and British Society, 1871–1971*. Basingstoke: Macmillan.

Holmes, C. (1991). *A Tolerant Country? Immigrants, Refugees and Minorities in Britain*. London: Faber and Faber.

Home Office (1965). *Immigration from the Commonwealth*. White Paper. Cmnd 2739. London: Home Office.

Home Office (1972). Press Release, 4 October 1972. London: Home Office.

Home Office (1979). *Control of Immigration: Statistics United Kingdom 1978*. Cmnd 7565. London: Home Office.

Home Office (1984). *Control of Immigration: Statistics United Kingdom 1983*. Cmnd 9246. London: Home Office.

Home Office (1985). *Control of Immigration: Statistics United Kingdom 1984*. Cmnd 9544. London: Home Office.

Home Office (1990). *Control of Immigration: Statistics United Kingdon 1989*. London: Home Office.

Home Office (1995). *Control of Immigration: Statistics United Kingdon 1994*. London: Home Office.

Home Office (1998). *Fairer, Faster and Firmer. A Modern Approach to Immigration and Asylum*. White Paper. Cmnd 4018. London: Home Office.

Home Office (2001). *Control of Immigration: Statistics United Kingdom 2000*. Cmnd 5315. London: Home Office.

Home Office (2002). *Secure Borders, Safe Haven. Integration with Diversity in Modern Britain*. White Paper. Cmnd 5387. London: Home Office.

Home Office (2003). *Control of Immigration: Statistics United Kingdom 2002*. Cmnd 6053. London: Home Office.

Home Office (2005a). *Control of Immigration: Statistics United Kingdom 2004*. Cmnd 6690. London: Home Office.

Home Office (2005b). *Illegal Working Taskforce Regulatory Impact Assessment for Immigration, Asylum and Nationality Bill*. London: Home Office.

Home Office (2005c). *Controlling our Borders: Making Migration Work for Britain. Five Year Strategy for Asylum and Immigration*. Cmnd 6472. London: Home Office.

Home Office (2006a). *Control of Immigration: Statistics United Kingdom 2005*. Cmnd 6904. London: Home Office.

Home Office (2006b). *Fair, Effective, Transparent and Trusted. Rebuilding Confidence in our Immigration System*. London: Home Office.

Home Office (2006c). *A Five Year Strategy for Protecting the Public and Reducing Re-Offending*. Cmnd 6717. London: Home Office.

Home Office (2007a). *Securing the UK Border. Our Vision and Strategy for the Future.* London: Home Office.

Home Office (2007b). *Enforcing the Rules. A Strategy to Ensure and Enforce Compliance with our Immigration Laws.* London: Home Office.

Home Office (2007c). *Simplifying Immigration Law: An Initial Consultation.* London: Home Office.

Home Office (2008a). *Control of Immigration: Statistics United Kingdom 2007.* 10/08. London: Home Office.

Home Office (2008b). *Enforcing the Deal. Our Plans for Enforcing the Immigration Laws in the United Kingdom's Communities.* London: Home Office.

Home Office (2008c). *Prevention of Illegal Working. Comprehensive Guidance for Employers on Preventing Illegal Working.* London: Home Office.

Home Office (2009a). *Control of Immigration: Statistics United Kingdom 2008.* 14/09. London: Home Office.

Home Office (2009b). *Making Change Stick. An Introduction to the Immigration and Citizenship Bill.* London: Home Office.

Home Office (2009c). *UK Border Agency Business Plan April 2008–March 2011.* London: Home Office.

Home Office (2010a). *Consultation on Changes to Immigration-Related Home Office Statistical Outputs.* London: Home Office. Available at: http://www.homeoffice.gov. uk/publications/science-research-statistics/research-statistics/immigration-asylum-research/immigration-consultation-2011?view=Binary (accessed: 27 November 2012).

Home Office (2010b). *Control of Immigration: Statistics United Kingdom 2009.* 15/10. London: Home Office.

Home Office (2010c). Building the Crime Directorate. Capability, Capacity and Performance. A Strategy to Enable Effective Use of Investigation and Prosecution to Achieve UKBA Objectives. Unpublished document. London: Home Office/ UKBA.

Home Office (2010d). *Protecting our Border, Protecting the Public. The UK Border Agency's Five Year Strategy for Enforcing Our Immigration Rules and Addressing Immigration and Cross Border Crime.* London: Home Office.

Home Office (2010e). *UK Border Agency Business Plan April 2009–March 2012.* London: Home Office.

Home Office (2011a). *UK Border Agency Business Plan 2011–15. Delivering our Commitments with a Smaller, More Efficient Agency.* London: Home Office.

Home Office (2011b). *Immigration Statistics April–June 2011.* London: Home Office. Available at: http://www.homeoffice.gov.uk/publications/science-research-statistics/research-statistics/immigration-asylum-research/immigration-q2-2011/ (accessed: 19 October 2012).

Home Office (2011c). *Human Trafficking: The Government's Strategy.* London: Home Office.

Home Office (2012). *Immigration Statistics April–June 2012.* London: Home Office. Available at: http://www.homeoffice.gov.uk/publications/science-research-statistics/research-statistics/immigration-asylum-research/immigration-tabs-q2-2012/ (accessed: 19 October 2012).

Hood, R. (1992). *Race and Sentencing.* Oxford: Oxford University Press/Clarendon Press.

Horder, J. (2012). Harmless Wrongdoing and Anticipatory Perspective on Criminalisation. In R. Sullivan and I. Dennis (eds) *Seeking Security. Pre-Empting the Commission of Criminal Harms.* Oxford: Hart, pp. 79–102.

House of Commons (2001). *First Report. Border Controls: Report and Proceedings of the Committee*. Home Affairs Committee. HC 163-II. London: TSO.

House of Commons (2004). *Asylum and Immigration (Treatment of Claimants, etc.) Bill, First Report of Session 2003–04*. Home Affairs Committee. HC 109 [Incorporating HC 692-ix, Session 2002–03]. London: TSO.

House of Commons (2006). *Immigration Control. Fifth Report of Session 2005–06. Vol. I*. Home Affairs Committee. London: TSO.

Hoyle, C., Bosworth, M. and Dempsey, M. (2011). Labelling the Victims of Sex Trafficking: Exploring the Borderland between Rhetoric and Reality. *Social & Legal Studies*, 20, 313–329.

Human Rights Council (2010). Report of the Working Group on Arbitrary Detention. A/HRC/13/30, 18 January 2010. United Nations. Available at: http://www2.ohchr. org/english/issues/detention/docs/A-HRC-13-30-Add2.pdf (accessed: 9 February 2013).

Human Rights Watch (2010). Fast-Tracked Unfairness. Detention and Denial of Women Asylum Seekers in the UK. New York: Human Rights Watch. Available at: http://www.hrw.org/sites/default/files/reports/uk0210webwcover.pdf (accessed: 21 November 2012).

Husak, D. (2004). The Criminal Law as a Last Resort. *Oxford Journal of Legal Studies*, 24, 207–235.

Husak, D. (2005). Strict Liability, Justice, and Proportionality. In A. Simester (ed.) *Appraising Strict Liability*. Oxford: Oxford University Press, pp. 81–103.

Husak, D. (2008). *Overcriminalization. The Limits of the Criminal Law*. New York: Oxford University Press.

Huysmans, J. (1995). Migrants as a Security Problem: Dangers of 'Securitizing' Societal Issues. In R. Miles and D. Thränhardt (eds) *Migration and European Integration: The Dynamics of Inclusion and Exclusion*. London: Pinters Publishers, pp. 53–73.

Huysmans, J. (2000). The European Union and the Securitization of Migration. *Journal of Common Market Studies*, 38, 751–777.

Huysmans, J. (2006). *The Politics of Insecurity. Fear, Migration and Asylum in the EU*. London and New York: Routledge.

Huysmans, J. and Buonfino, A. (2008). Politics of Exception and Unease: Immigration, Asylum and Terrorism in Parliamentary Debates in the UK. *Political Studies*, 56, 766–788.

IAS (1999). Memorandum from the Immigration Advisory Service. Hansard, House of Commons Debate, 17 March 1999.

Ibrahim, M. (2005). The Securitization of Migration: A Racial Discourse. *International Migration*, 43, 163–187.

ILPA (2011). Information on New Immigration Offences for Criminal Practitioners. London: Immigration Law Practitioners' Association. Available at: http://www.ilpa. org.uk/data/resources/13174/04.09.667.pdf (accessed: 6 February 2013).

International Centre for Prison Studies (2011). Prison Brief for United Kingdom: England and Wales. London: King's College London. Available at: http://www.kcl.ac.uk/depsta/law/research/icps/worldbrief/wpb_country.php?country=169 (accessed: 9 February 2013).

Ipsos Mori (2002). *Political Monitor*. 31 January 2002. Available at: http://www.ipsos-mori.com/researchpublications/researcharchive/1088/MORI-Political-Monitor-February-2002.aspx (accessed: 9 February 2013).

Israel, M. (2004). Strictly Confidential? Integrity and Disclosure of Criminological and Socio-Legal Research. *British Journal of Criminology*, 44, 715–740.

JCWI (1999). Memorandum from the Joint Council for the Welfare of Immigrants. Hansard, House of Commons Debate, 16 March 1999.

John, G. (2003). *Race for Justice. A Review of CPS Decision Making for Possible Racial Bias at Each Stage of the Prosecution Process*. London: Gus John Partnership Limited.

Johnson, T. (2011). On Silence, Sexuality and Skeletons: Reconceptualizing Narrative in Asylum Hearings. *Social & Legal Studies*, 20, 57–78.

Joppke, C. (1999). *Immigration and the Nation-State: The United States, Germany, and Great Britain*. Oxford: Oxford University Press.

Joppke, C. (2005). *Selecting by Origin: Ethnic Migration in the Liberal State*. Cambridge, MA: Harvard University Press.

Jordan, B. and Düvell, F. (2002). *Irregular Migration: The Dilemmas of Transnational Mobility*. Cheltenham: Edward Elgar.

Jubany-Baucells, O. (2003). Constructing Truths in a Culture of Disbelief: Screening Asylum Seekers in the UK and Spain. Unpublished PhD thesis, London School of Economics.

Junkert, C. and Kreienbrink, A. (2008). Irregular Employment of Migrant Workers in Germany – Legal Situation and Approaches to Tackling the Phenomenon. In M. Kupiszewski and H. Mattila (eds) *Addressing the Irregular Employment of Immigrants in the European Union: Between Sanctions and Rights*. Budapest: IOM, pp. 13–88.

Juss, S. (1997). *Discretion and Deviation in the Administration of Immigration Control*. London: Sweet & Maxwell.

Juss, S. (2005). The Decline and Decay of European Refugee Policy. *Oxford Journal of Legal Studies*, 25, 749–792.

Kadish, S. (1967). The Crisis of Overcriminalization. *The Annals of the American Academy of Political and Social Science*, 374, 157–170.

Kamenka, E. and Tay, A. (1975). Beyond Bourgeois Individualism: The Contemporary Crisis in Law and Legal Ideology. In E. Kamenka and R. Neale (eds) *Feudalism, Capitalism and Beyond*. London: Edward Arnold, pp. 127–144.

Kanstroom, D. (2000). Deportation, Social Control, and Punishment: Some Thoughts about Why Hard Laws Make Bad Cases. *Harvard Law Review*, 113, 1890–1935.

Kanstroom, D. (2004). Criminalizing the Undocumented: Ironic Boundaries of the Post-September 11th 'Pale of Law'. Boston College Law School Legal Studies Research Paper Series, Research Paper 2004–02, pp. 1–33.

Kanstroom, D. (2006). The Better Part of Valor: The REAL ID Act, Discretion, and the 'Rule' of Immigration Law. *New York Law School Law Review*, 51, 161–206.

Kay, D. and Miles, R. (1988). Refugees or Migrant Workers? The Case of the European Volunteer Workers in Britain (1946–1951). *Journal of Refugee Studies*, 1, 214–236.

Kaye, R. (1999). The Politics of Exclusion: The Withdrawal of Social Welfare Benefits from Asylum Seekers in the UK. *Contemporary Politics*, 5, 25–45.

Khosravi, S. (2010). *'Illegal' Traveller: An Auto-Ethnography of Borders*. Basingstoke and New York: Palgrave Macmillan.

Klein, S. (1999). Redrawing the Criminal–Civil Boundary. *Buffalo Criminal Law Review*, 2, 679–721.

Kostakopoulou, D. (2006). Trafficking and Smuggling Human Beings: The British Perspective. In E. Guild and P. Minderhoud (eds) *Immigration and Criminal Law in the European Union. The Legal Measures and Social Consequences of Criminal Law in Member States on Trafficking and Smuggling in Human Beings*. Leiden: Martinus Nijhoff, pp. 345–370.

Lacey, N. (1995). Contingency and Criminalisation. In I. Loveland (ed.) *The Frontiers of Criminality*. London: Sweet & Maxwell, pp. 1–27.

Lacey, N. (2004). Criminalization as Regulation: The Role of Criminal Law. In C. Parker, C. Scott, N. Lacey and J. Braithwaite (eds) *Regulating Law*. Oxford: Oxford University Press, pp. 144–167.

Lacey, N. (2008). *The Prisoners' Dilemma: Political Economy and Punishment in Contemporary Democracies*. New York: Cambridge University Press.

Lacey, N. (2009). Historicising Criminalisation: Conceptual and Empirical Issues. *Modern Law Review*, 72, 936–960.

Lacey, N. (2012). Principles, Policies, and Politics of Criminal Law. In L. Zedner and J. Roberts (eds) *Principles and Values in Criminal Law and Criminal Justice. Essays in Honour of Andrew Ashworth*. Oxford: Oxford University Press, pp. 19–36.

Lahav, G. (1998). Immigration and the State: The Devolution and Privatization of Immigration Control in the EU. *Journal of Ethnic and Migration Studies*, 24, 675–694.

Latimer, M. (1999). When Labour Played the Racist Card. *New Statesman*. 22 January 1999. Available at: http://www.newstatesman.com/when-labour-played-racist-card (accessed: 9 February 2013).

Law Commission (2010). Criminal Liability in Regulatory Contexts. A Consultation Paper. Consultation Paper No. 195. London: Law Commission.

Layton-Henry, Z. (1992). *The Politics of Immigration: Immigration, 'Race' and 'Race' Relations in Post-War Britain*. Oxford: Blackwell.

Layton-Henry, Z. (1994). Britain: The Would-be Zero-Immigration Country. In W. Cornelius, P. Martin and J. Hollifield (eds) *Controlling Immigration: A Global Perspective*. Stanford, CA: Stanford University Press, pp. 273–296.

Lee, M. (2005). Human Trade and the Criminalization of Irregular Migration. *International Journal of the Sociology of Law*, 33, 1–15.

Legal Services Commission (2006). *Legal Aid Reform: The Way Ahead*. London: Department for Constitutional Affairs and the Legal Services Commission.

Legomsky, S. (2007). The New Path of Immigration Law: Asymmetric Incorporation of Criminal Justice Norms. *Washington and Lee Law Review*, 64, 469–528.

Leigh, L. (1982). *Strict and Vicarious Liability: A Study in Administrative Criminal Law*. London: Sweet & Maxwell.

Lester, A. (2002). Thirty Years On: The East African Case Revisited. *Public Law*, Spring, 52–72.

Loader, I. (2002). Policing, Securitization and Democratization in Europe. *Theoretical Criminology*, 2, 125–153.

Loader, I. (2009). Ice Cream and Incarceration. *Punishment & Society*, 11, 241–257.

Loader, I. (2010a). For Penal Moderation. *Theoretical Criminology*, 14, 349–367.

Loader, I. (2010b). Consuming Security? *Theoretical Criminology*, 14, 3–30.

Loader, I. and Zedner, L. (2007). Review Essay. Police Beyond Law? *New Criminal Law Review*, 10, 142–152.

Loftus, B. (2009). *Police Culture in a Changing World*. Oxford: Oxford University Press.

London Detainee Support Group (2009). *Detained Lives. The Real Cost of Indefinite Immigration Detention*. London: LDSG.

Lowe, R. (2005). *The Welfare State in Britain since 1945*. Basingstoke: Palgrave Macmillan.

Lydgate, J. (2010). Assembly-Line Justice: A Review of Operation Streamline. *Policy Brief January 2010*. The Chief Justice Earl Warren Institute on Race, Ethnicity & Diversity. Berkeley, CA: University of California at Berkeley.

Lyon, D. (2009). *Identifying Citizens. ID Cards as Surveillance*. Cambridge: Polity Press.

McCulloch, J. and Pickering, S. (2009). Pre-Crime and Counter-Terrorism: Imagining Future Crime in the 'War on Terror'. *British Journal of Criminology*, 49, 628–645.

Macdonald, I. (1969). *Race Relations and Immigration Law*. London: Butterworths.

Macdonald, I. (2010). *MacDonald's Immigration Law and Practice*. London: LexisNexis.

McLaren, L. and Johnson, M. (2007). Resources, Group Conflict and Symbols: Explaining Anti-Immigration Hostility in Britain. *Political Studies*, 55, 709–732.

Macrory, R. (2006). *Regulatory Justice: Making Sanctions Effective*. Final Report. London: Cabinet Office.

McSherry, B., Norrie, A. and Bronitt, S. (2009). Regulating Deviance. The Redirection of Criminalisation and the Futures of Criminal Law. In B. McSherry, A. Norrie and S. Bronitt (eds) *Regulating Deviance. The Redirection of Criminalisation and the Futures of Criminal Law*. Oxford: Hart, pp. 3–10.

Malkin, B. (2007). Migrants 'Should Pay for our Services'. *The Telegraph*. 24 September 2007. Available at: http://www.telegraph.co.uk/news/uknews/1564013/Migrants-should-pay-for-our-services.html (accessed: 9 February 2013).

Malloch, M. and Stanley, E. (2005). The Detention of Asylum Seekers in the UK: Representing Risk, Managing the Dangerous. *Punishment & Society*, 7, 53–71.

Markowitz, P. (2008). Straddling the Civil–Criminal Divide: A Bifurcated Approach to Understanding the Nature of Immigration Removal Proceedings. *Harvard Civil Rights–Civil Liberties Law Review*, 43, 289–351.

Martin, P. and Miller, M. (2000). *Employer Sanctions: French, German and US Experiences*. Geneva: International Migration Branch, International Labour Office.

Martínez Escamilla, M. (2009). Inmigración, Derechos Humanos y Política Criminal: ¿Hasta Dónde Estamos Dispuestos a Llegar? *Revista para el Análisis del Derecho*, 3, 1–45.

Matthews, R. (2005). The Myth of Punitiveness. *Theoretical Criminology*, 9, 175–201.

Maxwell, J. (2005). *Qualitative Research Design. An Interactive Approach*. Thousand Oaks, CA: Sage.

Medina, I. (1997). The Criminalization of Immigration Law: Employment Sanctions and Marriage Fraud. *George Mason Law Review*, 5, 669–731.

Medina, I. (2011). *Migration Law in the USA*. Alphen aan den Rijn, the Netherlands: Kluwer Law International.

Melossi, D. (2000). The Other in the New Europe: Migrations, Deviance, Social Order. In P. Green and A. Rutherford (eds) *Criminal Policy in Transition*. Oxford: Hart, pp. 151–166.

Melossi, D. (2002). *Stato, Controllo Sociale, Devianza*. Milan: Bruno Mondatori.

Melossi, D. (2003). 'In a Peaceful Life': Migration and the Crime of Modernity in Europe/Italy. *Punishment & Society*, 5, 371–397.

Melossi, D. (2005). Security, Social Control, Democracy and Migration within the 'Constitution' of the EU. *European Law Journal*, 11, 5–21.

Merlino, M. (2009). The Italian (In)Security Package. Security vs. Rule of Law and Fundamental Rights in the EU. CEPS Challenge Programme, Research Paper No. 14. Available at: http://aei.pitt.edu/10764/1/1809.pdf (accessed: 2 February 2013).

Messier, F. (1999). Alien Defendants in Criminal Proceedings: Justice Shrugs. *American Criminal Law Review*, 36, 1395–1419.

Mill, J. S. ([1859] 1978). *On Liberty*. Indianapolis, IN: Hackett Publishing Co., Inc.

Miller, T. (2003). Citizenship and Severity. Recent Immigration Reforms and the New Penology. *Georgetown Immigration Law Journal*, 17, 611–666.

Miller, T. (2005). Blurring the Boundaries between Immigration and Crime Control after September 11th. *Boston College Third World Law Journal*, 25, 81–124.

Ministry of Justice (2007). *Autumn Performance Report 2007*. Cmnd 7271. London: HMSO.

Ministry of Justice (2010a). *Offender Management Caseload Statistics 2009*. London: Ministry of Justice.

Ministry of Justice (2010b). *Simple Cautions for Foreign National Offenders Pilot Policy Statement*. London: Ministry of Justice.

Monclús Maso, M. (2009). *La Gestión Penal de la Inmigración*. Buenos Aires: Del Puerto.

Morgan, K. (2001). *Britain since 1945. The People's Peace*. Oxford: Oxford University Press.

Morris, H. (1997). Zero Tolerance: The Increasing Criminalization of Immigration Law. *Interpreter Releases*, 74, 1317.

Morris, L. (1998). Governing at a Distance: The Elaboration of Controls in British Immigration. *International Migration Review*, 32, 949–973.

Morris, N. (2006). New Offences, Created for the Same Old Reasons. *The Independent*. 16 August 2006.

Moss, J. (2011). Trafficking: A Human Rights Abuse, Not an Immigration Offence. *openDemocracy*. 17 August 2011.

Muller, B. (2004). (Dis)qualified Bodies: Securitization, Citizenship and 'Identity Management'. *Citizenship Studies*, 8, 279–294.

Naffine, N. (2009). Moral Uncertainties of Rape and Murder. Problems at the Core of Criminal Law Theory. In B. McSherry, A. Norrie and S. Bronitt (eds) *Regulating Deviance. The Redirection of Criminalisation and the Futures of Criminal Law*. Oxford: Hart, pp. 212–232.

NAO (2009a). *The Home Office. Management of Asylum Applications by the UK Border Agency*. HC 124 Session 2008–2009. 23 January 2009. London: TSO.

NAO (2009b). *The Procurement of Criminal Legal Aid in England and Wales by the Legal Services Commission*. HC 29, Session 2009–2010. 27 November 2009. London: TSO.

Neal, A. (2009). Securitization and Risk at the EU Border: The Origins of FRONTEX. *Journal of Common Market Studies*, 47, 333–356.

Nelken, D. (2009). Comparative Criminal Justice: Beyond Ethnocentrism and Relativism. *European Journal of Criminology*, 6, 291–311.

Nelken, D. (2010). Human Trafficking and Legal Culture. *Israel Law Review*, 43, 479–513.

Newsam, F. (1954). *The Home Office*. London: Allen & Unwin.

Noaks, L. and Wincup, E. (2004). *Criminological Research. Understanding Qualitative Methods*. London: Sage.

Norrie, A. (2009). Citizenship, Authoritarianism and the Changing Shape of the Criminal Law. In B. McSherry, A. Norrie and S. Bronitt (eds) *Regulating Deviance. The Redirection of Criminalisation and the Futures of Criminal Law*. Oxford: Hart, pp. 13–34.

Ogus, A. (2010). Regulation and Its Relationship with the Criminal Justice System. In H. Quirk, T. Seddon and G. Smith (eds) *Regulation and Criminal Justice: Innovations in Policy and Research*. Cambridge: Cambridge University Press, pp. 27–41.

OHCHR (2009). *High Commissioner's Strategic Management Plan 2010–2011*. Geneva: United Nations Human Rights High Commissioner.

O'Malley, P. (1992). Risk, Power and Crime Prevention. *Economy and Society*, 21, 252–275.

O'Malley, P. (1999). Volatile and Contradictory Punishment. *Theoretical Criminology*, 3, 175–196.

O'Malley, P. (2000). Criminologies of Catastrophe? Understanding Criminal Justice on the Edge of the New Millennium. *The Australian and New Zealand Journal of Criminology*, 33, 153–167.

O'Malley, P. (2001). Policing Crime Risks in the Neo-Liberal Era. In K. Stenson and R. Sullivan (eds) *Crime, Risk and Justice: The Politics of Crime Control in Liberal Democracies*. Cullompton, Devon: Willan, pp. 89–103.

O'Malley, P. (2002). Globalizing Risk? Distinguishing Styles of 'Neo-Liberal' Criminal Justice in Australia and the USA. *Criminal Justice*, 2, 205–222.

O'Malley, P. (2004). The Uncertain Promise of Risk. *The Australian and New Zealand Journal of Criminology*, 37, 323–343.

O'Malley, P. (2013) The Politics of Mass Preventive Justice. In A. Ashworth, L. Zedner and P. Tomlin (eds) *Prevention and the Limits of the Criminal Law*. Oxford: Oxford University Press, pp. 273–296.

O'Neill, S., Hussain, Z. and Evans, M. (2009). Pakistani 'Terror Plot Suspects' to Be Deported Rather than Charged. *The Sunday Times*. 13 April 2009.

Panayi, P. (1996). *Racial Violence in Britain in the Nineteenth and Twentieth Centuries*. London: Leicester University Press.

Pantazis, C. (2008). The Problem with Criminalisation. *Criminal Justice Matters*, 74, 10–12.

Park, R. (1928). Human Migration and the Marginal Man. *The American Journal of Sociology*, 33, 881–893.

Parker, C., Scott, C., Lacey, N. and Braithwaite, J. (2004). Introduction. In C. Parker, C. Scott, N. Lacey and J. Braithwaite (eds) *Regulating Law*. Oxford: Oxford University Press, pp. 1–12.

Pastor, D. (2005). La Deriva Neopunitivista de Organismos y Activistas como Causa del Desprestigio Actual de los Derechos Humanos. *Nueva Doctrina Penal*, 2005/A, 73–114.

Pastore, F. (2004). Visas, Borders, Immigration: Formation, Structure and Current Evolution of the EU Entry Control System. In N. Walker (ed.) *Europe's Area of Freedom, Security, and Justice*. Oxford: Oxford University Press, pp. 89–142.

Paul, K. (1997). *Whitewashing Britain: Race and Citizenship in the Postwar Era*. Ithaca, NY and London: Cornell University Press.

Payne, G. and Williams, M. (2005). Generalization in Qualitative Research. *Sociology*, 39, 295–314.

Pellew, J. (1989). The Home Office and the Aliens Act, 1905. *Historical Journal*, 32, 369–385.

Pham, H. (2008). Private Enforcement of Immigration Laws. *Georgetown Law Journal*, 96, 777–826.

Pham, H. (2009). When Immigration Borders Move. *Florida Law Review*, 61, 1115–1164.

Porter, B. (1979). *The Refugee Question in Mid-Victorian Politics*. Cambridge: Cambridge University Press.

Pratt, A. (2005). *Securing Borders. Detention and Deportation in Canada*. Vancouver: University of British Columbia Press.

Pratt, A. and Valverde, M. (2002). From Deserving Victims to 'Masters of Confusion': Redefining Refugees in the 1990s. *The Canadian Journal of Sociology*, 27, 135–161.

Pratt, J. (2006). *Penal Populism*. London: Routledge.

Quassoli, F. (2004). Making the Neighbourhood Safer: Social Alarm, Police Practices and

Immigrant Exclusion in Italy. *Journal of Ethnic and Migration Studies*, 30, 1163–1181.

Ramsay, P. (2006). The Responsible Subject as Citizen: Criminal Law, Democracy and the Welfare State. *Modern Law Review*, 69, 29–58.

Ramsay, P. (2010). Overcriminalization as Vulnerable Citizenship. *New Criminal Law Review*, 13, 262–285.

Reiner, R. (2007). *Law and Order. An Honest Citizen's Guide to Crime and Control.* Cambridge: Polity Press.

Roberts, J., Stalans, L., Indermaur, D. and Hough, M. (2003). *Penal Populism and Public Opinion: Lessons from Five Countries.* New York: Oxford University Press.

Rodriguez, J. (2006). *Civilizing Argentina: Science, Medicine, and the Modern State.* Chapel Hill, NC: University of North Carolina Press.

Routh, G. (1987). *Occupations of the People of Great Britain, 1801–1981.* Basingstoke: Macmillan.

Ruggiero, V. (1997). Trafficking in Human Beings: Slaves in Contemporary Europe. *International Journal of the Sociology of Law*, 25, 231–244.

Ruhs, M. and Anderson, B. (2010). Semi-Compliance and Illegality in Migrant Labour Markets: An Analysis of Migrants, Employers and the State in the UK. *Population, Space and Place*, 16, 195–211.

Ryan, B. (2006). The Evolving Legal Regime on Unauthorized Work by Migrants in Britain. *Law & Policy Journal*, 27, 27–58.

Sale, R. (2002). The Deserving and the Undeserving? Refugees, Asylum Seekers and Welfare in Britain. *Critical Social Policy*, 22, 456–478.

Salt, J. and Kitching, R. (1990). Labour Migration and the Work Permit System in the United Kingdom. *International Migration*, 28, 267–294.

Salt, J. and Stein, J. (1997). Migration as a Business: The Case of Trafficking. *International Migration*, 35, 467–494.

Sanders, A. (2010). Reconciling the Apparently Different Goals of Criminal Justice and Regulation: The 'Freedom' Perspective. In H. Quirk, T. Seddon and G. Smith (eds) *Regulation and Criminal Justice: Innovations in Policy and Research.* Cambridge: Cambridge University Press, pp. 42–71.

Sarat, A., Douglas, L. and Merrill Umphrey, M. (2011). On the Blurred Boundary between Regulation and Punishment. In A. Sarat (ed.) *Law as Punishment/Law as Regulation.* Stanford, CA: Stanford University Press, pp. 1–18.

Sassen, S. (2002). Governance Hotspots: Challenges we Must Confront in the Post-September 11 World. *Theory Culture & Society*, 19, 233–244.

Schloenhardt, A. (2008). Illegal Immigration and Migrant Smuggling in the Asia-Pacific: Balancing Regional Security and Human Rights. In M. Curley and S. Wong (eds) *Security and Migration in Asia: The Dynamics of Securitisation.* London and New York: Routledge, pp. 35–56.

Schuck, P. (1984). The Transformation of Immigration Law. *Columbia Law Review*, 84, 1–90.

Schuster, L. and Solomos, J. (2004). Race, Immigration and Asylum: New Labour's Agenda and its Consequences. *Ethnicities*, 4, 267–300.

Sciortino, G. and Pastore, F. (2004). Immigration and European Immigration Policy: Myths and Realities. In J. Apap (ed.) *Justice and Home Affairs in the EU. Liberty and Security Issues after Enlargement.* Cheltenham: Edward Elgar Publishing, pp. 191–209.

Scott, R. and Stuntz, W. (1992). Plea Bargaining as Contract. *The Yale Law Journal*, 101, 1909–1968.

Sebba, L. (2009). 'Victim-Driven' Criminalisation? Some Recent Trends in the Expansion of the Criminal Law. In B. McSherry, A. Norrie and S. Bronitt (eds) *Regulating Deviance. The Redirection of Criminalisation and the Futures of Criminal Law.* Oxford: Hart, pp. 59–84.

Segrave, M. (2009). Human Trafficking and Human Rights. *Australian Journal of Human Rights*, 14, 71–94.

Seldon, A. (1994). Consensus: A Debate too Long? *Parliamentary Affairs*, 4, 501–514.

Sentencing Guidelines Council (2004). *Overarching Principles: Seriousness.* London: Sentencing Guidelines Council.

Sentencing Guidelines Council (2005). *Guideline Judgments. Case Compendium.* London: Sentencing Guidelines Council.

Sentencing Guidelines Council (2007). *Reduction in Sentence for a Guilty Plea. Definitive Guideline.* London: Sentencing Guidelines Council.

Shyllon, F. (1977). *Black People in Britain 1555–1833.* London: Institute of Race Relations/Oxford University Press.

Silveira Gorski, H. (2009). Estados Expulsores y Semipersonas en la Unión Europea. *Anales de la Cátedra Francisco Suárez*, 43, 117–139.

Sim, A. (2008). The Cultural Economy of Illegal Migration. Migrant Workers Who Overstay in Hong Kong. In M. Curley and W. Siu-Iun (eds) *Security and Migration in Asia: The Dynamics of Securitisation.* London and New York: Routledge, pp. 120–147.

Sim, P. (1962). The Involuntary Actus Reus. *Modern Law Review*, 25, 741–744.

Simester, A., Spencer, J., Sullivan, R. and Virgo, G. (2010). *Simester and Sullivan's Criminal Law. Theory and Doctrine.* Oxford: Hart.

Simon, J. (1988). The Ideological Effects of Actuarial Practices. *Law & Society Review*, 22, 771–800.

Simon, J. (1998). Refugees in a Carceral Age: The Rebirth of Immigration Prisons in the United States. *Public Culture*, 10, 577–607.

Simon, J. (2007). *Governing through Crime. How the War on Crime Transformed American Democracy and Created a Culture of Fear.* Oxford: Oxford University Press.

Singh Bhui, H. (2007). Alien Experience: Foreign National Prisoners After the Deportation Crisis. *Probation Journal*, 54, 368–382.

Sivanandan, A. (1976). Race, Class and the State: The Black Experience in Britain. *Race and Class*, XVII, 347–368.

Sklansky, D. (2012). Crime, Immigration, and Ad Hoc Instrumentalism. *New Criminal Law Review*, 15, 157–223.

Slack, P. (1974). Vagrants and Vagrancy in England, 1598–1664. *The Economic History Review*, 27, 360–379.

Smith, D. (2005). Ethnic Differences in Intergenerational Crime Patterns. *Crime and Justice*, 32, 59–130.

Snacken, S. (2010). Resisting Punitiveness in Europe? *Theoretical Criminology*, 14, 273–292.

Snell, K. (1992). Settlement, Poor Law and the Rural Historian: New Approaches and Opportunities. *Rural History*, 3, 145–172.

Solomos, J. (1989). *Race and Racism in Contemporary Britain.* Basingstoke: Macmillan.

Somerville, W. (2007). *Immigration under New Labour.* Bristol: Policy Press.

Soysal, Y. (1994). *Limits of Citizenship. Migrants and Postnational Membership in Europe.* London: University of Chicago Press.

Sparks, C. and Spencer, S. (2002). *Them and Us? The Public, Offenders and the Criminal Justice System.* London: Institute for Public Policy Research.

Spencer, I. (1997). *British Immigration Policy since 1939: The Making of Multi-Racial Britain*. London: Routledge.

Spencer, S. (2007). Immigration. In A. Seldon (ed.) *Blair's Britain 1997–2007*. Cambridge: Cambridge University Press, pp. 341–360.

Spencer, S. (2011). *The Migration Debate*. Bristol: Policy Press.

Steiker, C. (1997). Punishment and Procedure: Punishment Theory and the Criminal–Civil Procedural Divide. *Annual Review of Criminal Procedure*, 26, 775–819.

Steiker, C. (1998). Foreword: The Limits of the Preventive State. *The Journal of Criminal Law and Criminology*, 88, 771–808.

Steiker, C. (2010). Criminalization and the Criminal Process: Prudential Mercy as a Limit on Penal Sanctions in an Era of Mass Incarceration. In: R. A. Duff, L. Farmer, S. E. Marshall, M. Renzo and V. Tadros (eds) *The Boundaries of the Criminal Law*. Oxford: Oxford University Press, pp. 27–58.

Stenson, K. (2001). The New Politics of Crime Control. In K. Stenson and R. Sullivan (eds) *Crime, Risk and Justice: The Politics of Crime Control in Liberal Democracies*. Cullompton, Devon: Willan, pp. 15–28.

Stephen-Smith, S. (2008). *Prisoners with No Crime. Detention of Trafficked Women in the UK*. London: The Poppy Project.

Stoyanova, V. (2012). Smuggling of Asylum-Seekers and Criminal Justice. Working Paper No. 5, Refugee Law Initiative. Available at: http://www.sas.ac.uk/sites/default/files/files/RLI/RLI%20Working%20Paper%20No%205.pdf (accessed: 9 February 2013).

Stumpf, J. (2007). The Crimmigration Crisis: Immigrants, Crime, and Sovereign State. *Lewis & Clark Law School Legal Research Paper Series*, 2007-2, 1–44.

Stumpf, J. (2009). Fitting Punishment. *Washington and Lee Law Review*, 66, 1683–1741.

Stumpf, J. (2011). Doing Time: Crimmigration Law and the Perils of Haste. *UCLA Law Review*, 58, 1705–1748.

Stuntz, W. (1996). Substance, Process, and the Civil–Criminal Line. *Journal of Contemporary Legal Issues*, 7, 1–41.

Stuntz, W. (2001). The Pathological Politics of Criminal Law. *Michigan Law Review*, 100, 505–600.

Stuntz, W. (2008). Unequal Justice. *Harvard Law Review*, 121, 1977–2040.

Stuntz, W. (2011). *The Collapse of American Criminal Justice*. Cambridge, MA: Harvard University Press.

Tadros, V. (2007). *Criminal Responsibility*. Oxford: Oxford University Press.

Tadros, V. (2010). Criminalization and Regulation. In R. A. Duff, L. Farmer, S. E. Marshall, M. Renzo and V. Tadros (eds) *The Boundaries of the Criminal Law*. Oxford: Oxford University Press, pp. 163–190.

Tansey, O. (2007). Process Tracing and Elite Interviewing: A Case for Non-Probability Sampling. *Political Science & Politics*, 40, 765–772.

Taylor, J. (1976). The Impact of Pauper Settlement 1691–1834. *Past & Present*, 42–74.

The Economist (2009a). Attitudes to Immigration. This Sceptical Isle. 9 December 2009. Available at: http://www.economist.com/node/15017461 (accessed: 9 February 2013).

The Economist (2009b). After the Backlog, a Backlog. As One Mountain of Old Asylum Claims is Demolished, a New One Grows. 18 September 2009. Available at: http://www.economist.com/node/13863415 (accessed: 9 February 2013).

Thomas, R. (2011). *Administrative Justice and Asylum Appeals*. Oxford: Hart.

Toner, H. (2009). Foreign National Prisoners, Deportation, and Gender. In H. Stalford, S. Curie and S. Velluti (eds) *Gender and Migration in 21st Century Europe*. Farnham, Surrey and Burlington, VT: Ashgate, pp. 183–208.

Tonry, M. (1997). Ethnicity, Crime, and Immigration. *Crime and Justice*, 21, 1–29.

Tonry, M. (2004a). Criminology and Criminal Justice in Europe. In G. Bruinsma, H. Elffers and J. de Keijser (eds) *Punishment, Places and Perpetrators: Developments in Criminology and Criminal Justice Research*. Cullompton, Devon: Willan, pp. 21–37.

Tonry, M. (2004b). *Thinking about Crime: Sense and Sensibility in American Penal Culture*. New York: Oxford University Press.

Torpey, J. (2000). States and the Regulation of Migration in the Twentieth-Century North Atlantic World. In P. Andreas and T. Snyder (eds) *The Wall around the West. State Borders and Immigration Controls in North America and Europe*. Oxford: Rowman & Littlefield Publishers Inc., pp. 31–54.

Tranter, N. (1996). *British Population in the Twentieth Century*. Basingstoke: Macmillan Press Ltd.

Travis, A. (2002a). After 44 Years Secret Papers Reveal Truth about Five Nights of Violence in Notting Hill. *The Guardian*. 24 August 2002. Available at: http://www.guardian.co.uk/uk/2002/aug/24/artsandhumanities.nottinghillcarnival2002 (accessed: 9 February 2013).

Travis, A. (2002b). Ministers Saw Law's 'Racism' as Defensible. Powell Wielded Influence over Bill's Direction. *The Guardian*. 1 January 2002. Available at: http://www.guardian.co.uk/politics/2002/jan/01/uk.race (accessed: 9 February 2013).

Travis, A. (2010). Huge Rise in Unresolved Asylum Cases Revealed. Watchdog Says Government Targets Unachievable, Leaving Labour Facing Election Unable to Claim Asylum Issue Is Fixed. *The Guardian*. 26 February 2010. Available at: http://www.guardian.co.uk/uk/2010/feb/26/immigration (accessed: 9 February 2013).

Travis, A. (2011). Sex Trafficking Victim Wins Substantial Damages from Home Office. *The Guardian*. 11 April 2011. Available at: http://www.guardian.co.uk/uk/2011/apr/11/sex-trafficking-home-office-damages (accessed: 9 February 2013).

Troup, C. (1925). *The Home Office*. London and New York: G. P. Putnam's Sons Ltd.

Tumlin, K. (2004). Suspect First: How Terrorism Policy Is Reshaping Immigration Policy. *California Law Review*, 92, 1173–1239.

United Nations (2008). Trends in Total Migrant Stock: The 2008 Revision Population Database. New York: UN, Department of Economic and Social Affairs, Population Division.

Valier, C. (2003). Foreigners, Crime and Changing Mobilities. *British Journal of Criminology*, 43, 1–21.

Valverde, M. (2010). Practices of Citizenship and Scales of Governance. *New Criminal Law Review*, 13, 216–240.

van Kalmthout, A., Hofstee-van der Meulen, F. and Dünkel, F. (2007). *Foreigners in European Prisons*. Nijmegen: Wolf Legal Publishers.

Ventrella McCreight, M. (2006). Crimes of Assisting Illegal Immigration and Trafficking in Human Beings in Italian Law: Illegal Immigration between Administrative Infringement and Criminal Offence. In E. Guild and P. Minderhoud (eds) *Immigration and Criminal Law in the European Union. The Legal Measures and Social Consequences of Criminal Law in Member States on Trafficking and Smuggling in Human Beings*. Leiden: Martinus Nijhoff, pp. 141–168.

Vine, J. (2010). *UK Border Agency's Operations in the North West of England. An Inspection of the Civil Penalties Compliance Team – Illegal Working*. London: Independent Chief Inspector of the UKBA.

Vine, J. (2011). *A Short-Notice Inspection of a UK Border Agency Arrest Team (Croydon)*. London: Independent Chief Inspector of the UKBA.

Vogel, D., McDonald, W., Düvell, F., Jordan, B., Kovacheva, V. and Vollmer, B. (2009). Police Cooperation in Internal Enforcement of Immigration Control: Learning from International Comparison. *Sociology of Crime, Law and Deviance*, 13, 207–244.

von Hirsch, A. (1976). *Doing Justice: The Choice of Punishments*. New York: Hill and Wang.

von Hirsch, A. and Roberts, J. (2004). Legislating Sentencing Principles: The Provisions of the Criminal Justice Act 2003 Relating to Sentencing Purposes and the Role of Previous Convictions. *Criminal Law Review*, 639–652.

Vorspan, R. (1977). Vagrancy and the New Poor Law in Late-Victorian and Edwardian England. *The English Historical Review*, 92, 59–81.

Wacquant, L. (1999). 'Suitable Enemies': Foreigners and Immigrants in the Prisons of Europe. *Punishment & Society*, 1, 215–222.

Wacquant, L. (2005). Enemies of the Wholesome Part of the Nation. Postcolonial Migrants in the Prisons of Europe. *Sociologie*, 1, 31–51.

Wacquant, L. (2006). Penalization, Depoliticization, Racialization: On the Over-Incarceration of Immigrants in the European Union. In S. Armstrong and L. McAra (eds) *Perspectives on Punishment*. New York: Oxford University Press, pp. 83–100.

Wadham, J., Gallagher, C. and Chrolavicius, N. (2006). *Blackstone's Guide to the Identity Cards Act 2006*. Oxford: Oxford University Press.

Walvin, J. (1973). *Black and White: The Negro and English Society 1555–1945*. London: Allen Lane, The Penguin Press.

Webb, S. and Burrows, J. (2009). Organised Immigration Crime: A Post-Conviction Study. Research Report No. 15. London: Home Office.

Webber, F. (2008). *Border Wars and Asylum Crimes*. London: Statewatch.

Webber, F. (2009). Crusade against the Undocumented. Comment, 5 February 2009, Institute of Race Relations website. Available at: http://www.irr.org.uk/news/crusade-against-the-undocumented/ (accessed: 29 January 2013).

Weber, L. (2003). Decisions to Detain Asylum Seekers: Routine, Duty or Individual Choice? In L. Gelsthorpe and N. Padfield (eds) *Exercising Discretion: Decision-Making in the Criminal Justice System and Beyond*. Cullompton, Devon: Willan, pp. 164–185.

Weber, L. (2007). Policing the Virtual Border: Punitive Preemption in Australian Offshore Migration Control. *Social Justice*, 34, 77–93.

Weber, L. and Bowling, B. (2004). Policing Migration: A Framework for Investigating the Regulation of Global Mobility. *Policing and Society*, 14, 195–212.

Weber, L. and Grewcock, M. (2012). Criminalizing People Smuggling: Preventing or Globalizing Harm? In F. Allum and S. Gilmour (eds) *The Routledge Handbook of Transnational Organized Crime*. London: Routledge, pp. 379–390.

Weber, L. and Landman, T. (2002). *Deciding to Detain: The Organisational Context for Decisions to Detain Asylum Seekers at UK ports*. Colchester: Human Rights Centre, University of Essex.

Weber, L. and Pickering, S. (2011). *Globalization and Borders. Death at the Global Frontier*. Basingstoke: Palgrave Macmillan.

Welch, M. (2003). Ironies of Social Control and the Criminalization of Immigrants. *Crime, Law and Social Change*, 39, 319–337.

Welch, M. and Schuster, L. (2005a). Detention of Asylum Seekers in the UK and USA. *Punishment & Society*, 7, 397–417.

Welch, M. and Schuster, L. (2005b). Detention of Asylum Seekers in the US, UK, France, Germany, and Italy. *Criminal Justice*, 5, 331–355.

Wells, C. (2005). *Corporations and Criminal Liability*. Oxford: Oxford University Press.

Whitehead, T. (2008). Rural Communities Struggling to Cope with Immigration, Prince Charles Report Warns. *The Telegraph*. 20 November 2008. Available at: http://www.telegraph.co.uk/news/politics/3491829/Rural-communities-struggling-to-cope-with-immigration-Prince-Charles-report-warns.html (accessed: 9 February 2013).

Whitman, J. (2003). *Harsh Justice: Criminal Punishment and the Widening Divide Between America and Europe*. New York: Oxford University Press.

Williams, S. (1984). A Guide to Interviewing MPs: How to Avoid Relegation to the Bin. *Public Administration Bulletin*, 45, 44–52.

Wilson, D. and Weber, L. (2008). Surveillance, Risk and Preemption on the Australian Border. *Surveillance & Society*, 5, 124–141.

Woodbridge, J., Burgum, D. and Heath, T. (2000). Asylum Statistics United Kingdom 1999. 17/00. London: Home Office.

Wrench, J. (2000). British Unions and Racism: Organisational Dilemmas in an Unsympathetic Climate. In R. Penninx and J. Roosblad (eds) *Trade Unions, Immigration, and Immigrants in Europe, 1960–1993: A Comparative Study of the Attitudes and Actions of Trade Unions in Seven West European Countries*. Oxford: Berghahn Books, pp. 135–155.

Young, J. (2003). To These Wet and Windy Shores. *Punishment & Society*, 5, 449–462.

Zedner, L. (1995). In Pursuit of the Vernacular: Comparing Law and Order Discourse in Britain and Germany. *Social & Legal Studies*, 4, 517–534.

Zedner, L. (2002). Dangers of Dystopias in Penal Theory. *Oxford Journal of Legal Studies*, 22, 341–366.

Zedner, L. (2004). *Criminal Justice*. Oxford: Oxford University Press.

Zedner, L. (2005). Securing Liberty in the Face of Terror: Reflections from Criminal Justice. *Journal of Law and Society*, 32, 507–533.

Zedner, L. (2007). Preventive Justice or Pre-Punishment? The Case of Control Orders. In C. O'Cinneide and J. Holder (eds) *Current Legal Problems*. Oxford: Oxford University Press, pp. 173–203.

Zedner, L. (2009). Fixing the Future? The Pre-emptive Turn in Criminal Justice. In B. McSherry, A. Norrie and S. Bronitt (eds) *Regulating Deviance. The Redirection of Criminalisation and the Futures of Criminal Law*. Oxford: Hart, pp. 35–58.

Zedner, L. (2010). Security, the State, and the Citizen: The Changing Architecture of Crime Control. *New Criminal Law Review*, 13, 379–403.

Index